Seizing Freedom

Seizing Freedom

Slave Emancipation and Liberty for All

DAVID ROEDIGER

VERSO

London • New York

First published by Verso 2014
© David Roediger 2014

1 3 5 7 9 10 8 6 4 2

Verso
UK: 6 Meard Street, London W1F 0EG
US: 20 Jay Street, Suite 1010, Brooklyn, NY 11201
www.versobooks.com

Verso is the imprint of New Left Books

ISBN-13: 978-1-78168-609-6 (HB)
eISBN-13: 978-1-78168-610-2 (US)
eISBN-13: 978-1-78168-705-5 (UK)

British Library Cataloguing in Publication Data
A catalogue record for this book is available from the British Library

Library of Congress Cataloging-in-Publication Data
A catalog record for this book is available from the Library of Congress

Typeset in Garamond Premier Pro by Hewer Text UK Ltd, Edinburgh, Scotland
Printed in the US by Maple Press

It is more difficult to honor the memory of the anonymous than it is to honor the memory of the famous . . . The historical construction is dedicated to the memory of the anonymous.

Walter Benjamin, "Paralipomena to 'On the Concept of History'" (1940)

Contents

Introduction:

Plotting Jubilee

We are not to be saved by the captain . . . but by the crew.
Frederick Douglass (1863)

As perhaps the most "embedded" of the Union war correspondents, the Civil War journalist Charles Carleton Coffin could report from wherever he wished within Union-controlled areas. In spring 1863, Coffin used his access to Abraham Lincoln, to transportation, and to officers to chronicle the preparation for a Yankee attempt to recapture Confederate-held Fort Sumter. He described in particular the magnificence of the "ironsides in action," as the armored Union vessels shelled Rebel positions. His thinking was clear: Fort Sumter's capture had begun the war two years before and retaking it would be of great symbolic value, especially insofar as the innovations in naval warfare exposed Confederate weaknesses. The reality was less dramatic than Coffin anticipated. The ironclads did inflict damage but also suffered losses. It would not be until September that an attempt to retake the fort was essayed, and that battle would end with the Confederate flag still flying. By then, Coffin had moved on to Pennsylvania, following sounder instincts regarding where the military action would be that year.[1]

---

1 The epigraph is from Douglass's "Address Delivered in Philadelphia, Pennsylvania, on 4 December 1863" as reprinted in *The Frederick Douglass Papers, Series One: Speeches, Debates, and Interviews, Volume 3, 1855–63*, eds. John Blassingame and others (New Haven, CT: Yale University Press, 1985),

Nevertheless, his springtime in the Sea Islands of South Carolina produced the best of his wartime writing. Coffin captured a human triumph that might have seemed small in the shadow of the ironclad artillery. However, with a little distance, that seemingly smaller drama was the more magnificent and portentous. As Rebel positions were shelled, he wrote, the owner of the surrounding land sent an overseer "to hurry up the negroes" so that the master could retain his enslaved property. No slave could be found. As Coffin described the events, "The colored people had heard the thundering down the bay. They knew its meaning." The slave Sam had overheard plans for evacuation and ran to spread the word, five minutes ahead of the overseer. The cry "To the woods! To the woods!" organized the self-emancipation of the slaves and the overseer found "his drove of human cattle gone." Only empty cabins remained. The lesson that Coffin drew was not only the possibility of the world turning upside down in a moment of liberation, but also the vulnerability of the Confederacy in the face of the knowledge, judgment, and organization of the unfree: "The planter and his overseer were obliged to do their own hasty packing up."[2]

Coffin described this moment in the history of the South Carolina coast as the transformation of a people, of a region, of a nation, and of himself. Coffin's preservation of the public speech of a "pure, full-blooded negro, Sancho" captured the drama as impossibly wonderful. Sancho said he "neber 'spected to see such a day as dis yere. For twenty years I hired my time of old massa I was 'bleeged to pay him twelve dollars a month in advance, and if I did n't hab de money ready, he wolloped me. But I's a free man now. De good Lord hab done it all." Coffin wanted to understand

---

608; Charles Carleton Coffin, *Four Years of Fighting: A Volume of Personal Observation with the Army and Navy* (Boston: Ticknor and Fields), 227–308. On his relations with Lincoln, see Coffin's *Abraham Lincoln* (New York: Harper and Brothers, 1893). Thanks to JoAnn Zeise of the South Carolina State Museum for directing my attention to Coffin in her spring 2012 University of South Carolina seminar paper, "'This Is Not a History': War Journalist Charles Carleton Coffin's Account of the Port Royal Area in *Four Years of Fighting*."
2 Coffin, *Four Years of Fighting*, 227–8 and 16.

the individual heroism and community organization he had witnessed in order to argue that the "splendidly" performing Black Union troops were a key to the moral and military fortunes of the Union. To ground his thinking, he offered one of the finest accounts of the music so central to what historian Sterling Stuckey has called "slave culture."

Coffin heard the slave spiritual "Roll, Jordan, Roll" as a work of rare beauty and force—both traditional and improvised—with the African-American dancing of the "ring shout" as compelling as the song itself:

> As the song goes on the enthusiasm rises. They sing louder and stronger. The recitative is given with increased vigor, and the chorus swells with increasing volume. They beat time, at first, with their hands, then their feet. They rise from their seats. William begins to shuffle his feet. Anna, a short, thick-set woman, wearing a checkered dress, and an apron, which once was a window-curtain, claps her hands, makes a short, quick jerk of her body, stamps her feet on the un-accented part of the measure, keeping exact syncopation. Catherine and Sancho catch the inspiration. They go round in a circle, shuffling, jerking, shouting louder and louder, while those outside of the circle respond with increasing vigor, all stamping, clapping their hands, and rolling out the chorus.[3]

Just after placing Sam, Sancho, slave culture, and self-emancipation at the center of Civil War history, Coffin described meeting a thin Black woman in the headquarters of the Union's commanding officer in the area. He learned that she had helped carry many away from slavery, moving through swamps, eluding Rebels, and providing important information to Union forces. She was introduced as "our Sojourner Truth."[4]

---

3 Coffin, *Four Years of Fighting*, 229 for the first two quotations, 247 ("splendidly"), 231 (for the description of the ring shout) and 227–32; cf. Sterling Stuckey, *Slave Culture: Nationalist Theory and the Foundations of Black America* (New York: Oxford University Press, 1988), esp. 10–61.
4 Coffin, *Four Years of Fighting*, 234. For Truth's own wartime heroism, see Nell Irvin Painter,

Coffin's chapter then takes a still more remarkable turn. Having established that the example of New York's ex-slave and direct action abolitionist Sojourner Truth lived in the consciousness of those helping to liberate slaves in South Carolina, he felt the need to introduce Truth to some of his presumably Northern readers. He reported sitting near the blazing fireplace of the reformer Francis Dana Gage, who was in the Sea Islands to nurse disabled Union veterans and to organize support for freedpeople. In listening to Gage, Coffin heard Truth's story from a leading feminist who provided one surviving text of Truth's celebrated "Ar'n't I a Woman?" speech on race, gender, and class given at the women's rights convention in Akron in 1851. Gage recounted to Coffin Truth's heroism in penetrating the South to aid in slave resistance and in facing down those who screamed "Women's Rights and Niggers!" as she began to speak in the North. Coffin portrayed Truth as "a wonderful woman [who] lives in modern art," sampling at great length best-selling writer Harriet Beecher Stowe's discussion of Truth and of the "Libyan Sibyl" statue of her. He then reproduced for readers Gage's version of Truth's speech at Akron, interrupting the chapter's journalism for nine pages of small type that biographers of Truth analyze to this day in sorting through connections of women's freedom to abolition.[5]

Both the central idea and the most important innovation of this book are visible in Coffin's Sea Island reporting. Structuring the story of *Seizing Freedom* is what the eminent historian of the war and Reconstruction W. E. B. Du Bois called the "general strike of the slaves."[6] The massive defection from slavery that Du Bois gave such an apt name took myriad

---

Sojourner Truth: A Life, A Symbol (New York: Norton, 1996), 177–86.
5 Coffin, *Four Years of Fighting*, 234–43 with the quoted passages at 241 and 235; Cheryl Harris, "Finding Sojourner's Truth: Race, Gender and the Institution of Property," *Cardozo Law Review* 18 (November 1996): 309–409; Painter, *Sojourner Truth*, 162–75. For Gage in the 1860s, see Ellen DuBois, *Feminism and Suffrage: The Emergence of an Independent Women's Movement in America* (Ithaca, NY: Cornell University Press, 1978), 68–9.
6 W.E.B. Du Bois, *Black Reconstruction in America, 1860–1880* (New York: Atheneum, 1998 [1935]), 55–83 and 128.

forms, involving the flight of perhaps half a million slaves and daily mutiny by a far greater number who stayed but resisted plantation labor. Hundreds of thousands of slaves gained freedom during the war, depriving the Confederacy of their labor and eroding the confidence of masters. Perhaps 100,000 made the transition from slavery to service in the Union army or navy, but many more gave information as they crossed behind Union lines. More subtly on strike were those who, like Sam in Coffin's columns, listened for clues as to the prospects of freedom, those who took advantage of disarray on the Rebel home front to become more and more unmanageable even while still enslaved, those who maintained dignity as Sancho did, and those who danced communally in joy and defiance.[7]

The innovation in my analysis flows from Coffin's turn from weighing abolition to thinking about feminism. In the inspired presence of the self-emancipation of slaves, hundreds of thousands of women and white workers began to think very differently about their own possibilities and desires. The stories of their attempts to seize freedom are systematically connected for the first time to the general strike of the slaves in these pages. Indeed, this book is about the fascinating brew of issues that Coffin's time in the Sea Islands brought together: how the very meaning of the Civil War shifted in response to the motion of slaves; what it meant to witness incredible transformations; how the representation of race changed; how white women mattered in the war effort, and how class, sex, and race differences appeared among those championing freedom.

As late as 1995, it would have been unnecessary to insist that slaves freed themselves. In an essay published that year, leading Civil War historian James McPherson bemoaned the spread of what he called the "self emancipation thesis," casting himself in the role of underdog in his effort to persuade historians that Lincoln freed the slaves. The theologian,

---

7 Armstead L. Robinson, *Bitter Fruits of Bondage: The Demise of Slavery and the Collapse of the Confederacy, 1861–1865* (Charlottesville, VA: University of Virginia Press, 2005), esp. 134, 181, and 283; Bruce Levine, *The Fall of the House of Dixie: The Civil War and the Social Revolution that Transformed the South* (New York: Random House, 2013), 94–8, 153, and 167.

movement leader, and historian Vincent Harding had provided, according
to McPherson, "almost a Bible for the [self-emancipation] argument." As
Harding wrote, "While Lincoln continued to hesitate . . . the relentless
movement of the self-liberated fugitives into the Union lines . . . took their
freedom into their own hands." The editors at the authoritative Freedmen
and Southern Society Project of documentary history, McPherson worried, made slaves "the prime movers in securing their own liberty." One of
those editors, Barbara Fields, appeared as an expert witness for the idea of
self-emancipation in the celebrated 1990 Ken Burns documentary film
The Civil War. In her companion essay to the film, "Who Freed the Slaves?"
Fields made her case with force and eloquence, adding that it was
self-emancipation that gave the carnage a moral sense and meaning, while
war for preserving the Union without abolishing slavery would have ultimately been exposed as "a goal too shallow to be worth the sacrifice of a
single life."[8]

Times have changed and it is necessary to ask now what has happened
to the general strike of the slaves in historical writing and in popular
understandings of the Civil War. Blockbuster books and films of the
recent past appreciate the general strike of slaves perhaps less than at
any time in the last half-century. In the period of the sesquicentennial
of emancipation, the only major celebration of the general strike of the
slaves has come not from the field of history but rather from the cultural
theorist Gayatri Spivak's 2009 lectures at Harvard on Du Bois's ideas
and the importance of general strikes. The impressive 2011 *Historical
Materialism* symposium on the US Civil War and slavery, featuring the
work of seven leading left scholars, offers a fair barometer of the state
of the art. Du Bois is cited just once, in a passage noting him as one
exception to the absence of appreciation of the self-emancipation of the

---

8 James McPherson, "Who Freed the Slaves?", *Proceedings of the American Philosophical Society* 139
(March 1995), 1–10 with the Harding quotations at 1 and Freedmen and Southern Society Project
quote at 2. Barbara Fields, "Who Freed the Slaves?" in *The Civil War: An Illustrated History*, ed.
Geoffrey Ward (New York: Knopf, 1990), 178 and 179–81.

slaves in early Marxist accounts. But the symposium articles themselves say little on self-emancipation. Meanwhile, in the most praised recent account of the coming of freedom, historian James Oakes attempts to show that Republicans had an emancipationist perspective from the moment they took office in 1860. Oakes eschews serious discussion of how taking such a position puts him in conflict with the leading US historian of the twentieth century, Du Bois, and with the leading African-American activists of the early war, especially Frederick Douglass. Even Oakes's brief accounts of "self-emancipation" leave no room for seeing slaves as the catalysts for the drama of the coming of freedom, instead dwelling on the generals on one side and "Lincoln and the lawmakers" on the other. There is scant space for Sam or Sojourner Truth in such a story.[9]

One useful point of departure in refusing to take inspired federal policy and Lincoln's leadership as the most important factors in emancipation is to think comparatively. Britain was not an antislavery nation during the American Revolution and only partly so at the time of the War of 1812. Nevertheless, capitalizing on slaves' desire for liberty by aggressively encouraging their flight and rebellion so clearly conferred military and political advantage that appeals for slave resistance became a cornerstone of British strategy. Indeed Britain made such calls preemptively with such force that Thomas Jefferson's draft Declaration of Independence already counted "exciting [slaves] to rise in arms among us" among the terrible crimes of the British king. That the United States moved with such excruciatingly deliberate speed to pressing the same military advantages in the Civil War bespeaks a longstanding respect for slave property and slaveholders' interests that hardly comports with the idea of a Republican Party

9 Gayatri Spivak, "Du Bois and the General Strike," a lecture delivered at the W.E.B. Du Bois Lecture Series at Harvard University (2009) and archived at dubois.fas.harvard.edu/node/780; James Oakes, "A War of Emancipation," *Jacobin* (September 25, 2012) at jacobinmag.com; Oakes, *Freedom National: The Destruction of Slavery in the United States, 1861–1865* (New York: W.W. Norton, 2012), 211 and 192–223. See also "A Symposium on the American Civil War and Slavery" in *Historical Materialism*, 19 (2011), 33–205.

and its president necessarily bound for freedom without profound pushes from the slaves themselves.[10]

The idea of the general strike of the slaves has been not so much contested as marginalized. Difficulty in seeing how broadly diverging forms of resistance all fit within the idea of a general strike, a misplaced belief that typical general strikes are formally called by workers' organizations, and an incredible overvaluation of the role of Abraham Lincoln and the Republican Party in emancipation underwrite moving the general strike offstage.[11] Lerone Bennett's 2000 study *Forced into Glory*, a drama in which slaves actually set Lincoln into motion, was roundly ignored by professional historians, much as Du Bois's *Black Reconstruction* had been fifty-five years before. The leading historian of the period, Eric Foner, in his classic 1989 study *Reconstruction: An Unfinished Revolution*, began with strong tributes to Du Bois, assenting to the latter's judgment in *Black Reconstruction* that "with perplexed and laggard steps the United States government followed in the steps of the black slave" where freedom was concerned. However, in part because he began his story only in 1863, Foner's study of Reconstruction gave little sense of any epoch-making general strike of the slaves, so central to Du Bois's narrative. When Foner more fully treated the early war in his recent study of Abraham Lincoln and race, even an index entry for Du Bois was absent.[12]

Even Steven Hahn's important inquiries into whether Civil War historians "missed" the world's greatest "slave rebellion," which call on Du Bois's idea of a self-emancipatory mass movement of the slaves explicitly, too quickly abandon the term "general strike." In some measure, Hahn there-

---

10 David R. Roediger, *How Race Survived US History: From Settlement and Slavery to the Obama Phenomenon* (New York: Verso, 2008), 38 and 31–44.

11 Kim Moody, "General Strikes, Mass Strikes," *Against the Current* 160 (September–October 2012), 21–7, offers useful clarifications on the history of general strikes, including (21) that of the slaves.

12 Du Bois as quoted in Eric Foner, *Reconstruction: America's Unfinished Revolution* (New York: Harper Perennial, 2002 [1989]), 4; Du Bois, *Black Reconstruction in America*, 55–83; Eric Foner, *The Fiery Trial: Abraham Lincoln and American Slavery* (New York: Norton, 2011); Noel Ignatiev, "'The American Blindspot': Reconstruction According to Eric Foner and W.E.B. Du Bois," *Labour/Le Travail*, 31 (1993): 243–51 offers an important critique of Foner's earlier work.

fore loses the extent to which Du Bois used that phrase to cast the slaves as modern historical actors and as the cutting edge of "our labor movement." Seeing the Civil War as transformed into a freedom struggle by a slave uprising shows perfectly how it ended an era. But Du Bois hoped it was also inaugurating one. Hahn's interesting idea of a protracted process of emancipation stretching across decades similarly both raises and obscures important matters. Certainly emancipation was a central part of the long slave experience in the United States, stretching back to (and before) the self-emancipations that occurred when slaves fled to the British side in the Revolution and the War of 1812. Rebellion, defense of maroon encampments, incorporation into Indian communities, self-purchase, manumission, and above all flight made talk of emancipation concrete even when unity among whites was not disrupted by war. Indeed, it is likely, though not remarked on by historians, that a majority of all those born or transported into slavery in the United States, and the colonies that later constituted the United States, experienced emancipation. However, this remarkable reality occurred principally because four million emancipations happened in a highly concentrated burst of what historians of the French Revolution have called "revolutionary time"—a period in which the pace of change and the possibility of freedom accelerated the very experience of time. As critical as the traditions and realities of a long struggle for emancipation were, the years of agitation for freedom between 1800 and 1860 saw the quadrupling of the slave population. We thus must understand self-emancipation as both deeply rooted and glorious in its sudden maturation.[13]

---

13 Steven Hahn, *The Political Worlds of Slavery and Freedom* (Cambridge, MA: Harvard University Press, 2009), 55 and 1–115; Cf. Stephanie McCurry, *Confederate Reckoning: Power and Politics in the Civil War South* (Cambridge, MA: Harvard University Press, 2010), 239–57 offers a similarly useful analysis with less recognition of Du Bois. Paul Richards, "W.E.B. Du Bois and American Social History: The Evolution of a Marxist," *Radical America*, 3 (November 1970), 37–66.; Ferruccio Gambino, "W.E.B. Du Bois and the Proletariat in Black Reconstruction" at libcom.org; Lynn Hunt, "The World We Have Gained: The Future of the French Revolution," *The American Historical Review*, February 2003, at historycooperative.org; for "our labor movement," see Du Bois, *Black Reconstruction*, 727.

Beyond the historians, recent popular portrayals of emancipation are even further from glimpsing the general strike of the slaves. When the leading US popular historical filmmaker, Steven Spielberg, teamed with the nation's most celebrated left-liberal playwright, Tony Kushner, to make a blockbuster film on Lincoln on the 150th anniversary of emancipation, we saw both how much and how little things have changed. Kushner's screenplay for Spielberg's *Lincoln* thoroughly tackled questions of slavery. The film permitted no evasion of the extent to which slavery caused the war. But the ideas and actions of slaves and ex-slaves scarcely entered the picture at all. Douglass and Harriet Tubman did not appear, let alone slaves like Sam.[14] There ought to be room for more—for a history of emancipation geared to readers who still want and need emancipation. In Du Bois's language, we need to see the "unending tragedy of Reconstruction" in its "real significance, its national and world-wide implications."[15]

Nevertheless it is unproductive to blame individual historians, screenwriters, and directors for losing track of the general strike of the slaves. Most of the main tellers of the Civil War story, broadly speaking, come from the anti-racist left. However, the moment in which we live profoundly shapes what they write. Fascination with the Obama presidency, at a time of absence of powerful movements from below, contributes to the focus on the role of the leader expertly navigating electoral currents and legislative battles. For good measure, Obama's difficulties in getting much done makes for a profound appreciation of the role of presidential leadership in effecting emancipation.

The reasons that we do not get a bigger, broader, and more dramatic story of how freedom came to the United States in the 1860s are exhibited in an exchange that took place in the primaries before the 2008 election.

---

14 Kate Masur, "In Spielberg's 'Lincoln,' Passive Black Characters," *New York Times* (November 12, 2012). See also Aaron Bady, "*Lincoln* against the Radicals" in *Jacobin*, (November 26, 2012) at jacobinmag.com, and for a superb short response to the film by a rank-and-file transit activist, Tim Schermerhorn, "Review: 'Lincoln' Somehow Missed the General Strike" at the *Labor Notes* website (March 14, 2013) at labornotes.org.
15 Du Bois, *Black Reconstruction*, 708.

At that time, Hillary Clinton skewered Barack Obama's lack of political experience at the national level by saying that making change required a savvy insider, not just a visionary leader. We needed, she said, a Lyndon Johnson as well as a Martin Luther King. For a moment, debate about the way freedom comes in history threatened to break out in, of all places, a presidential campaign. Obama made the obvious point that King was the greater figure, but the discussion quickly lost steam. Neither candidate could give full-throated voice to a coherent position. Clinton, herself relatively inexperienced in elected office, appealed to a Democratic base that included at least some who remembered Johnson as prosecutor of a terrible imperial war, not as an architect of civil rights legislation. Obama's fierce efforts to portray himself as a tough-on-"terror" leader, willing to use force, departed from a central pillar of King's legacy decisively. Both were running to be Lyndon Johnson and they clashed at a time when both the popular and the historical imagination favored the story of great leaders and impoverished discussion of the role of social movements.[16]

Seizing Freedom's methodologies are old and new. Defending Du Bois's proposition regarding the general strike of slaves positions this dissenting study as a Marxist one, without supposing that Marx's own writings on the period can settle interpretive matters. Those writings, largely political and journalistic, contain brilliant episodic insights regarding emancipation and the radiating impulses toward freedom that it set into motion. They also reflect a period of great political growth for Marx, especially after the inspiring 1857 revolts in India pulled him away from the mechanistic assumption that slaves and colonized people would progress toward liberation only after being brought up to the speed of modernity within oppressive systems. Thus, even before the Civil War, Marx hoped that John Brown's attempt to start a slave uprising and the occurrence of a small slave revolt in Missouri signaled that US slaves were about to change the world.

---

16 Patrick Healy and Jeff Zeleny, "Clinton and Obama Spar over Remark about Dr. King," *New York Times* (January 13, 2008).

As early as January 1861, Marx identified the "movement of slaves" in the United States—not the election of Lincoln—as a key impulse toward freedom. However, the circumstances of producing journalism and agitational material based on scraps of available information that typically focused on political elites, generals, and battles, and of being in the midst of producing a classic study of capital based on theorizing its generality rather than historicizing its complicating racial dimensions, left Marx far from able to fully understand Black self-emancipation during the Civil War. His sympathetic writings on Lincoln lend themselves too easily to sampling in both liberal and radical histories that are hesitant to develop the insights of Du Bois on how the drama of liberation turned on Black self-activity.[17] In defending a Marxist approach, *Seizing Freedom* hearkens less to Marx than to *Black Reconstruction* as the most fully realized work of Marxist history of the United States yet produced and as an important study of how history moves.

A newer body of knowledge inspires another historiographical aspiration of this book. Building especially on the writing of Douglas Baynton, it seeks to place disability centrally in the history of the Civil War and Reconstruction. The habitual omission of disability is an odd one, in that the war left far more than half a million veterans disabled. The reconstruction of their bodies, minds, and spirits was a major task of Reconstruction. Making disability a critical part of the story entails of course considering the lives of the disabled and of those who cared for them. It also involves

17   Kevin Anderson, *Marx at the Margins: On Nationalism, Ethnicity, and Non-Western Societies* (Chicago: University of Chicago Press, 2010), esp. 32–7; Tom Jeannot, "Marx, Capitalism, and Race," *Radical Philosophy Today* 5 (2007), 72 ("movement") and 69–92. These defenses of Marx's approach suffer from an inability to speak to the tension between Marx's appreciation of the mass pressures for emancipation (and his anti-racism), on the one hand, and his tendency to submerge that insight when discussing Lincoln. See also Robin Blackburn, ed., *An Unfinished Revolution: Karl Marx and Abraham Lincoln* (New York: Verso, 2011). The lack of attention to African-American struggles during Reconstruction by Marx is seldom raised by those emphasizing his insights on race and the United States. Ironically, the Old Left historian Philip S. Foner comes closest to a measured critique. See his *American Socialism and Black Americans: From the Age of Jackson to World War II* (Westport, CT: Greenwood, 1977), 39–44. On Marx's *Capital* and race, see Michael A. Lebowitz, "The Politics of Assumption, the Assumption of Politics," *Historical Materialism* 14 (2006), 29–47.

showing how normalized assumptions linking white manhood with ability and fitness for citizenship gave way. They did so at the very time that women nurses and Black soldiers demonstrated that they possessed crucially needed abilities. Such a combination effected at least briefly an "emancipation from whiteness" enabling oppressed whites to seek freedom through structural changes rather than take comfort in being legally fit for privilege. Moreover, Baynton's work establishes that, for women, immigrant workers, and African Americans, making the claim to be "not disabled" (and therefore fit to exercise the intelligence, rationality, and strength that were presumed necessary for republican citizenship) was the price of the ticket for claiming rights. Thus disability as an issue suffuses all sections of the book, with concentrated attention in the second chapter.[18]

For those readers thinking about how worlds change and perhaps about how to change the world, two political interventions of the book deserve brief mention. The first relates to revolutionary time and to the very ways that I came to write on this topic. For thirty years, I have begun large lecture courses by placing postbellum freedom movements in the wake of the general strike of the slaves. In early 2011, as I began such a course, I briefly took note of the revolts in Tunisia. "Watch out for more news far beyond Tunisia," was my offhand prediction, with the observation segueing into discussion of how witnessing the impossibly successful freedom struggle of slaves had generated freedom dreams within other groups. Soon, the Arab uprisings matured in Egypt, Libya, Syria, Bahrain, and Kuwait. What started in Tunisia quickly influenced struggles in Spain, in London, in Wisconsin, and on Wall Street. The students from this course who enrolled the next term in my class on Herman Melville figured that

---

18 Douglas Baynton, "Disability and the Justification of Inequality in American History," in *The New Disability History: American Perspectives*, eds. Paul K. Longmore and Lauri Umansky (New York: New York University Press, 2001), 33–57; Colonel Emma E. Vogel, USA (Ret.), *Physical Therapists Before World War II (1917–40)* at the US Army Medical Department Office of Medical History website at history.amedd.army.mil, observes that during and after World War I, "reconstruction aides" became the term for the therapists working with disabled veterans.

I was something of a soothsayer and I was at first content to leave it at that. But, on reflection, it seemed important to acknowledge that, in considering the bursts of revolutionary time when profound and unimaginable changes explode, radical historians can best account for transformation because we know that when it proceeds from below, the good example of freedom struggles spreads in unpredictable ways. This insight has its limits. It may even imply that radicals are less able than others to apprehend the daily grind of misery that prevails outside of revolutionary time. But it does offer some sustenance to those of us horrified by that oppression to know that a slow grind is not the only gear in which history moves. *Seizing Freedom* seeks to dramatize that point.

Thus, the story told here is both exhilarating and sobering in equal measures. Far from predictable and piecemeal, change of the most liberating sort came in bursts after a long spell during which any hardheaded accounting of trends would have reckoned the possibility of immediate, unplanned, and uncompensated emancipation—not to mention the arming of slaves—as beyond remote. Change erupted when slaves, drawing on skills and commitments made in the long decades of circumscribed possibilities, withdrew themselves from plantation labor, sometimes by fleeing and sometimes by staying sullenly put. Change then reverberated across lines of race, gender—as Coffin's insertion of Sojourner Truth illustrates—and class. How the resulting hydra of liberation movements emerged and how each ran into its own sobering limits, confronting the fragility of alliances, the strength of enemies, and the limitations of friends, structures the final sections of the book.

In its second political intervention, *Seizing Freedom* hopes to offer useful reflections for those involved in thinking historically and practically about how coalitions among the oppressed work and stop working. When revolutionary time waned, the desire of each separate group within a fragile coalition to win its own demands, even as the coalition's demands seemed beyond reach, could become palpable. The deteriorating relations by the late 1860s between the advocates of Black manhood suffrage and those of women's suffrage revealed as much. That the oppressed were oppressed in very different ways made fissures common. In the decade after 1865, the greatest radicals in mid-nineteenth-century US history—Douglass, Elizabeth Cady Stanton, Wendell Phillips—fell out utterly with each other at times, especially when claims to rights seemed to compete.

Defending Du Bois's emphasis on a general strike by the slaves and applying disability studies to the history of Reconstruction represent no desire for this book to be mainly an intervention in historiographical battles. Nor are the political points it makes meant to overshadow the human dramas it portrays. It is a story about the most liberating and important period in US history. It is a story for students, dropouts, and occupiers, though its distinctive combination of concerns will interest historians. The book juxtaposes stories not usually told together, though they unfolded simultaneously. As such, it sets out again to follow Du Bois, whose historiographical chapter within *Black Reconstruction* dwelled on methodological mistakes of his predecessors but ended with an emphasis on their failure to appreciate the period as one of "magnificent drama" and as a "tragedy that beggared the Greek." No subsequent account has succeeded in portraying that drama, or that tragedy, as Du Bois did. Nor will this one. However, it will expand the discussion of issues that *Black Reconstruction* anticipated and add new dramas. Concentrating on how the self-organization of Black people changed the story of the United States, Du Bois was able to offer tantalizing accounts of the white worker in the North and poor whites in the South. His second chapter in *Black Reconstruction* offered the first serious history of the "white worker" ever written in United States.[19] Regarding the women's movement and the labor movement as part and parcel of the story of Reconstruction and as fully beholden to the self-emancipation of slaves expands the approach of Du Bois. Succeeding as a magnificent drama that revises the whole story of emancipation is likewise its goal.

---

19 Du Bois, *Black Reconstruction*, 17–31.

To bring such a range of stories together necessitates relying on generally excellent secondary literatures. In doing so, I have been especially drawn to studies that themselves have begun to expand the narrative of Reconstruction and to challenge boundaries separating one set of studies from others. Eric Foner's brief section on the North in his epic study of Reconstruction, Ellen DuBois's investigations of intersections among race, labor, and women's suffrage, and David Montgomery's effort to move the study of Reconstruction into the North and into working-class history in *Beyond Equality* count as leading examples. But, in every case, the expansion of concerns has remained somewhat circumscribed. The remarks of Montgomery, perhaps his generation's leading US historian, regarding *Beyond Equality* are illustrative of what we are all up against when bounded histories draw us back to old formulations even when we seek to move beyond boundaries. Montgomery prefaced the book by describing its goal as "to reassemble the scattered fragments of this epoch's historical interpretation in a new fashion." Asked by interviewers if he had a "model" when he began to write history, Montgomery replied, "Without a doubt, the most influential scholar was W.E.B. Du Bois. When I think of someone who just towered over everything throughout that period Du Bois comes to mind. That would even be the answer of why I went back to Reconstruction." But when he went back to that period in *Beyond Equality*, race was all but absent from the analysis. I say this not as part of an indictment of individual scholars—quite the opposite in Montgomery's case—but rather as rationale for bending the stick in an opposite direction, toward an account that risks all in order to accommodate the simultaneity of varied lived experiences.[20]

The compact preview of the magnificent drama and the deep tragedy of emancipation that follows serves as an entry to the chapters to come.

20 Ellen DuBois, *Feminism and Suffrage*; Foner, *Reconstruction*, 460–511; David Montgomery, *Beyond Equality: Labor and the Radical Republicans, 1862–1872* (New York: Knopf, 1967); the interview of Montgomery, published in *Radical History Review* in 1980 and conducted by Paul Buhle and Mark Naison, is archived at rhr.dukejournals.org, p. 50.

The revolutionary self-emancipation of US slaves flew in the face of all hardheaded political calculation and changed everything for a time. If anything seemed impossible in the 1850s political universe, it was the immediate, unplanned, and uncompensated emancipation of four million slaves. The case for such "immediatism" had long been ably made, but only a tiny minority of white voters were persuaded. In much of the country, it was perilous to even make the case. Indeed, the world's history underlined the impossibility of immediate freedom for slaves with no payment to masters; nowhere in history had so large a revolutionary seizure of property taken place as that eventuating from the general strike of slaves seeking their own freedom, which made possible the Emancipation Proclamation and the Thirteenth Amendment. By 1870, ex-slaves had become equal citizens constitutionally. No wonder freedpeople described a "Coming of the Lord" made flesh by their own actions. An impressive act of mass theology performed by a people denied literacy and kept from the Bible found them knowing just where to turn in Leviticus for a description of emancipation as part of Jubilee, a cyclical time of liberation, of abolition, and of mechanisms of redress that specifically included land redistribution. Referring to Jubilee, rather than simply emancipation and Reconstruction, in the plotting of *Seizing Freedom* emphasizes the role of slaves in both making freedom and making meaning of freedom.[21]

The frame for retelling the impossible drama of emancipation thus needs to be more surely focused on the centrality of slaves and freedpeople but also explosively expanded to account for how the impossible freedom of ex-slaves transformed and threatened to revolutionize the entire US nation. Unlike most general histories of Reconstruction, *Seizing Freedom* will include the histories of social movements among Indians, poor whites

---

21 Matthew James Zacharias Harper, "Living in God's Time: African-American Faith and Politics in Post-Emancipation North Carolina" (PhD dissertation: University of North Carolina at Chapel Hill, 2009). For "Coming of the Lord," see Du Bois, *Black Reconstruction*, 84. On immediatism, see David Brion Davis, "The Emergence of Immediatism in British and American Antislavery Thought," *The Mississippi Valley Historical Review* 49 (September 1962), 209–30.

in the South, Irish nationalists in the United States, and especially wage
laborers and women. The last two of these groups are especially central
for the ways that they were directly and systematically inspired by the Civil
War and emancipation to consider what a Jubilee would consist of for
them. Both the women's suffrage movement and the labor movement were
completely renewed, in some ways even created, by such revolutionary
inspirations. Liberation coincided with the carnage of the war, which
created hosts of disabled veterans and severed the hard-wired connections
of white manhood to ability and independence on which the republicanism of the early United States had been premised. The resulting
emancipation from whiteness was broad and deep.

Prior to the Civil War, if there was an idea rivaling the immediate emancipation of slaves for sheer implausibility in US politics, it was the notion
that women would vote. At the inaugural 1848 women's rights convention
in Seneca Falls, suffrage almost seemed too much to demand to even the
few hundred activist delegates. Frederick Douglass's pro-suffrage appear-
ance helped ensure that a suffrage plank passed but with the slimmest
hopes of success. The unpaid women's work of caring labor and social
reproduction, along with their keeping farms and workshops productive,
had been a less-than-acknowledged reality in the antebellum years. The
Civil War changed that, as the heroism of women in "loyal" organizations
volunteering to nurse, sew, fund-raise, and more led to the casting of wom-
en's rights as recompense for patriotic labor. Association with abolitionists
put feminist leaders like Susan B. Anthony and Elizabeth Cady Stanton
in proximity to the impossible triumph and moral authority of emancipation as they were transforming women's organizations from war work
to women's rights activism. Suffrage became the key to a Jubilee for women
for Anthony, Stanton, and those around their *Revolution* newspaper.[22]

---

22 Frederick Douglass, "The Rights of Women," *The North Star* (July 28, 1848). Marjorie Spruill
Wheeler, ed., *One Woman, One Vote: Rediscovering the Women's Suffrage Movement* (Troutdale, OR:
NewSage Press, 1995), 9; Ellen DuBois, *Feminism and Suffrage,* 53–125; LeeAnn Whites, *Gender
Matters: Civil War, Reconstruction, and the Making of the New South* (New York: Palgrave, 2005), 25–44.

At the same time, the organized labor movement began to develop a sense that its patriotism ought to deliver a Jubilee for wage workers. The experience of patriotic and coerced wartime sacrifices generated debates in the labor press on the nation's obligation to workingmen even as fighting continued. Very quickly, the eight-hour working day became the centerpiece of dreams about and demands for the impossible. (The ten-hour day was at the time the reasonable and established goal.) The establishment of a third of the day, and half of waking hours, as time controlled by workers seemed a step toward enabling the education, dignity, and organization on which all further reform might rest. Ira Steward, a machinist and old antislavery fighter, became with his wife Mary the unschooled intellectuals for a movement attracting hundreds of thousands into Eight-Hour Leagues and laying the basis for the National Labor Union (NLU). The Stewards developed the idea that the shorter day was a continuation of antislavery work, a position bolstered by the support of Wendell Phillips and other abolitionist leaders. By the late 1860s, many industrial and industrializing states had passed eight-hour laws, however bereft of enforcement provisions.[23]

These war- and emancipation-inspired insurgencies—one could add others, including the formation of a pro-Union mobilization of Indians from the Five Tribes who, often in defiance of leaders supporting the Confederacy, united across tribal and racial lines into a fighting force and the stirring eight-hour strike of Chinese workers on the Transcontinental Railroad—raised possibilities for something like a nineteenth-century Rainbow Coalition, seeking to bring together the nation's aggrieved. Organic and longstanding ties, personified in figures like Stanton, Douglass, Phillips, the Stewards, and Anthony, brought disparate movements into inspired contact, if not unity.[24]

---

23 David Roediger, "Ira Steward and the Anti-Slavery Origins of American Eight Hour Theory," *Labor History* 27 (Summer 1986), esp. 421–2; David A. Zonderman, *Uneasy Allies: Working for Labor Reform in Nineteenth-Century Boston* (Amherst, MA: University of Massachusetts Press, 2011), 76–178; Montgomery, *Beyond Equality*, 296–334; Thomas N. Brown, *Irish-American Nationalism, 1870–1890* (Philadelphia: J. B. Lippincott Company, 1966), 43–4.

24 Mark Lause, *Race and Radicalism in the Union Army* (Urbana, IL: University of Illinois Press,

The links and gaps are best made dramatic and human through a series of glorious and tragic stories in which attempts to bring groups together revealed common inspirations, lived relationships, and real differences. Both Douglass's son and the "lady printers" of *Revolution*, for example, tried to join the typographical union, sparking extended controversies. The NLU opened its meetings, but not its ranks, to Black workers, and its acceptance of a few women workers ended badly. The failure of Reconstruction-era constitutional amendments to provide for women's rights did not keep Douglass from supporting those amendments. Although Douglass personally retained close relationships to women's suffrage activists, distance grew between the movements for African-American freedom and women's rights. Explaining the failure of a Rainbow Coalition to gain traction allows for the reinterpretation of the political history that is the staple of Reconstruction historiography, without losing the context of the force of social movements. If freedpeople, white women, and wage workers were to coalesce and find ways to weigh competing claims, some outside force with independent organizational resources was likely required. This was especially true because far more than half of the potential coalition—women and, in many times and places, African Americans—could not vote. They needed a force not only to bring them into coalition but also into political life.[25]

That outside force—and again this suggests the impossibility of the times and measures our distance from it—came from the Republican Party. New, relatively unformed, and bereft of Lincoln, that party generated in Reconstruction a powerful self-styled "Radical" wing. Often formerly abolitionist, the Radical leaders spearheaded (and then retreated from) efforts to empower women and even to protect Chinese civil rights.

2009); David Montgomery, *The Fall of the House of Labor: The Workplace, the State, and American Labor Activism, 1865–1925* (Cambridge, UK: Cambridge University Press, 1987), 67–8; Manu Vimalassery, "Skew Tracks: Racial Capitalism and the First Transcontinental Railroad" (PhD dissertation, New York University, 2010), 47.

25 See below, Chapter 4.

In the bipartisan campaigns for eight-hour laws and policies, Republicans at times mobilized key support in Northern states. At the same time, as Du Bois marvelously detailed, the Republican Party had another "soul." It was the party not only of racial justice and righteous anti-planter hatred, but also of "big business," of expanding industry, and often of what Alexander Saxton terms "hard" racism against Native Americans. If there had merely been two wings of the Republican Party—one pro-justice and the other pro-development—that would have produced drama enough. Instead, the party's "warring ideals" often existed also inside the brain of the same individual Republican leader or voter. Committed at once to capitalist expansion and to destroying planter power, these allies of the freedpeople far more consistently championed private property than new emancipatory initiatives. They therefore were notoriously slow to support redistribution of land to ex-slaves. Their support for eight-hour laws confined itself to symbolism, with resulting legislation putting the sanctity of contracts above the enforcement of the eight-hour standard.[26]

The more we see the possibility of a broad politics of Jubilee applying, the deeper and broader becomes the tragedy of Reconstruction's unraveling. Black soldiers were relocated from the South long before the 1877 withdrawal of the dwindling presence of federal troops protecting civil rights in the region. African-American "Buffalo Soldiers" ended up famously patrolling the West on behalf of occupations of Native lands. The women's movement, stymied by suffrage's failure, developed sporadic alliances with openly white supremacist Democrats. With land reform forsaken, Black Republicans in the South at times turned to tax increases, not only as a way to fund education but also as a way to break up large estates. But the first victims of such initiatives were often poor whites subsisting largely outside the cash economy. The "revolutionary time" of Jubilee dissipated as dramatically as it had arisen.

---

26 Du Bois, *Black Reconstruction*, 182–235; Montgomery, *Beyond Equality*, 296–334, and Chapter 4 below; Alexander Saxton, *The Rise and Fall of the White Republic: Class Politics and Mass Culture in Nineteenth-Century America* (New York: Verso, 2003 [1990]), 148–53.

The central concerns of the book—telling a good set of stories usually kept apart, showing how the general strike of the slaves changed everything, establishing revolutionary time as a reality in US history, charting the coexistence of drama and tragedy, and thinking through the rise and fall of coalitions—are pursued over its four thematically organized chapters and afterword. Only the first of these, "Turning a World Upside Down: The General Strike of the Slaves, Jubilee, and the Making of a Revolutionary Civil War," takes up the story of a single group. After the stage-setting, world-changing activities of African Americans are understood, their ramifying impact is considered in "Emancipation from Whiteness: Witnessing Disability and Jubilee." The third chapter, "After the Impossible: Eight Hours, Black Labor, Women's Suffrage, and Freedom for All," shows how the self-emancipation of slaves inspired new freedom dreams. The fate of these inspired mobilizations, as they tried to make one freedom movement relate to others and as they retreated from solidarity, forms the subject of a fourth chapter, "Falling Apart: The First Rainbow Coalition and the Waning of Revolutionary Time." An afterword, "Dreams Deferred: Social Tragedies and Hidden Histories in the Longer Run," totals the losses.

But not all was destroyed. Terrible as chain gangs, debt peonage, and Jim Crow were, no "new slavery" followed the defeat of Jubilee. Such an overly pessimistic idea, ironically developing from some of the best recent work on the United States, rests on a loose equation between slavery and the system of segregation, peonage, and convict labor after it, and then between the postwar Jim Crow regime and the current "carceral state" keeping millions of people of color in jail and on probation. Important as this work is, for the history of the late nineteenth century, we need to take seriously Du Bois's characterization of moves "back toward slavery" but not a reinstitution of that horror. Sharecropping was not slavery, and to suppose that it was risks imagining history without moments of lasting self-emancipation. Understanding the broader tragedy of failed solidarities among differently oppressed groups demands that we be more charitable to historical actors (and to ourselves) in the face of defeats. We also see in this history the possibility that realism actually demands more commitment to maintaining alliances, even at the cost of foregoing immediate gains, or of preserving existing advantages for groups constituting the coalition. This possibility—that we often can only win meaningful changes in unshakeable coalition—underpins Angela Davis's recent call to base "the identity on politics rather than the politics on identity." Jubilee, at its best involving both self-emancipation and solidarity, made starts in that direction.[27]

---

27   Douglas A. Blackmon, *Slavery by Another Name: The Re-Enslavement of Black People in America from the Civil War to World War II* (New York: Doubleday, 2008); Michelle Alexander, *The New Jim Crow: Mass Incarceration in the Age of Colorblindness* (New York: The New Press, 2010); Du Bois, *Black Reconstruction*, 580 and 581–710; Marie Gottschalk, "Hiding in Plain Sight: American Politics and the Carceral State," *Annual Review of Political Science* 11 (June 2008), 235–60; Angela Davis, as interviewed by Lisa Lowe, "Reflections on Race, Class, and Gender in the USA," in *The Politics of Culture in the Shadow of Capital*, eds. Lowe and David Lloyd (Durham, NC: Duke University Press, 1997), 318.

Chapter 1

Turning a World Upside Down:
The General Strike of the Slaves, Jubilee, and the Making of a Revolutionary Civil War

*And ye shall hallow the fiftieth year, and proclaim liberty throughout
all the land unto all the inhabitants thereof: it shall be a jubilee unto
you; and ye shall return every man unto his possession, and ye shall
return every man unto his family.*
Leviticus 25:10

On the eve of the Civil War, but two years before the Emancipation Proclamation, the radical abolitionist Wendell Phillips expressed hope but also registered a grim reality. Detailing what the Republican Party was up against if it hoped to "undermine the Slave Power," Phillips argued

> that power is composed, 1st, of the inevitable influence of wealth,
> $2,000,000,000, —the worth of the slaves in the Union,—so much
> capital drawing to it the sympathy of all other capital; 2d, of the
> artificial aristocracy created by the three-fifths slave basis of the
> Constitution; &d, by the potent and baleful prejudice of color.

In fact Phillips underestimated. The actual figure was $3 billion in 1860, equal to the combined value of all capital invested in manufacturing, railroads, and banks, as well as all currency in circulation and all federal

expenditures. Wealth in slaves and real estate in the slaveholding states—
the law little distinguished between the two—exceeded wealth in real
estate in the free states by about a fifth.[1]

Phillips's appreciation of the forces arrayed against liberation reflected
a knowledge of the recent past and of the broader record of the nation.
His nuanced position typified that of abolitionists generally. The long
slouch of US history toward emancipation had resulted in a profoundly
ingrained strain of pessimism among their number, and the years just
before 1860 drove the message home. In 1850, the North acquiesced to a
Fugitive Slave Act. In the *Dred Scott* decision of 1857, the Supreme Court
ruled in favor of the property rights of masters who had transported slaves
to free states but held them in bondage upon return to slaveholding areas.
The Court famously went further, adding that Black Americans had "no
rights which the white man is bound to respect."[2] The Southern dignitaries
who gathered for the execution of the abolitionist John Brown for his
seemingly forlorn 1859 attempt to foment slave rebellion had reason, as
historian William McKee Evans observes, "to crow." No one would have
predicted that, three years later, the federal government would begin doing
"what spectators in 1859 [at Brown's execution] considered criminal or
insane, the freeing and arming of slaves."[3]

Douglass himself greatly admired Brown but knew the impossibility of
the Harpers Ferry raid succeeding in the face of repression and popular
opinion. He decided not to join the adventure but nonetheless was a target
of the backlash. Douglass's associations with the planners of the Harpers
Ferry raid made it likely enough that he would himself be indicted that

---

1   Wendell Phillips, *Lectures, Speeches, and Letters* (Boston: Lee and Shepard, 1894), 362–3 reprinting
his January 20, 1861 lecture "Disunion." For the figures on wealth, see Steven Deyle, "The Domestic
Slave Trade in America" in *The Chattel Principle*, ed. Walter Johnson (New Haven, CT: Yale University Press, 2004), 96.

2   For an acute elaboration of these points, see Stephen Kantrowitz, "The Other Thirteenth Amendment: Free African Americans and the Constitution That Wasn't," *Marquette Law Review* 93 (Summer
2010), 1366–71; *Dred Scott v. Sandford* (1857), 60 US (19 How.), 393 and 406–7.

3   William McKee Evans, *Open Wound: The Long View of Race in America* (Urbana, IL: University
of Illinois Press, 2009), 148 and 147–61.

he fled into Canada and then Britain, finding safety from the "Slave Power" within the US government for six months in the wake of Brown's capture.[4] Nonviolent strategies for emancipation seemed hardly more promising. At the very moment when electoral politics opened unprecedented fissures between North and South in 1860, abolitionist celebration had to be muted. Just before Lincoln's inauguration, a proposed Thirteenth Amendment made it through Congress with the required two-thirds majority for constitutional change and began ratification by states. Unlike the emancipationist Thirteenth Amendment that became law four years later, its predecessor threatened to make slavery endless. The measure, historian Stephen Kantrowitz writes, "prohibited any amendment to the Constitution giving Congress the power to interfere with or abolish slavery where it was currently lawful." Proposed legislation explicitly barring Black voting and office-holding at any level of government and authorizing federal-state cooperation to forcibly colonize "such free negroes and mulattoes as the several states may wish to have removed" followed. These planks garnered more than 40 percent of Congress's votes in late February 1861, despite many slave-state representatives absenting themselves from Congress by that time. Far from being only a time of promise, the period just before and just after the election of Lincoln was one in which slavery and white supremacy at times threatened to become more entrenched.[5]

Although some historians now argue that Republicans entered office with a strategy for the emancipation of slaves in place, such positions reflect wishful thinking much advantaged by hindsight. General William Tecumseh Sherman's polemic with a Confederate general captured moderate Northern views at the start of the war all too well. He wrote that Rebels had attacked Union troops whose very job was "to protect your people from negroes and Indians." The pro-Lincoln satire and news

---

4 William S. McFeely, *Frederick Douglass* (New York: W.W. Norton, 1991), 186–209.
5 Kantrowitz, "The Other Thirteenth Amendment," 1371 and 1367–74.

magazine *Vanity Fair* delighted in the president's rebuffing of abolitionists through much of 1862. Its September cartoon *The Monotonous
Minstrel* (see p. 94) showed the president dismissing a horn-playing
Horace Greeley with a pet monkey or a Black child in tow. The caption
had Lincoln saying, "Go away you tiresome vagrant! It's always the same
old croaking tune, 'Abolition, Abolition, Marching On.'" The magazine's
editorial poem "Abe and Abolition" began, "Cheers for old Abe—in
him the nation trusts/Unmoved by Abolition's hue and cry."[6]

The forces arrayed against freedom were longstanding and powerfully
supported by material realities. Lincoln's first inaugural address made no
objection to the logic of the proposed proslavery Thirteenth Amendment,
calling it "implied constitutional law."[7] From 1790 onward and more
explicitly in the 1850s, the nation based itself on respect for slave property,
making the decision in the *Dred Scott* case as plausible as it was chilling.
Indeed, the steep imbalance of the national economy toward wealth in
slaves combined with respect for and full legal recognition of slave property to render the accepted "realistic" alternatives to the John Brown idea
of how freedom would come even more fanciful than they had been when
put forward by the Founding Fathers. Any politically imaginable emancipation had to be gradual, planned, and compensated, as Britain's had
been. The incredible growth in slave population and prices in the nineteenth century left compensation especially problematic. Much of the
profit of the slave system, managerial advice literature insisted, lay in the
"increase" in slaves' numbers and value. That increase made the problem
of abolition all the more intractable. While Lincoln and Congress con-
templated compensated emancipation schemes in the Border States early
in the war and included compensation to "loyal" slaveholders in 1862 in

---

6 Sherman as quoted in Edmund Wilson, *Patriotic Gore: Studies in the Literature of the American
Civil War* (New York: Oxford University Press, 1962), 189. For the most extreme expression of the
"emancipation from above" position, see James Oakes, "A War of Emancipation," *Jacobin* (September
25, 2012) at jacobinmag.com. "The Monotonous Minstrel" is in *Vanity Fair* 6 (September 6, 2012),
120; for "Abe and Abolition," see *Vanity Fair* 5 (June 7, 1862), 274.
7 Kantrowitz, "The Other Thirteenth Amendment," 1371.

the legislation freeing slaves in the District of Columbia, mathematics very much militated against applying such a solution nationally.[8]

Realism in politics meant support for the idea of sacred property rights over slaves, to the return of fugitives, and to the permissibility of fighting the expansion, but not the existence, of the slave system. The policy of returning slaves to masters, which Lincoln for a time approved, changed rather speedily on paper with an August 1861 order from the secretary of war. However, local applications varied greatly and the abandonment by Union forces of refugee women and children in undefended camps led to their return to slavery, or worse. Abolitionists, for all their petitioning, brilliance, and direct-action successes in creating prewar support for escaped slaves facing recapture, had not dented the consensus that immediate, uncompensated emancipation was the third rail of US politics, consigning its supporters to marginality in Northern elections and keeping them from running or even speaking in the South. Douglass announced in the summer of 1860 that he would "sincerely hope" for a Republican triumph in that year's presidential election but added that he could not support Lincoln. Douglass opted instead for the radical abolitionist candidacy of Gerrit Smith. In doing so, he accepted marginality but not because he was a gloomy and rigid figure trapped in the irrational "posthumous hold" of John Brown, as one recent account charges. Instead, Douglass was registering the reality that the emerging political possibilities had not yet overcome assumptions that made abolition impossible.[9]

---

8 Kate Masur, *An Example for All the Land: Emancipation and the Struggle over Equality in Washington, D.C.* (Chapel Hill, NC: University of North Carolina Press, 2010), 25; on failed Border States' efforts at compensated emancipation, see Eugene H. Berwanger, "Lincoln's Constitutional Dilemma: Emancipation and Black Suffrage," *Journal of the Abraham Lincoln Association* 5 (1983). For a discussion of the "increase," see Elizabeth Esch and David Roediger, *The Production of Difference: Race and the Management of Labor in US History* (New York: Oxford University Press, 2012), 45. On Britain, see Nicholas Draper, *The Price of Emancipation: Slave-Ownership, Compensation, and British Society at the End of Slavery* (Cambridge, UK: Cambridge University Press, 2010).

9 James Oakes, *The Radical and the Republican: Frederick Douglass, Abraham Lincoln, and the Triumph of Antislavery Politics* (New York: W.W. Norton, 2007), 99 and 87–132; for less judgmental accounts, see McFeely, *Frederick Douglass*, 208, and David W. Blight, *Frederick Douglass' Civil War: Keeping Faith in Jubilee* (Baton Rouge, LA: Louisiana State University Press, 1989), 56–62; Douglass,

Indeed, this chapter takes Douglass's situated wisdom as a point of entry into how war became revolution and then dramatizes how slaves secured and experienced freedom and learned its limits.

A SMALL JOKE AND THE LINCOLN-DOUGLASS DEBATE

When the war began, Lincoln vindicated Douglass's pessimism. The president's position well into the conflict, even as military challenges mounted, remained that the "paramount object in this struggle is to save the Union, and is not either to save or to destroy slavery. If I could save the Union without freeing any slave I would do it, and if I could save it by freeing all the slaves I would do it; and if I could save it by freeing some and leaving others alone I would also do that."[10] Douglass took to describing the conflict as a "war in the interests of slavery on both sides," with the South openly fighting for its peculiar institution and Lincoln promising not to interfere with it where it existed. "The slave who loved us," Douglass wrote, "was hated . . . as the nation went in search of the means of defeat." Such biting critiques began to connect military and moral decisions immediately. In May 1861 Douglass editorialized on "How to End the War," insisting that *carrying the war into Africa* was the key to peace and freedom. In doing so, he both adopted John Brown's strategy of liberating

---

"Slavery and the Irrepressible Conflict: An Address Delivered in Geneva, New York, on 1 August 1860" reprinted in *The Frederick Douglass Papers: Speeches, Debates, and Interviews, 1855–63*, Series 1, Volume 3, eds. Blassingame and others (New Haven, CT: Yale University Press, 1985), 380–1. See also Oakes, *Freedom National: The Destruction of Slavery in the United States, 1861–1865* (New York: W.W. Norton, 2012), 210. On returning slaves, see Barbara Jeanne Fields, *Slavery and Freedom on the Middle Ground: Maryland during the Nineteenth Century* (New Haven, CT: Yale University Press, 1985), 107–8; Thavolia Glymph, "Under the Shields of the Law of Nations," lecture to the Sesquicentennial of Emancipation Lecture Series at University of Illinois—Urbana-Champaign, January 31, 2013.

10   Abraham Lincoln, "Letter to Horace Greeley" (August 22, 1862) reprinted in *The Collected Works of Abraham Lincoln*, Volume 5, ed. Roy P. Basler, 388. More generally see the provocative, neglected account of the early war in Lerone Bennett, *Forced into Glory: Abraham Lincoln's White Dream* (Chicago: Johnson Publishing Company, 2000), 337–87 with useful remarks on Douglass at 340.

and arming slaves and italicized the phrase to signal that he was directly echoing Brown's own words.[11]

A month later, in castigating Lincoln's policies as weak, Douglass challenged the idea that whiteness held the key to able and manly citizenship. The Union was "fighting with one hand" because it abjured emancipation: "What a spectacle of blind, unreasoning prejudice and pusillanimity is this!" With the "national edifice . . . on fire," Douglass held, "every man who can carry a bucket of water, or remove a brick, is wanted." Nevertheless, he continued, "those who have the care of the building, having a profound respect for the feeling of the national burglars who set the building on fire, are determined that the flames shall only be extinguished by Indo-Caucasian hands, and to have the building burnt rather than save it by means of any other."[12] The real Lincoln-Douglass debate was then on, focusing squarely on what was possible.

Douglass's position in this pivotal time deserves close attention, as he was the most celebrated and forceful figure arguing in print for turning the Civil War into a revolution. (On the ground, Harriet Tubman was the key figure in such initiatives.) As an ex-slave, Douglass could make his case with special force, insisting that he knew the slave's desire for freedom, and the rigidity of the master class, could create the possibility for just such a transformation in the war's meaning. Douglass appreciated both the ways that longstanding property-driven bargains with injustice exerted pressure to keep abolition impossible and how the present movement of slaves made attacking slavery logical and even necessary. In registering both truths, he often appears to modern historians as contradictory. Recent

---

11   Frederick Douglass, *The Life and Times of Frederick Douglass* (Hartford, CT: Park Publishing, 1882), 427; Douglass, "How to End the War," *Douglass' Monthly*, reprinted in *The Life and Writings of Frederick Douglass*, Volume 3, ed. Philip S. Foner (New York: International Publishers, 1952), 94–6; for Brown's promise to "carry the war into Africa," see David Reynolds, *John Brown, Abolitionist* (New York: Vintage, 2006), 202. See Du Bois, *Black Reconstruction in America* (New York: The Free Press, 1992 [1935]), 61, for a brilliant recollection of Douglass's words and logic on the war and the preservation of slavery.

12   Douglass, "Fighting Rebels with Only One Hand," *Douglass' Monthly* (September 1861), reprinted in *The Life and Writings of Frederick Douglass*, Volume 3, ed. Foner, 152 and 151–4.

scholarship on the relationship of Lincoln and Douglass searches in the psychology of the two men—mostly Douglass—to explain the wide gulf between them through much of 1862. Douglass, seen as practicing the "politics of hope" in the 1850s, is cast by David Blight and James Oakes as moody and mercurial in the early war. In their view, he indulged in impatient millennial hope and misunderstood the president's determination to press matters to their conclusion. Douglass's religious views and his psychology, forged in the relation of master and slave, allegedly made for a fear of compromise. Blight's emphases are particularly puzzling in that, at times, he realizes that more economical and elegant explanations are available. Douglass, he more persuasively wrote at one point, sought "remorseless revolutionary struggle," just what Lincoln "did not want."[13]

Indeed, for all his pessimism, Douglass proved far more able than Lincoln to anticipate the impossible speed with which liberation would come. He could imagine that the Civil War might see the suspension of long-standing proslavery political and economic common sense. He saw that events could unfold at the breakneck, millennial pace of what historians of the French Revolution have called "revolutionary time," transforming the very notion of how history moved.[14] Douglass had a double advantage in seeing the end of impossibility because he knew firsthand the vulnerability of the master class, the desire for freedom among slaves, and the connections between the two.

Douglass's insights into the weaknesses of masters are perhaps best illustrated by his embrace of a complicated little joke. With the Civil War scarcely six months old, Union successes in the low country of South Carolina had opened the possibility of a new world. Frederick Douglass

---

13   Oakes, *The Radical and the Republican*, 159–65; Blight, *Frederick Douglass' Civil War*, 26–121, esp. 82, n. 4; David W. Blight, *Frederick Douglass and Abraham Lincoln: A Relationship in Language, Politics, and Memory* (Milwaukee, WI: Marquette University Press, 2001), 10; on Tubman, see Clinton, *Harriet Tubman*, 140–61.

14   Lynn Hunt, "The World We Have Gained: The Future of the French Revolution," *The American Historical Review* 108: 1 (February 2003).

captured as much when *Douglass' Monthly* printed this waggish advertisement from Beaufort, South Carolina:

> $500 REWARD.—Rund away from me on de 7th ob dis month, my massa Julian Rhett. Massa Rhett am five feet 'leven inches high, big shoulders, brack har, curly shaggy whiskers, low forehead, an' dark face. He make big fuss when he go 'mong de gemmen, he talk ver big, and use de name ob de Lord all de time. Calls heself "Suddern gemmen," but I suppose will try now to pass heself off as a brack man or mulatter. Massa Rhett has a deep scar on his shoulder from a fight [and a] scratch cross de left eye, made by my Dinah when he tried to whip her.

The best-known citation of this incredible prank suggests that Frederick Douglass's publication broke the story in the North, and the text certainly reflects Douglass's early desire to show that the unwillingness of the North to attack slavery could not withstand the pressures of combat and the indomitability of slaves. It would even be easy to imagine Douglass as the author of the pointed joke.[15]

However, the mocking offer of a reward dated from November 9, 1861, long before *Douglass' Monthly* featured it in January 1862. In the interim, its circulation in the white mainstream press illustrated the fact that openings toward African-American freedom were not only rapturously experienced but also endlessly represented, for a considerable time fascinating white readers. Republications of the Rhett text—the authorship remains unknown, although a South Carolina ex-slave named Sambo Rhett does appear as a petitioner in South Carolina records in 1863—anticipated the various ways that modern scholars of humor, social history, and even folklore would later interpret it. To an anti-African-American

15 As reproduced and discussed in Leon F. Litwack, *Been in the Storm So Long: The Aftermath of Slavery* (New York: Vintage, 1980), 112–13; for Douglass's publication of the ad, see *Douglass' Monthly* 5 (January 1862), 580.

paper like the *New York Evening Express*, the ad signaled the consequences of failures to always return runaway slaves to masters. It seemed ominous reportage, not parody. The advertisement's first publication in a book regarded it as "clever travestie" by an ex-slave. A military camp publication could likewise catch the humor.[16]

In other media as well, the figure of the runaway master found a place. The classic expression of the serious implications of his absence and of the new ways in which slaves were present appears in Henry P. Moore's 1862 photograph "J.P. Seabrook's Flower Garden." Taken on South Carolina's Edisto Island, by then under Union control, the shot looks down from the high point of the plantation's Big House—the panoptical spot from which the master would survey his flowers and the slaves' labor. But there is no master. Instead, work proceeds quite well without him. From a pedestal that "might have been intended for a neoclassical statue," a young African American salutes a Union officer. As visual theorist Nicholas Mirzoeff points out in his discussion of the photograph, the gesture expresses the "impossible" transformation that had occurred and the role of African Americans in making meaning of that change. The runaway master was likewise a figure of fun in Henry Work's popular 1862 song "Kingdom Coming."[17]

Douglass's own reprinting of the Sambo Rhett joke, told in the minstrel tones he generally despised, was by far its most interesting use. In *Douglass'*

---

16   For Sambo Rhett in a South Carolina petition in 1863, see Digital Library of American Slavery at library.uncg.edu; for the *Evening Express* version and one from the *Waterville Times* reprints, see fultonhistory.com; for "clever travestie," see Frank Moore, *Rebellion Record: A Diary of American Events: Poetry and Incidents*, Volume 3 (New York: Van Nostrand, 1862) and *Black River Herald* (December 20, 1861); B.A. Botkin, ed., *A Civil War Treasury of Tales, Legends, and Folklore* (Lincoln, NE: University of Nebraska Press, 2000 [1960]), 57–8; for a widely circulated version from *Leslie's Illustrated Newspaper* (January 11, 1862), see Cameron C. Nickels, *Civil War Humor* (Jackson, MS: University of Mississippi Press, 2010), 116–17.

17   Nicholas Mirzoeff, *The Right to Look: A Counterhistory of Visuality* (Durham, NC: Duke University Press, 2011), 167 and (for the quotations) 168. The words and sheet music to "Kingdom Coming" are available at masshist.org. For the runaway master in another venue, see "A New Plantation Song," *Vanity Fair* 5 (March 16, 1862), 129 and "The Latest Contraband of War" in the digital American Memory collection of the Library of Congress at memory.loc.gov.

Monthly, the advertisement acknowledged magnificent but uneven transformation at the very time that the publication's editorial line was
understandably unsmiling in its bitter denunciations of the timidity of
the Lincoln administration. As such, the humor illustrated Sigmund
Freud's contention that jokes function in ways that are inherently related
to rebellion in their refusal to accept the existing order's miseries. The
joke insisted on the possibility of something different emerging even
when that possibility appeared totally blocked from logical realization.
Indeed, it apprehended that the world had turned upside down but that
the master's return still seemed a threat. Its closing paragraph offered a
$100 reward for the master's safe return but $500 if he were shown dead.
The master, in the case of Sambo Rhett, was gone, and the slaves could
rejoice. But their freedom was not recognized. Indeed, as South Carolina
historian and archivist JoAnn Zeise has observed, Union forces kept
meticulous records of wages owed for labor by slaves in occupied areas
of South Carolina early in the war not in order to pay the slaves but to
be able to eventually repay their masters.[18] As Douglass's hopes soared,
he had work to do.

   More important than his appreciation of the vulnerability of slave-
owners was Douglass's knowledge that slaves were ready to conduct
remorseless struggle and had begun to wage it. Douglass's own views took
the slave as a guiding star; he sought to keep faith with and to trust in
them. His recollections of the dawn of the war in the last of his three
autobiographies spoke with startling candor: "From the first, I, for one
saw in this war the end of slavery and truth requires me to say that my
interest in the success of the North was largely due to this belief." This
view was not unique. An African-American newspaper in New York
headed its reaction to the early war with "Second American Revolution"

---

18   Sigmund Freud, *Jokes and Their Relation to the Unconscious* (New York: W.W. Norton, 1990
[1905]), 154; JoAnn Zeise, "Dawn of Freedom: The Freedmen's Town of Mitchelville on Hilton Head
Island, South Carolina" presented to the Institute for African-American Research Seminar, University
of South Carolina (October 24, 2012).

and assured readers, "This Revolution has begun, and is in progress. We say so because the *Nation* has come into direct physical conflict with the slaveholders!" For Douglass, the war not only changed the prospects for slaves being freed but also raised the possibility that they would free themselves, in the process deciding the war and transforming the nation. Weeks after the shooting started, he offered a prescription for moral and military success: "*Let the slaves and free colored people be called into service, and formed into a liberating army*, to march into the South and raise the banner of Emancipation among the slaves." Even his insistence that he should be able to be glad amid frustration and forlorn amid joy kept faith with Douglass's fiercely dialectical understanding of the moods and rhythms of slave culture and its blues sensibilities, brilliantly explicated in Sterling Stuckey's recent work.[19]

For Douglass, what slaves thought of the meaning of the war mattered more than what Lincoln thought. Douglass's own life bespoke the fact that the actions of a relatively few slaves could be catalytic. Stealing himself away from slavery and then standing against it, he had taken up the role of the militant fugitive, a role that the Trinidadian historian C.L.R. James described as the "self-expressive presence . . . embodying the nationally traumatic experience of bondage and freedom, [without whom] anti-slavery would have been a sentiment only."[20] Douglass knew that slaves could be counted on to show up as opportunities for freedom arose. They showed up early, while the federal government was still toying with returning fugitives to their masters.

---

19 Douglass, *The Life and Times of Frederick Douglass*, 335 ("from the first"); David Roediger, "Why Douglass Knew" in *The Meaning of Slavery in the North*, eds. Roediger and Martin Blatt (New York: Garland, 1998), 177–85; Evans, *Open Wound*, 150 ("Second American Revolution"); Douglass, "How to End the War," 94; Stuckey, "The Great Form before Frederick Douglass" a public lecture at the University of South Carolina History Center (March 23, 2012) as keynote of the Whiteness, Blackness, Racial Formation in Comparative Perspective Conference.
20   C.L.R. James, "The Atlantic Slave Trade and Slavery" in *Amistad 1*, eds. John A. Williams and Charles F. Harris (New York: Vintage, 1970), 142.

WHAT SLAVES DECIDED

Before major battles had even been fought, slaves left slavery—just three at first, fleeing into the Virginia camp of Union general Benjamin Butler. The general could see slaves being used to construct Rebel military fortifications across the lines dividing the two forces. A local Confederate commander owned the slaves who fled to the Union side. Butler, needing "able-bodied" men, could not bring himself to return the fugitives. Instead he sent the master a receipt for the slaves, nominating them as "contraband of war." Douglass skewered the new language as morally opaque in the extreme, finding "contraband" to be "a name that will apply better to a pistol than a human being." Lewis Lockwood, a missionary to refugees at Fortress Monroe, similarly denounced "contrabandism" as "government slavery." Later approved by the secretary of war, the policy preserved the norms of slave property even as it opened new possibilities to resist bondage. Slaves were putatively to be returned or the disloyal owner compensated after an armistice. As did commanders in South Carolina, Butler's subordinates recorded hours of labor by contrabands, with the convoluted rationale that masters were entitled to compensation for labor done to put down the rebellion they pursued. The North's military necessities governed the process, which was avowedly not emancipatory, though Harriet Tubman's assistance of General Butler illustrated the ways that African Americans struggled to use the contraband policy to expand freedom. Such policy did not apply everywhere or consistently protect those who had left slavery. The nurse Cornelia Hancock wrote to her sister on the day the Emancipation Proclamation took effect that she had recently encountered slave catchers operating in the northern Virginia camp in which she worked. They prowled about protected by a pass given by the general in charge. Douglass complained that even Butler was complicit in the slave-catching and in suppressing slave revolts. Tubman, equally skeptical of Lincoln's slowgoing policies on emancipation, nonetheless went to the Sea Islands of South Carolina long before freedom was announced, possessed of a spiritual vision that the war would end slavery. She functioned as a nurse armed with a rifle, as a spy for Union forces, and as an organizer and strategist abetting mass escapes by slaves.[21]

Had flight from slavery been rare, decisions to seize contraband might have been bureaucratic procedures following captures of slaves in Union victories. But slaves came by the thousands and, ultimately, the hundreds of thousands. Their uneven, protracted, and thoughtful motion—what W.E.B. Du Bois called "the general strike of the slaves"—placed slaves' humanity and ability at history's center. In May 1862, the South Carolina slave Robert Smalls commandeered a Confederate military transport named the the *Planter*, delivering it, artillery, an important Rebel code book, and himself to the Union side. The skill of piloting, an ingenious disguise, and the fascinating defection of a slave presumed to be privileged and loyal fueled newspaper interest in the sensational story. Other dramas were witnessed within a smaller circle, but knowledge of them likewise diffused. The commander in Memphis in the early war began with hopes of keeping slavery from being an issue in a war for union, but the desires

21   Louis S. Gerteis, *From Contraband to Freedman: Federal Policy Toward Southern Blacks, 1861–1865* (Westport, CT: Greenwood, 1973), 12–19; Oakes, *The Radical and the Republican*, 144 ("able-bodied") and 143–9; Douglass, "Our Army Still Slave-Catching," *Douglass' Monthly* (September 1861) reprinted in *The Life and Writings of Frederick Douglass*, Volume 3, ed. Foner, 151–4; see also Douglass, "Negroes and the National War Effort," reprinted in *The Frederick Douglass Papers*, Volume 3, eds. Blassingame et al., 594; "Cornelia Hancock to Her Sister" (January 1, 1863) in Cornelia Hancock Letters at Clements Library at University of Michigan; Clinton, *Harriet Tubman*, 147–9; Earl Conrad, *Harriet Tubman: Negro Soldier and Abolitionist* (New York: International Publishers, 1942), 33–42. For Douglass on contraband, see his "Fighting the Rebels with One Hand: An Address Delivered in Philadelphia, Pennsylvania, on 14 January 1862," reprinted in *The Frederick Douglass Papers*, Volume 3, eds. Blassingame et al., 478. Lockwood reprinted from a January 29, 1862 letter in Ira Berlin et al., eds., *Freedom: A Documentary History of Emancipation, 1861–1867*, Series 1, Volume 2, *The Wartime Genesis of Free Labor: The Upper South* (Cambridge, UK: Cambridge University Press, 1993), 112; on reimbursing masters, see Butler's pronouncement of May 27, 1861, in Berlin et al, eds., *Free at Last: A Documentary History of Slavery, Freedom, and the Civil War* (New York: New Press, 1992), 9–10; Zeise, "Dawn of Freedom." For the extent of slaves escaping bondage under the new conditions of war, see Yael A. Sternhell, *Routes of War: The World of Movement in the Confederate South* (Cambridge, MA: Harvard University Press, 2012), 95–107.

for labor, and for depriving the South of labor, soon transformed Memphis into a center of contrabands and then of Black troops.[22]

The passing of the Second Confiscation Act and the Militia Act in July 1862 committed Lincoln to more or less the John Brown strategy of permanently liberating and arming slaves. But the long delay by Lincoln ensured that the public's debates over whether emancipation was impossible and/or imperative matured. Freedom followed from the slave's own heroism. Emancipation contributed to the national interest, to victory, and to making meaning of a protracted bloodbath that had come to seem more disabling than ennobling. The idiosyncratic but influential intellectual Orestes Brownson so appreciated the popular need for such meaning that he welcomed the Emancipation Proclamation as a war measure even though he insisted that he did not support emancipation.[23]

Because of the motion of slaves—even in the face of highly public executions such as those following slave rebellions—the war had become something different. After the Second Confiscation Act, Karl Marx predicted, "So far we have witnessed the first act of the Civil War—the constitutional waging of war. The second act, the revolutionary waging of war is now at hand." The Pennsylvania Republican Thaddeus Stevens urged just before the Emancipation Proclamation, "Free every slave—slay every traitor—burn every rebel mansion" in a conflict that he now saw as a "radical revolution" destined to "remodel our institutions." That revolution would ultimately confiscate more property—the freed slaves had been just that—than any revolution in all history prior to the twentieth century. Douglass became a military recruiter of Black troops.

---

22 Du Bois, *Black Reconstruction*, 55–83 and 128; Andrew Billingsley, *Yearning to Breathe Free: Robert Smalls of South Carolina and His Families* (Columbia, SC: University of South Carolina Press, 2007), 53–74; Kevin R. Hardwick, "'Your Old Father Abe Lincoln Is Dead and Damned': Black Soldiers and the Memphis Race Riot of 1866," *Journal of Social History* 18 (Fall 1993), 111.

23 Evans, *Open Wound*, 153–62; Fredrickson, *Inner Civil War*, 114–15; for Douglass glorying in troops' songs of Brown, see his "Pictures and Progress: An Address Delivered in Boston, Massachusetts, on 3 December 1861," in *The Frederick Douglass Papers*, Volume 3, eds. Blassingame et al., 471.

Nearly 200,000 African Americans joined the army or navy in the cause
of the Union, 81 percent of whom were from the slaveholding states,
many newly emancipated and armed. Douglass maintained that January
1, when the Emancipation Proclamation took effect, was "incomparably
greater" than July 4.[24]

The impossibility of the slave's motion from bondage to soldiering had
seemed clear well into the war. As late as 1862, Lieutenant Charles Francis
Adams, whose family represented the intersecting power of high culture
and politics in the United States, registered how little sense the idea of
Black soldiers still made to even some Yankee elites. He thought that with
great and wasteful expense "a soldiery equal to the native Hindoo regiments" could be created in about five years. He added, "It won't pay." But,
by July 1864, the same Adams had begun to admire Black troops whom
he saw in action. He wrote, "They seem to have behaved just as well and
as badly as the rest and to have suffered far more severely." Others, seeing
the brutal wage discrimination such troops faced and their courage both
in confronting the Rebel enemy and in their direct attempts to emancipate
slaves, had a still higher opinion of African-American soldiers. Among
freedpeople, such soldiers enjoyed prestige reflecting their valor in battle
and their roles in defending civil rights at home. The great historian of
African-American troops, Dudley Taylor Cornish, wrote, "The Negro
soldier proved that a slave could become a man." Douglass's own 1863
broadside "Men of Color to Arms" insisted that African-Americans would
emancipate themselves.[25]

---

24 Deyle, "The Domestic Slave Trade in America," 96; Evans, *Open Wound*, 154 (quoting Stevens);
for Marx, see Richard Enmale, ed., *The Civil War in the United States* (New York: International Publishers, 1937), 200; John David Smith, ed., *Black Soldiers in Blue: African-American Troops in the Civil
War* (Chapel Hill, NC: University of North Carolina Press, 2002), 8; Mitch Kachun, *Festivals of
Freedom: Memory and Meaning in African-American Emancipation Celebrations, 1808–1915*
(Amherst, MA: University of Massachusetts Press, 2003), 209 ("incomparably greater"). On public
executions of those fleeing slavery, see Sternhell, *Routes of War*, 127.
25 Ira Berlin et al, eds., *Freedom's Soldiers: The Black Military Experience in the Civil War* (Cambridge,
UK: Cambridge University Press, 1998), 18–19, 28–9, 86–7, and 172–3; Dudley Taylor Cornish,
The Sable Arm: Negro Troops in the Union Army (New York: Longman's, Green and Company, 1956),

The self-emancipatory acts of slaves during wartime powerfully affected masters' psyches. Douglass's pleas to end the Union's policy of fighting "with one hand" and turn the war into a revolution of course emphasized the benefits of labor lost to the Confederacy and gained for the Union war effort, but more was at stake psychologically. As Douglass once phrased it, any "proclamation of emancipation" would "act on the masters" as well as the slaves. A sense of how brittle and apt to turn into hysteria the slave-owning class's claims to mastery proved in the face of resistance suffused his autobiographical writings.[26] During the war, such deep vulnerabilities characterized the reactions of masters and mistresses whose slaves ran away or stayed and disobeyed. The flight of trusted household slaves particularly drained confidence. When the washerwoman Dolly, whose owners categorized her as an "invalid" in plantation records, ran away, one of the leading families in Georgia lost not only their laundress but also their faith in the future and some of their confidence that they had ever mastered slaves. "The Negro women marched off," Louisiana plantation mistress Kate Stone lamented, "in their mistresses' dresses." Stone was on the losing end of "the war within" plantation households, a contest shaking Confederate morale.[27]

The magnificent drama of slaves' movement toward a freedom by no means guaranteed by federal policy played out before and even after Lincoln's proclamation. Many slaves suffered in Border States loyal to the Union but with significant pro-Confederate sympathies, especially among slaveholders. Well after accepting Butler's contraband policy in Virginia,

---

291 ("man"), 49 ("Hindoo"), and 287 ("behaved").

26 Douglass, "The Slaveholders' Rebellion: An Address Delivered in Himrod's, New York, on 4 July 1862," in *The Frederick Douglass Papers*, Volume 3, eds. Blassingame et al., 542 Cf; Douglass, *Narrative of the Life of Frederick Douglass* (Boston: The Anti-Slavery Office, 1845), 60–81.

27 "Eliza Jane Atkins to her husband Robert M. Walker," September 25, 1864, Atkins family papers in University of Georgia's Hargrett Library; Karen Cook Bell, "'Lincoln,' Self-Emancipation, and the Continuing Saga of the 'Great Emancipator'" at H-Afro-Am (November 27, 2012), link no longer available; Thavolia Glymph, *Out of the House of Bondage: The Transformation of the Plantation Household* (Cambridge, UK: Cambridge: University Press, 2008), 97 (for Stone and for "the war within") and 98–136; Tera Hunter, *To 'Joy My Freedom: Southern Black Women's Lives and Labors after the Civil War* (Cambridge, UK: Cambridge University Press, 1997), 15.

Lincoln still attempted to placate masters in the border regions and beyond, rejecting General John C. Frémont's order emancipating Missouri slaves of disloyal masters, removing Frémont from his command, and floating ideas regarding exceedingly gradual, compensated emancipation. Defiant protests such as those directed at the War Department from border regions by General O.M. Mitchel in May 1862 helped shape debates over emancipation. Mitchel reported that continuing the policy of returning fugitives to masters had become impossible: "My River front [the Tennessee] is 120 miles long and if the Government disapprove of what I have done I must receive heavy re-enforcements or abandon my position. With the assistance of the Negroes in watching the River I feel myself sufficiently strong to defy the enemy." But, well into 1863, the policy of returning slaves to "loyal" owners applied in the Border States. St. Louis used its city jail to hold recalcitrant slaves. A short distance away was Benton Barracks, where Blacks joined the Union army.[28]

The processes that Butler began and that Frémont sought to broaden repeated themselves in many places, with those in the field staking out a variety of positions and Lincoln responding vigorously or not. The proposals and responses shifted as military fortunes ebbed and flowed and as laws changed. The current emphasis on Lincoln's status as a moral exemplar and political genius makes for a flattened history, one that supposes that drama adheres to great men and too readily reads itself backward from its results. Thus, we get a Lincoln biding his time for the opportune moment to decisively strike blows at a slave system he detested. In the case of Frémont's order, Lincoln is seen as shrewdly resisting an adventurist, politically driven general in the interest of the rule of law and of keeping Missouri and Kentucky slaveholders loyal to the Union.[29] However, in 1862, when

28 Leslie A. Schwalm, *Emancipation's Diaspora: Race and Reconstruction in the Upper Midwest* (Chapel Hill, NC: University of North Carolina Press, 2009), 51–4; Evans, *Open Wound*, 154 and 159 (Mitchel); Eric Foner, *The Fiery Trial: Abraham Lincoln and American Slavery* (New York: W.W. Norton, 2010), 176–7.

29 William C. Harris, *Lincoln and the Border States: Preserving the Union* (Lawrence, KS: University Press of Kansas, 2011), 96–104 and the introduction to this book. The least predictable and most

the "abolitionist general" David Hunter implemented a South Carolina emancipation and draft of freedmen after great preparation within the channels of government, Lincoln countermanded that order as well. Part of the context was a simultaneous debate over compensated emancipation in the Border States, which caused Lincoln to regard emancipationist appeals as "embarrassing." Frémont's successor was likewise removed for being too pro-emancipation. When Lincoln called the major general and railway engineer Grenville Dodge to Washington to discuss building the Transcontinental Railroad, Dodge feared he was to be the subject of disciplinary action for arming ex-slaves. The point here is not to deny that Lincoln faced enormous political problems and confronted longstanding habits of federal government respect for slave property. But it is necessary to insist that the drama of Lincoln slowly and gloriously changing be taken in the round, with slaves acting to teach commanders that their labor and loyalty could be decisive for the war effort. As the editors at the Freedmen and Southern Society Project remind us, "While Lincoln and his subordinates courted slaveholders, slaves demonstrated their readiness to risk all for freedom and to do whatever they could to aid their owner's enemy."[30]

LIVING THROUGH JUBILEE

In freedom, the impossible transformation of former slaves continued to capture popular imagination with both exhilaration and tragedy. Northern racists, often Democrats opposing Lincoln and full prosecution of the war, ironically helped to ensure as much, generating a voluminous "black scare"

---

interesting of the recent works on Lincoln is George M. Fredrickson's excellent *Big Enough to Be Inconsistent: Abraham Lincoln Confronts Slavery and Race* (Cambridge, MA: Harvard University Press, 2008), 85–119.

30 Harris, *Lincoln and the Border States*, 23 and 167 ("embarrassing") and 173–6; Edward A. Miller, Jr., *Lincoln's Abolitionist General: The Biography of David Hunter* (Columbia, SC: University of South Carolina Press, 1997), esp. 99–115; Cornish, *The Sable Arm*, 33–41; on Dodge, see Esch and Roediger, *The Production of Difference*, 72.

SEIZING FREEDOM

literature obsessing on the spectacular gains made by African Americans. Those gains proliferated with the Thirteenth, Fourteenth, and Fifteenth Amendments from 1865 to 1870. The Constitution registered the full extent of impossible triumph: from slaves to free, equal, voting citizens— constitutionally at least—in less than a decade. The freedpeople's story also commanded attention because it included a fair share of publicized tragedy, privation, disability, and death. If historians are only recently recovering this dimension of Reconstruction, it received dramatic publicity at the time.[31]

Freedpeople performed freedom, interpreting its coming as Jubilee. Here again, their own actions were critical. Staging dignified pageants of Jubilee, they impressed listeners with music heard as strange, wild, and moving. Jubilee provided a name for their ceremonies of celebration, thanksgiving, remembrance, and revelry in a way that modern historical accounts apprehend too one-sidedly as simply festivity. Jubilee's other dimension was a serious intervention in theology, which historians thus largely miss. In hearkening back to Old Testament accounts of Jubilee in Leviticus, African Americans found in the Bible the precise passages portraying emancipation as part of God's plan. In October 1861, Douglass's calls for a revolutionary Civil War took the form of professing a desire "to sing the glad song of Jubilee to the sable millions." Jubilee theologically explained why victory over slavery was possible and grounded hopes for further victory. Not exactly millennial, the verses on Jubilee in Leviticus describe regular calendars of liberation and reparation culminating every fiftieth year in an emancipation of Jewish slaves accompanied by redistribution of land. The term had frequently appeared in abolitionist and

---

31 Jim Downs, *Sick from Freedom: African-American Illness and Suffering during the Civil War and Reconstruction* (New York: Oxford University Press, 2012); Forrest G. Wood, *Black Scare: The Racist Response to Emancipation & Reconstruction* (Berkeley, CA: University of California Press, 1968); Mary Frances Berry, *My Face Is Black It Is True: Callie House and the Ex-Slave Reparations Movement* (New York: Vintage, 2006), 98–101. For the most compelling new work on the misery of freedpeople and those in the process of freeing themselves, see Thavolia Glymph's forthcoming book on the Civil War "refugee crisis" of women and children as adumbrated in Glymph, "Under the Shields of the Law of Nations."

proslavery discourse contesting whether or not God supported bondage, but its spread during and after the war was remarkable. Its usage connected freedpeople with a long tradition of transatlantic and maritime uses of the term by "jubilating" radicals spreading visions of new worlds grounded in old ones. Above all, Jubilee expressed the combination of deep emotional release and mature expectation of having a place in a changed world.[32]

Before Du Bois's *Black Reconstruction*, the greatest evocation of what was at play in Jubilee came in a song composed in the wake of emancipation. In "No More Auction Block," freedpeople sang:

> No more auction block for me.
> No more auction block for me.
> No more auction block for me
> Many thousand gone.

Other verses added other atrocities suddenly and ecstatically to be left behind—"No more driver's lash," for example, and the haunting "No more mistress' call"—always with the sobering ballast of "Many thousand gone." That recurring last line, so resonant with the mixing of joy and sorrow in slave music, recalled those recently sold away on auction blocks. It further memorialized ancestors and deceased friends who did not live to see freedom, but who set the stage for it. The song registered the sharp break between the grinding on of the days of slavery and the coming of revolu-

---

32 Matthew James Zacharias Harper, "Living in God's Time: African-American Faith and Politics in Post-Emancipation North Carolina" (PhD diss., University of North Carolina at Chapel Hill, 2009), 110–60, esp. 112–14; Thomas Wentworth Higginson, *Army Life in a Black Regiment* (Boston: Fields, Osgood and Co., 1870), 41 and passim; Peter Linebaugh, "Jubilating; Or, How the Atlantic Working Class Used the Biblical Jubilee against Capitalism, with Some Success," *Midnight Notes* (Fall 1990); Blight includes "Jubilee" in the subtitle to his *Frederick Douglass' Civil War* but without attention to the theological import of the term; cf. Litwack, *Been in the Storm*, esp. 177–8; Douglass used "Jubilee" often. See, for example, Blight, *Frederick Douglass' Civil War*, epigraph on vii; Schwalm, *Emancipation's Diaspora*, 74; Douglass, *The Life and Times of Frederick Douglass*, 351–4; see also Douglass, "To My British Antislavery Friends," *Douglass' Monthly* (June 1860), reprinted in *Frederick Douglass*, ed. Foner, as adapted and abridged by Yuval Taylor, 392.

tionary time, memorializing both.[33] It echoed the other classic of
freedpeople's music, "Oh Freedom," in its litany of those left behind. But
while "Oh, Freedom" juxtaposes "No more moanin'," and "No more
weepin'" with references to the Lord, "No More Auction Block" sounds
like a secular song until we apprehend how deeply connected to West
African spirituality its memory of ancestors is. Thus both songs celebrate
at once a sharp break with the past and the ways—spiritual, aesthetic, and
historical—in which the long history and long memory of slave culture
made such a break possible.[34]

When performed by Bob Dylan, Odetta, and others in the recent past,
some verses of "No More Auction Block" are bound to have puzzled
modern listeners. What can stanzas announcing "No more peck of corn"
and "No more pint of salt" mean? In both instances, freedpeople sang of
the sad and necessary concern with materiality that could not be sus-
pended even in the euphoria of Jubilee. The missing salt and corn were
rations, provided periodically by masters to feed slaves. Those too were
coming no more, leaving how food would be provided a central concern
after freedom. While "Oh, Freedom" posed the existential dilemma of the
slave rebel and the self-emancipated soldier—"Before I'll be a slave,/I'll
be buried in my grave"—the burden of "No More Auction Block" was to
express joy and the persisting challenge of survival.[35]

What slaves did with their joys and their challenges made them continue to be the most dramatically transformed and transformative group

---

33 For "No More Auction Block," see Eileen Southern, *The Music of Black Americans: A History*
(New York: W.W. Norton, 1997), 160–1; the early text referred to here is from William F. Allen and
others, *Slave Songs of the United States* (New York: A. Simpson, 1867), 48, under the title "Many
Thousand Go." See also Stuckey: "The Great Form before Frederick Douglass"; Douglass, *Narrative
of the Life of Frederick Douglass*, 13–15.

34 Kim Ruehl, "'Oh, Freedom': History of an American Folk Song" at folkmusic.about.com includes
the lyrics; Allen and others, *Slave Songs of the United States*, 48; Sterling Stuckey, *Slave Culture:
Nationalist Theory and the Foundations of Black America* (New York: Oxford University Press, 1988),
esp. 10–61. Stuckey's emphasis is not only on the existence of slave culture at the intersection of race
and class but also on its aesthetic, political, and moral sophistication.

35 Allen and others, *Slave Songs of the United States*, 48; Ruehl, "'Oh Freedom.'"

in the nation well past emancipation. It is tempting to see them, as some historians have, as insisting—insofar as was possible and even when it seemed impossible—on all the things slavery forbade to slaves: mobility, free speech, political rights and power, independent worship, education, family, and, above all, land and control over one's own labor. All of that is correct enough, but a more dramatic and telling formulation is also possible. The historian of the Black family before and after emancipation, Herbert Gutman, glimpsed the possibility. He once described a book that he died before completing as premised on apprehending Reconstruction by insisting that "beliefs nourished but often barely articulated prior to the Civil War found expression during and just after that conflict." That is, most of what freedpeople seized in the war's wake built on what historian Thavolia Glymph has called "small freedoms" and on triumphs of humanity wrested from slavery. The best study of slavery, emancipation, and Reconstruction, Glymph's *Out of the House of Bondage*, soars because its structure and its argument insist that we cannot know the story of emancipation without knowing the story of slavery. It equally shows that the ways slaves emancipated themselves, and what they did with freedom, ought to make us reimagine the history of slavery itself.[36]

A return to Robert Smalls's commandeering of the *Planter* provides a wonderful example. Smalls, as a ship pilot, belonged during slavery to the small group of slaves whose skill in that craft gave them perhaps the most social power of any group of workers in the South. They could shut down the ports through which the cotton, rice, and sugar kingdoms sustained themselves. They could do so by declaring the sea impassable. The skills that underwrote such power flowed from an unsurpassed knowledge of the sea, often brought from West Africa but also nourished in fishing, diving, catching turtles, and canoeing as New World slaves. Sometimes this was work assigned by masters, but in the coastal Carolina area where

---

36 Glymph, *Out of the House of Bondage*, esp. 209, offers a very useful commentary relating "small rights to large ones," which underpins the framing of matters here. Herbert G. Gutman, *The Black Family in Slavery and Freedom, 1750–1925* (New York: Pantheon, 1976), 366.

Smalls lived, knowledge of the ocean spread more widely. That is, South
Carolina and Georgia low country slaves, who were managed under the
task system rather than driven in gangs, could finish assigned work in rice
production early and find a few hours—and longer stretches on Sun-
days—to fish, catch turtles, and market their catch. The select few, as
Kevin Dawson has shown, who parlayed the individual and collective
knowledge of the sea thus gained into becoming pilots received implicit
recognition as the men best qualified to bring valuable oceangoing ships
and priceless cargoes to shore, navigating wind, tide, and the ocean floor.
They held effective command as they did so, not bossed by their often
faraway owner and typically deferred to by the ship captain. Often
wearing motley but impressive captain's clothes, they remained slaves but
with enormous status in the eyes of those in authority in ports and those
in Black communities, where pilots chose to remain with families despite
myriad avenues of escape.[37]

Thus we should imagine Smalls as having ability and confidence to plan
and pilot the taking of the *Planter*—to adopt a disguise as a Confederate
officer and the bearing of that figure—developed within slavery. Very soon
after gaining freedom, Smalls became a central political leader in South
Carolina and the symbol of Black political power most able to endure in
office long after Jubilee had suffered defeat almost everywhere else. His
long career bespoke the ability of enslaved pilots to construct a niche in
which their mastery competed with that of the master. And the instances
in which Smalls as a politician was only partly attuned to the demands of
ordinary African-American laborers on the land were not perhaps
unmoored from the particular origins of his ideas in his own experiences
of slavery.[38]

---

37 Kevin Dawson, "Enslaved Ship Pilots in the Age of Revolutions: Challenging Perceptions of Race
and Slavery Between the Boundaries of Maritime and Terrestrial Bondage," in *Journal of Social History*
47 (Fall 2013), 71–100, brilliantly studies these matters.
38 Billingsley, *Yearning to Breathe Free*, 43 and passim; see also Dorothy Sterling, *Captain of The
Planter: The Story of Robert Smalls* (Garden City, NY: Doubleday and Company, 1958); Edward A.
Miller, *Gullah Statesman: Robert Smalls from Slavery to Congress, 1839–1915* (Columbia, SC: Uni-

The theology of Jubilee similarly illustrates how the moment and the realization of emancipation flowed from the prior achievements of slaves and from the ethos of a slave culture. That culture was far from monolithic, but it was united in its ability to challenge the worldview of masters. The interpretation of Reconstruction as Jubilee suggested much about that ethos. An ex-slave called Aunt Aggy, running into Mary Livermore, a former governess from her plantation during the war, shared sentiments that would have been impossible to speak months before. Livermore, by then having undergone transformations herself to become a Union army nurse, reported Aggy as professing to be unfazed by "white folks' blood . . . a-runnin' on the ground like a riber." Aggy said why: "It was a-comin'. I allers 'spected to see white folks heaped up dead. An' de Lor', he's kept his promise, and 'venged his people, jes' as I knowed he would."[39] This particularly blood-centered prophecy may not have been shared by many slaves, but the idea of deliverance was. As the leading account of Recon-struction and Jubilee observes, slaves often invoked Jubilee at the birth of a child, hoping the newborn's was the generation of freedom. From such a tradition, it was not a great leap to see the opportunities presented by the Civil War as a "divinely appointed climax of history."[40] Emancipation, the epitome of planlessness for many whites, seemed firmly in God's plan to slaves.

No slave ethos could chart one unified path after emancipation, though broadly shared commonalities continued. Indeed, the very idea of living in God's time could lead to militancy or to passively waiting for deliverance in the postwar period. Denominational religious differences proved both

versity of South Carolina Press, 1995), 13–17 and passim; Glymph, *Out of the House of Bondage*, 209. On Smalls and labor, see also Eric Foner, *Nothing But Freedom: Emancipation and Its Legacy* (Baton Rouge, LA: Louisiana State University Press, 1984), 97–108.

39   Drew Gilpin Faust, *This Republic of Suffering: Death and the American Civil War* (New York: Vintage, 2008), 54, retells the Livermore and Aunt Aggy story.

40   Harper, "Living in God's Time," 2009, 25 ("divinely appointed"), 27, 42, and 57. On childbirth and Jubilee, see Ira Berlin and Leslie S. Rowland, eds., *Families and Freedom: A Documentary History of African-American Kinship in the Civil War Era* (New York: New Press, 1997), 10.

expressive of and contributors to class divisions among freedpeople, as
well as between freedpeople and African Americans already free before
the Civil War. Nevertheless, the desire for an independent African-
American faith, however expressed in competing churches, made its way
from a sense of Jubilee to a determination after freedom to avoid domi-
nation by white religious bodies. The African Methodist Episcopal (AME)
and AME Zion faiths made great gains despite their Northern origins.
They held the considerable advantage of seeing racial separation as "essential to God's plan for the race," literally turning segregation into
congregation. Those gains came at the expense of the white-led Baptist,
Methodist, and Presbyterian denominations, in which slaves had wor-
shipped at the sufferance of their masters. The attempts of such churches
to retain Black worshippers chronically undershot the mark so much that
a careful recent account identifies no less than five successive phases in
which white authorities tried and mostly failed to catch up with African-
American demands for autonomy.[41]

The roots of the freedpeople's passion for education grew out of slavery
in complicated ways. Of the passion, there can be no doubt. A Virginia
educator of the emancipated first wrote privately of their being "*anxious
to learn*" before settling instead on "*crazy* to learn," describing the ways
Jubilee informed post-slavery campaigns for literacy among African Americans. Determined to foster literacy in their children, ex-slaves also
embarked on adult education in a massive way. Du Bois captured some of
the passion as the "crusade of the New England schoolmarm." Such

---

41 Harper, "Living in God's Time," 61 ("God's time"), 27, 57, and 58–110; Michael W. Fitzgerald,
Urban Emancipation: Popular Politics in Reconstruction Mobile, 1860–1890 (Baton Rouge, LA:
Louisiana State University Press, 2002), 49–131; Daniel W. Stowell, *Rebuilding Zion: The Religious
Reconstruction of the South, 1863–1877* (New York: Oxford University Press, 1998), 85–9; Edward
Blum, *Reforging the White Republic: Race, Religion, and American Nationalism, 1865–1898* (Baton
Rouge, LA: Louisiana State University Press, 2007), best provides context. On segregation and con-
gregation, see Earl Lewis, *In Their Own Interests: Race, Class and Power in Twentieth-Century Norfolk,
Virginia* (Berkeley, CA: University of California Press, 1991), 109. Here and elsewhere in the chapter,
I take the idea of a slave ethos from Sterling Stuckey, "Through the Prism of Folklore: The Black Ethos
in Slavery," *Massachusetts Review* 9 (Summer 1968), 417–37.

teachers worked: "Behind the mists of ruin and rapine [and] after the hoarse mouthings of the field guns rang the rhythm of the alphabet." The extraordinary receptivity of freedpeople to these missionary white women educators bespoke a sense that in literacy lay the key to everything: autonomous religious practice, not being cheated on the job, political organizing, and more. The masters, by their frequent and brutal efforts to deny slaves literacy, had taught well, if inadvertently, that education was connected to liberation. As the best-selling antislavery writer Harriet Beecher Stowe put it, ex-slaves "rushed not to the grog-shop but to the schoolroom. They cried for the spelling-book as bread, and pleaded for teachers as a necessity of life." The grandeur of the changes wrought was daunting. In New Orleans, a Frederick Douglass School for freedpeople arose in the former confines of a pen where slaves had been sold. The globe stand of the classroom sat on the former auction block. Much of Southern education, Black and white, was to be transformed by the passion of ex-slaves. Public education there, Du Bois wrote, was a "Negro idea."[42]

In our appreciation of the role of the repressive power of the master and the crusade of missionary educators, we risk missing important nuances in the history of slavery that help account for how quickly self-reliance became a hallmark of Black education in the South. Slaves read. The very fact that the denial of education galled slaves is known because it also goaded them into stealing knowledge they were not supposed to have, often learning from white children. Frederick Douglass most famously brought forward this story, bemoaning denial of slave literacy and detailing how he learned to read in an eloquent autobiography. Gaining some knowledge from a briefly sympathetic mistress and some from white youths in Baltimore, he quickly became a teacher of reading to other slaves. In some places and times in the South, masters also voluntarily educated

---

42 James Anderson, *The Education of Blacks in the South* (Chapel Hill, NC: University of North Carolina Press, 1988), 5 (Stowe) and 4–32; Litwack, *Been in the Storm*, 475; Du Bois, *Black Reconstruction*, 638 ("Negro idea"); Du Bois, *The Souls of Black Folk* (Chicago: McClurg and Company, 1903), 25 ("crusade" and "calico").

slaves, sometimes providing education for their own children with slave women, sometimes seeing economic advantage in having a few literate and numerate slaves, and sometimes acting on Christian principles holding that all God's children needed access to at least some of the Bible. The knowledge that Leviticus was the place to turn to find freedom talk in scripture doubtless came disproportionately from the small but important core of literate slaves and ex-slaves as well as those educated in free African-American families.[43]

The crisis of the United States from 1850 to 1865 demonstrated to slaves how vital such skills were. The creole of color Jean Baptiste Roudanez recalled in an 1864 report to an inquiry on freedpeople that as an engineer on Louisiana sugar plantations he was told the details of John Brown's execution shortly after the event. The information came from a slave. Having secretly learned to read, the informant asked for a newspaper to clean machinery in the sugarhouse, gaining and spreading knowledge of its contents. Roudanez, for his part, published the *New Orleans Tribune*, a voice of Jubilee and the nation's first African-American daily newspaper. Enjoying unprecedented freedom of assembly and of speech, Black Southerners also massed together in contraband camps and later in the army, where they could learn, and in some cases teach each other, to read. In South Carolina, Du Bois hazarded that perhaps half of all free Blacks could read and write by emancipation and as many as one slave in twenty. Modern estimates range higher by a factor of two or more for slaves, and literacy rates for free Blacks were high far beyond South Carolina. The later campaigns to build and staff schools often reflected strong desires for autonomy with a cadre of activists who had been literate in the slavery period playing key roles.[44]

43 Douglass, *Narrative of the Life of Frederick Douglass*, 36–44.

44 Christopher Span, *From Cotton Field to Schoolhouse: African-American Education in Mississippi, 1862-1875* (Chapel Hill, NC: University of North Carolina Press, 2009), 3, 33–4, 63, and 80; Ronald Butchart, *Schooling the Freed People: Teaching, Learning, and the Struggle for Black Freedom, 1861–1876* (Chapel Hill, NC: University of North Carolina Press, 2010). For Roudanez, see Ira Berlin et al., eds., *Freedom: A Documentary History of Emancipation, 1861–1867*, Series 1, Volume 3, *The*

Pursuit of family ties likewise became a unifying and sometimes fractious passion during Jubilee for reasons stemming from a hard-won ethos and practice developed during slavery. Gutman's pioneering investigations of the Black family showed a tremendous postbellum passion to marry or, more frequently, to register with the state existing marriages performed in slave ceremonies or churches before emancipation. The committed relationships thus recognized had survived over long periods in many cases. For example, in two Virginia counties studied by Gutman, a majority of marriages of freedpeople during 1866 were of couples already together over ten years and in almost a third of the cases over twenty years. Slave children, Ira Berlin and Leslie Rowland write, typically "were born into two-parent households, generally with the help of a slave midwife." They further enjoyed the support of extensive kin networks, real and fictive, that drew on practices in west and central Africa and thrived by virtue of the necessity to love and nurture even as slave sales broke up families.[45]

Of course the violence directed against slaves ought to caution against any simple view that the slave family survived and thrived. In registering their marriages, sometimes with the blessing and encouragement of Freedmen's Bureau government officials and of missionaries from the North, freedpeople hoped to make permanent a relationship the slave market had threatened daily. At the same time, they were attempting to address the loss of family caused by slave sales and by the war. If the newspaper advertisement seeking return of the "runaway master" by Sambo Rhett had a triumphal jocularity, postwar ads seeking information on family members

Wartime Genesis of Free Labor: The Lower South (Cambridge, UK: Cambridge University Press, 1990), 523–5 and Jean-Charles Houzeau, *My Passage at the New Orleans Tribune: A Memoir of the Civil War Era* (Baton Rouge, LA: Louisiana State University Press, 1984), 25, n. 34; Du Bois, *Black Reconstruction*, 638. For a sophisticated reckoning of slave literacy that supports and amplifies Du Bois's estimates, see Janet Duitsman Cornelius, *"When I Can Read My Title Clear": Literacy, Slavery, and Religion in the Antebellum South* (Columbia, SC: University of South Carolina Press, 1991), esp. 6–10. See also Willie Lee Rose, *Rehearsal for Reconstruction: The Port Royal Experiment* (Indianapolis, IN: Bobbs-Merrill Company, 1964), 86–7 and 229–35 and Litwack, *Been in the Storm*, 487–500.

45 Gutman, *The Black Family in Slavery and Freedom*, 12, 3–37, and 363–431; Berlin and Rowland, eds., *Families and Freedom*, 8; Litwack, *Been in the Storm*, 231–9.

sold away years and even decades before bespoke tragedy: "Sam Dove wishes to know the whereabouts of his mother, Areno, his sisters Maria, Neziah, and Peggy, and his brother Edmond," read a typically heart-breaking one. In what may be the period's greatest short story, Mark Twain's "A True Story" (1874), all of the drama hinged on a slave woman's search for a child, a quest Twain claimed to have rendered verbatim from an ex-slave's own words of oral history. Twain's heroine jubilated at renewing ties with one of seven children sold away from her. Six others were lost forever. At the same time, freedpeople often moved their families, if only to a nearby dwelling, in order to assert rights to mobility denied before emancipation and to provide distance from old memories.[46]

In wartime contraband camps and in the ranks of the army, African Americans realized that new opportunities for freedom included reaching back into Rebel-held territory to rescue loved ones. One white commander referred to such heroism as "carrying on their contraband affairs." When the hospitalized soldier and literate freedman Spotswood Rice wrote two letters from Benton Barracks in Missouri in September 1864, old ties and new possibilities animated them. In one, he wrote to his children: "I have not forgot you and that I want to see you as bad as ever . . . be assured that I will have you if it cost me my life daughter: you call my children your property. Not so with me my Children is my own and I expect to get them and when I get ready to come . . . I will have bout a powrer and autherity to bring hear away and to [exact] vengeance on them that holds my Child you will then know how to talke to me." Making dreams like Rice's real often involved cooperation with white soldiers, underlining the fact that direct abolitionist action could be as important as the spread of enlightened racial attitudes.[47]

---

46 Litwack, *Been in the Storm So Long*, 232 for the advertisement and 172 and 193–235; Berlin and Rowland, eds., *Families and Freedom*, 17–18; Twain, "A True Story, Repeated Word for Word as I Heard It," *Atlantic Monthly* (November 1874), 591–4.
47 Berlin and Rowland, eds., *Families and Freedom*, 27–9 ("affairs"), 47, and 195–7 (for Rice's letters); Berlin et al., eds., *Free at Last*, 16, 19, and 27–8.

Emancipation decisively changed daily realities for families, ending specific forms of intimate terror associated with the slave system that were perhaps too horrific to even be specifically memorialized in a song like "No More Auction Block." The practices of beating family members in front of each other, and in particular of beating parents in front of their children and children in front of their parents, represented particularly stark assaults on the slave family. "No more driver's lash," exalted over the end of such abuse for the "children of Jubilee."[48] The end of slavery also materially changed the vulnerability to rape and sexual coercion at the hands of masters and overseers. Freedwomen and children gained distance from the power and proximity of slave-owners and at least briefly secured opportunities to appeal to the Freedmen's Bureau, to the law, and to the presence of armed Black veterans when sexual exploitation did occur.[49]

However, a brutal war introduced its own problems, and afterward, old and new vulnerabilities to white authority and tensions within the African-American gender system coexisted with a spirit of Jubilee. The self-interested military inspirations of the North's contraband policy, the later desire for Black male soldiers, and the haphazard decisions of masters fleeing with their property in slaves all made for a variety of wartime strains on African-American families. In general, the Union's desire for contraband labor early in the fighting focused on those capable of heavy work, and men were preferentially recruited from General Butler's first experiments forward. While some female service labor was sought, the presence of children served armies poorly. Commanders' brutality focused especially on Black women escaping slavery and later settling as "camp-followers" of soldiers. If women and children stayed behind, they faced danger from vengeful masters contributing to a hesitancy of enslaved men to leave and

48 Peter Bardaglio, "The Children of Jubilee: African-American Childhood in Wartime," in *Divided Houses: Gender and the Civil War*, eds. Catherine Clinton and Nina Silber (New York: Oxford University Press, 1992), 212–29.
49 Gutman, *The Black Family in Slavery and Freedom*, 388–99; Hunter, *To 'Joy My Freedom*, 12; Chandra Manning, *What This Cruel War Was Over: Soldiers, Slavery and the Civil War* (New York: Vintage, 2008), 44–78; Berlin and Rowland, eds., *Families and Freedom*, 47 and 96–7.

fight. If they made it to camps, slave women were often treated with contempt
and with even more suspicion of sexual promiscuity than camp-following
white women faced. One commander broached the "problem" of female
slaves finding freedom as the "Nigger Woman Question."[50]

General Thomas Sherman, perhaps the most outspoken opponent of
taking on contrabands, particularly deplored women, children, and elderly
refugees from slavery—that is, families. He saw them as "a great many
useless mouths." Even when he began to support the use of Black troops
in the summer of 1862, Sherman remained at pains to point out that "We
never harbor women and children—we give employment to men." Others
instrumentally used relatively humane treatment to attract more labor
from freedpeople constituted in family units, but even abolitionist generals, such as Rufus Saxton and David Hunter, were sometimes part of the
problem. The former particularly fretted about slave women's sexual activities with white soldiers, targeting not the frequent rapes in war zones but
consensual acts, for which he blamed promiscuous Black women. The
Second Confiscation Act accelerated the search for "able-bodied" men for
employment by the military, making single Black women still more vulnerable. Military policy also countenanced exploitative apprenticing of
African-American children by the Union forces.[51]

The movement toward freedom of so many women and children was
perhaps the most magnificent drama of the general strike of the slaves and
the occasion of its most harsh tragedies. Only episodically protected and
inadequately provisioned even when doing profitable agricultural labor,
they suffered under commanders who feared their "wild notions of

50 Gutman, *The Black Family in Slavery and Freedom,* 371 ("Question") and 371–84.

51 Darrel E. Bigham, *On Jordan's Banks: Emancipation and Its Aftermath in the Ohio River Valley*
(Lexington, KY: University Press of Kentucky, 2006), 66–8; on Saxton, see Leslie Schwalm, *A Hard
Fight for We: Women's Transition from Slavery to Freedom in South Carolina* (Urbana, IL: University
of Illinois Press, 1997), 101–4; Berlin and Rowland, eds., *Families and Freedom,* 31, 59, 65, 73; Berlin
and Rowland, eds., *Families and Freedom,* 210–24; Gutman, *The Black Family in Slavery and Freedom,*
402–12. For Sherman, see Berlin and others, eds., *Free at Last,* 15 and 68–9, and 70 ("harbor"); Berlin
and others, eds., *The Upper South,* 89 ("mouths"); on the Second Confiscation Act, disability, and
gender, see Downs, *Sick for Freedom,* 126–9.

freedom." Confederates saw them as vulnerable targets, especially as Union troops deployed away from areas where women and children were staying. Targeted brutal attacks, presaging the patterns and ferocity of postwar white terror by the Ku Klux Klan, were common. After the war, Southern opponents of Reconstruction, and employers of labor generally, used apprenticeship of children as a way to circumvent parental rights and to secure workers and used sexual violence to reassert control over workers.[52]

The poignant efforts to find mates lost in slavery and war sometimes ran up against the reality that a commitment to the idea of marriage could lead to starting new relationships after sales separated families. Recognition that some freedpeople were involved in "plural" and strained relationships made pursuit of divorce, or the decision to part by not formalizing marriages, a minor chord in the symphony of reconciliations and of recording marriages. Because the Freedmen's Bureau and allied religious reformers so championed marriage, they also fretted that African Americans did not conform to all dimensions of sexual morality championed by white middle-class Christians, especially where premarital sex was concerned. Freedwomen asserted rights within marriage in a new situation—the state now saw Black husbands as patriarchal authorities—using varied methods including litigation and the making public of grievances against spouses who were abusive.[53]

Because patriarchy could hardly have thrived among those caught in a slave system denying men authority and property, the relations between men and women in Jubilee moved into uncharted territories. The prominent role of women in the community of slaves would not easily give way after freedom.

---

52 Glymph, "Under the Shields of the Law of Nations;" Schwalm, *A Hard Fight for We*, 110–14 and Chapter 4 below.

53 Hunter, *To 'Joy My Freedom: Southern Black Women's Lives and Labors after the Civil War* (Cambridge, UK: Cambridge University Press, 1997). 38–40; Litwack, *Been in the Storm*, 242–3; Gutman, *The Black Family in Slavery and Freedom*, 366 ("plural"), 163 and 504–5, and Berlin and Rowland, eds., *Families and Freedom*, 170–1. See also Laura F. Edwards, "Women and the Law: Domestic Discord in North Carolina after the Civil War," in *Local Matters: Race, Crime, and Justice in the Nineteenth-Century South*, eds. Christopher Waldrep and Donald G. Nieman (Athens, GA: University of Georgia Press, 2001), 125–54.

As Elsa Barkley Brown's work on Reconstruction in Virginia shows, incredible commitments to direct democracy across gender lines featured freedwomen fully participating in community political meetings, shaping mandates on which male politicians were to act. Children, too, voted in some such meetings. In South Carolina, similar patterns applied alongside some African-American support for women's suffrage as a formal demand.[54] In Arkansas, freedmen and women for a time went beyond appeals to patriarchy in claiming rights. They built organizations in which women were sufficiently empowered publically that conservatives contesting the ratification of the state's new Reconstruction constitution in 1868 fantasized that the results had been swayed by cross-dressing Black women who voted as men.[55] At the same time, the US social order that freedpeople entered remained deeply patriarchal, and gains in voting and property-holding after emancipation particularly advantaged freedmen. Women's ability to control their own labor and bodies had to take account of old and new threats.

The best illustration of the crosscurrents involved at the intersections of race, gender, and Jubilee lies in the decision of many families to withdraw women from full-time work in field labor. While white planters and plantation mistresses could claim to see in such a decision only a vain attempt at "playing the lady," much more was at issue. The field had been a particular site of atrocity but also an arena in which the planters' enforcement of a rough equality of the sexes underlined Black women's strength and power. Abolitionist allies, though committed to the discipline provided by wage labor, supported the decision to curtail female labor in the fields out of an equally strong commitment to faith in bourgeois family forms as promoting uplift. The resulting pattern was necessarily complex.

---

54   Elsa Barkley Brown, "Negotiating and Transforming the Public Sphere: Political Life in the Transition from Slavery to Freedom," *Public Culture* (Fall 1994), 107–46; Steven Hahn, *A Nation under Our Feet: Black Political Struggles in the Rural South from Slavery to the Great Migration* (Cambridge, MA: Harvard University Press, 2003), 212–14; Berry, *My Face Is Black It Is True*, 24.
55   Hannah Rosen, *Terror in the Heart of Freedom: Citizenship, Sexual Violence, and the Meaning of Race in the Postemancipation South* (Chapel Hill, NC: University of North Carolina Press, 2009), 106–7 and 129–30.

Slave women withdrew only partially from field labor, "protected" from it but also at times engaging in such work according to their will and their families'. Former house slaves sometimes left domestic work for bouts of field labor, either for seasonally higher wages or to produce a crop on land owned or sharecropped by their families.[56]

LAND AND THE LIMITS OF FREEDOM

The Jubilee of formerly enslaved women thus unfolded in particular ways within general struggles to gain a living in an economy in which "no more peck of corn" would be forthcoming as a ration. Such struggles centered on gaining land. The Emancipation Proclamation's brief "policy" sections set the stage for contradictory future federal interventions structuring the struggle for survival. The document proclaimed that the "Executive government of the United States, including the military and naval authorities thereof, will recognize and maintain the freedom of said [freed] persons" who were enjoined "to abstain from all violence, unless in necessary self-defence and . . . in all cases when allowed . . . labor faithfully for reasonable wages."[57] Wage labor was thus joined to emancipation from the outset, but on the ground, commanders adopted a different strategy to "maintain freedom." With abandoned land and idle labor abundant, they allowed contraband and later freedpeople to cultivate land on vacated plantations. Best exemplifying that strategy were practices under General William Tecumseh Sherman's Special Field Orders Number 15 of January 1865, putting hundreds of thousands of acres of low country South Carolina and Georgia land into production and promising political control

---

56 Hahn, *A Nation under Our Feet*, 171; Litwack, *Been in the Storm*, 245 [playing] and 244–6; Gerald David Jaynes, *Branches Without Roots: Genesis of the Black Working Class in the American South, 1862–1882* (New York: Oxford University Press, 1986), 68–9; Berlin and Rowland, eds., *Families and Freedom*, 185–7.
57 The text of the proclamation (January 1, 1863) is at archives.gov; Jaynes, *Branches without Roots*, 19.

of the region for freedpeople. Allotments of forty-acre parcels often came with the use of a draft animal, making "forty acres and a mule" sum up aspirations for how Jubilee might be fulfilled and some of the damage of slavery repaired. Leviticus 25:23 had proposed: "The land shall not be sold for ever: for the land is mine, for ye were strangers and sojourners with me."[58] And Sherman had delivered, or so it seemed.

Written long before his extensive research into Reconstruction but closer to the experience of slavery, Du Bois's 1903 account of the postwar years in *The Souls of Black Folk* reflected perfectly the African-American sense of betrayal regarding land and freedom after Sherman's policy turned out to be temporary. Du Bois firmly understood the hope: "It had long been the more or less definitely expressed theory of the North that all the chief problems of Emancipation might be settled by establishing the slaves on the forfeited lands of their masters—a sort of poetic justice, said some." He likewise saw the mechanics of how such hope was dashed:

> But this poetry done into solemn prose meant either wholesale con-
> fiscation of private property in the South, or vast appropriations.
> Now Congress had not appropriated a cent, and [with] proclama-
> tions of general amnesty [for Rebel masters] eight hundred thousand
> acres of abandoned lands in the hands of the Freedmen's Bureau
> melted quickly away.[59]

The idea of Republicans redistributing the land of elite families to the poorest Americans will seem fanciful today. However, the impossible

---

58 Leviticus, 25:23; for Special Orders Number 15, see Berlin et al., eds., *The Lower South*, 338–40; Henry Louis Gates, Jr., "The Truth Behind Forty Acres and a Mule," *The Root* (January 7, 2013) at theroot.com. See also Edward Magdol, *A Right to the Land: Essays on the Freedmen's Community* (Westport, CT: Greenwood, 1977) for the centrality of the demand for land and, on the link to reparation, Paul Ortiz, "The Reparations Demand in History," *Against the Current*, 102, January–February 2003.

59 Eric Foner, *Reconstruction: America's Unfinished Revolution, 1863–1877* (New York: Harper and Row, 1988), 70–1. Du Bois, *Souls of Black Folk*, 18.

dispossession of planters from their slave property underlines that we should use our imaginations. This was also a time when Indian land in the West was being given to homesteading settlers and to land grant colleges and universities under the terms of laws passed at almost the same moment as the Second Confiscation Act, which undermined the holding of slave property. General Saxton, who implemented Special Orders Number 15, so firmly assumed that the land redistribution it turned on was permanent that he later expressed sharp regret that he had not insisted on assurances that the redistribution would last. A popular wartime song linked "Jubilo" to the prospect that freedpeople were about to "occupy the land." Indeed, during and just after the war, ex-slaves had already done so in many places, putting up stiff resistance to the return of runaway masters. Moreover, as no less an analyst than the revolutionary thinker Lenin wrote in his study of capitalism and agriculture in the United States, the average acreage of a Southern farm was cut by more than half between 1860 and 1880 because war and abolition directed "a decisive blow at the latifundia of the slave-owners."[60] But where land was concerned, the crisis of the planter did not lead to the completion of Jubilee for the slave.

The Freedmen's Bureau resolved conflicts between its tendency to see wage labor as the source of virtues and its forays toward "establishing the Negroes as peasant proprietors" overwhelmingly by tilting toward the former position. It did so for compelling reasons of political economy and white supremacy. The economics of the matter, like so much else, went back to the ethos slaves had developed in slavery. Owning little land, slaves had struggled successfully to control some by exchanging hard work during most of the daylight hours for time to cultivate small plots to supplement their diets and/or produce foodstuffs for local markets. The plots especially thrived under the task system, as slaves could complete the work tasked to them speedily, gaining time to tend their own crops. Although some

---

60 Rose, *Rehearsal for Reconstruction*, 330 and 290–84.; Litwack, *Been in the Storm*, 117 ("Jubilo"); V.I. Lenin, *Lenin on the United States: Selections from His Writings* (New York: International, 1970), 127–8.

staple crops marketed internationally grew on these plots, the pattern was one of production for family and local use. When able to secure land after freedom, the priorities were often the same, hardly surprisingly as the necessities of life were in such short supply. The Boston engineer Edward Philbrick, unevenly adopting a presumed African-American dialect, summarized for Congress the attitude of freedpeople to agricultural production in 1865: "Cotton is no good for the nigger. Corn good for nigger; ground nuts good for nigger; cotton good for massa . . . cotton make nigger perish." Indeed, even the original forty-acre allotments were considered less than ideal by many ex-slaves who preferred not to possess the "best" plantation land improved for commodity production but land with some woods, generally better suited for self-sufficiency. Had white Republicans wanted to see a peasantry of freedpeople develop as a counterweight to the planter class, or had they wished only to deal a punishing blow to the planter class, such a result might have been attractive. But their desire was also to improve freedpeople, regarding market relations and labor discipline as keys to doing so. African-American elites frequently shared such a view. Moreover, the deeply indebted postwar US state looked to resuming its number one export—cotton—as a key to securing gold and credit. In Louisiana, resumption of sugar exports similarly soon took priority over production for local use. Only a wing of Radical Republicans supported dispossessing the masters to create small units of independent production. In a few places in the South, local federal officials hearkened to the last words of the agency's full name, which charged it with administering "abandoned lands" and set up freedpeople on former plantation land.[61] Freedpeople grounded a case for just such a course in an impressive combination of mindfulness regarding ancestors and a most modern

61   Du Bois, *Souls of Black Folk*, 23; Jaynes, *Branches without Roots*, 13 and 3–19; William McKee Evans, *Ballots and Fence Rails: Reconstruction in Lower Cape Fear* (Chapel Hill, NC: University of North Carolina Press, 1966), 56–9; Julie Saville, *The Work of Reconstruction: From Slave to Wage Laborer in South Carolina, 1860–1870* (Cambridge, UK: Cambridge University Press, 1994), 5–12, 42 and 5–71; Jaynes, *Branches without Roots*, 66. On Louisiana, see Rebecca J. Scott, *Degrees of Freedom: Louisiana and Cuba after Slavery* (Cambridge, MA: Harvard University Press, 2005), 36.

appreciation of labor's role in creating value. "Our wives, our children, our husbands has been sold over and over again to purchase the lands we now locates on" ran one argument. Another emphasized that the claimants' enslaved fathers and mothers "drained those Swamps and Marshes" making production possible.[62]

The most mathematically precise solution came from the great Radical Republican Congressman Thaddeus Stevens, who proposed expropriating 70,000 "arch-traitors"—disloyal landowners whose roughly 400 million acres could work magic. About a tenth of the acreage could set up ex-slaves as independent proprietors with forty-acre tracts. The remaining 354 million acres could be quickly sold at ten dollars an acre, the proceeds used to recompense loyal citizens losing property in the war and to address the national debt incurred during the fighting. That the great bulk of the seized land would be the object of investment would presumably tie the region to commodity production. Though ingenious, this idea left open the possibility that the labor of freedpeople, just what was needed for such commodity production, would be focused on production for use. It also ignored capital's interest in gaining repayment of loans from indebted planters.[63]

The incredible movement of rumors and hopes that shook the South in the Christmas and New Year's season of 1865 to 1866, imagined what Stevens could not deliver. Across an astonishing expanse—Virginia, the Carolinas, Georgia, Alabama, Texas, Louisiana, Mississippi, Arkansas, and Tennessee—freedpeople told themselves and each other that the second act of Jubilee would come during the holidays. The movement brought much together. Stevens's speech in favor of confiscation and forty acres had circulated since September. Veterans of color were said to be responsible for spreading "enormous and incongruous notions of liberty" and

---

62 Dylan Penningroth, *The Claims of Kinfolk: African-American Property and Community in the Nineteenth Century* (Chapel Hill, NC: University of North Carolina Press, 2003), 158 for both quotations.
63 Jaynes, *Branches without Roots*, quoting Stevens on "arch-traitors" at 10; Du Bois, *Black Reconstruction*, 197–9.

for encouraging movements against year-long labor contracts. By
November, historian Steven Hahn writes, "the expectations of blacks and
the apprehensions of whites had been raised." Despite cautions from
Freedmen's Bureau officials and other white authorities that the idea had
no foundation, plans proceeded apace. In some areas, mass marriages took
place, as it was thought the land was to go to couples. One ex-slave, interviewed seven decades later, still remembered contemplating picking out
his mule in anticipation that it would come with the land. Enough freedpeople were thought to be planning to act if the holidays did not bring
land that some whites reported living through the "Christmas Insurrection
Scare of 1865." Deep connections to slave culture again mattered, as
Christmas was a time during which masters granted days off and often
provided food and alcohol to support celebrations. If they did not, slaves
might demand more. In southern Virginia and eastern North Carolina,
the African-inflected Jonkonnu festivities animated yuletide festivities.
Two years before, January 1 had witnessed the taking effect of the Emancipation Proclamation. Certainty that the land would not belong to the
planters made for concerted action to shun signing on as a worker or
sharecropper for the year of 1866.[64]

No such second Jubilee occurred. Frederick Douglass, given his doleful
experiences on the land as a slave, was, like many urban African-American
leaders, not at the time a particularly impassioned advocate of "forty acres
and a mule." Nonetheless, looking back a quarter century after emancipation, he wrote, "untold misery might have been prevented" by a just land
policy. Instead, a planter class soundly defeated by northern capital was
allowed to dominate Black labor in many places, not in anything like a slave

---

64 Hahn, *Nation under Our Feet*, 129, 146 and 127–59; Steven Hahn et al., eds., *Freedom: A Doc-
umentary History of Emancipation, 1861–1867*, Series 3, Volume 1, *Land and Labor, 1865* (Cambridge,
UK: Cambridge University Press, 2008), 895–901; Scott, *Degrees of Freedom*, 37; Harper, "Living in
God's Time," 111–19; Jaynes, *Branches without Roots*, 73–4 ("incongruous"). William H. Wiggins Jr.,
O Freedom!: Afro-American Emancipation Celebrations (Knoxville, TN: University of Tennessee Press,
1987), 29, observes interestingly that January 1 Emancipation Day celebrations themselves grew out
of slave celebrations of Christmas.

system but using sharecropping, wage labor, terror, convict labor, and coercive apprenticeship systems to rule. With fragilely held political freedoms, the right to quit, and collective labor action, freedpeople contested the terms of exploitation at every turn, as this book's third chapter emphasizes. Sometimes, as in parts of the Carolina low country in particular, they did secure land from a dying plantation order, often by pooling money from kin and community. Republican-led Reconstruction state governments at times abetted such efforts.[65] At other times, freedpeople won the prerogative from white landowners to farm "marginal lands" or at least resisted planter attempts to restrict use of common land and small plots to below the customs that prevailed during slavery.[66] Given these meager but real gains, often enough in the coming decades, freedpeople would turn to Exodus rather than Jubilee and seek land and freedom outside the South. They had transformed a war and a nation, but had not completed Jubilee.

---

65 Berry, *My Face Is Black It Is True*, 39; Blight, *Frederick Douglass' Civil War*, 179 and 200–3; Heather Cox Richardson, *The Death of Reconstruction: Race, Labor, and Politics in the Post-Civil War North, 1865–1901* (Cambridge, MA: Harvard University Press, 2001), 90. On the lack of purchase on the land issue among Black urban elites, see David Quigley, *Second Founding: New York City, Reconstruction, and the Making of American Democracy* (New York: Hill and Wang, 2004), 17 and 15–26.
66 Rose, *Rehearsal for Reconstruction*, 406; Saville, *Work of Reconstruction*, 121–30; Penningroth, *The Claims of Kinfolk*, 142–4 and 158–61.

Chapter 2

Emancipation from Whiteness:
Witnessing Disability and Jubilee

*The resulting emotional and intellectual rebound of the
nation made it nearly inconceivable in 1876 that ten years
earlier most men had believed in human equality.*
W.E.B. Du Bois (1935)

In concluding his pioneering study of slavery, the historian George
Rawick reflected on Reconstruction and on all US history. He argued
that "the pressure of blacks for equality" had "intensified" class conflict
generally in the nation's past.[1] Rawick's observation is an intriguing one,
but it leaves us with questions as to why this should be so. James Baldwin,
writing in the wake of the mid-twentieth-century Black freedom movement, sometimes called a "Second Reconstruction," perhaps offered a
fuller assessment. Baldwin trusted no automatic spread of impulses
toward freedom across the color line. Well after the high points of civil
rights struggles, he still felt the need to invite the "white man [to]
become a part of that suffering and dancing country he now watches
wistfully." Such a move toward joining the rest of humanity was a pre-
condition to changes in the outcomes of struggles for justice and in the

---

1 George P. Rawick, *From Sundown to Sunup: The Making of the Black Community* (Westport, CT:
Greenwood, 1972), 159. The epigraph is from W.E.B. Du Bois, *Black Reconstruction in America,
1860–1880* (1998), 727.

inner lives of whites, whom Baldwin regarded as both in misery and in denial.[2]

During the period under consideration in this book, a profound raising of the stakes in social struggles among whites did clearly occur. That is, in the period that historians called Reconstruction, but liberated slaves more tellingly called Jubilee, slaves not only won their own freedom, but white workers also built an unprecedented national labor movement around the visionary demand of an eight-hour working day. Women meanwhile mounted the first serious national campaign for suffrage and undertook an unprecedented public discussion of domestic violence in their own homes. These staggering developments were evidence of how beholden they were to what Karl Marx referred to in an address to US workers at the time as the "moral impetus . . . to your class movement" flowing from the slave's emancipation.[3]

Many whites did imagine freedom and moved toward it in the 1860s because they did to some extent join what Baldwin called "suffering and dancing" humanity. They could no longer take for granted the ideological connections of whiteness with independence and with ability that had been hard-wired into antebellum US nationalism. This chapter accounts for a brief period of "emancipation from whiteness" after the Civil War.[4] The aim is to further show that inspiration and misery were present at the same time. Both led to intensified capacities to imagine and to pursue new freedom dreams among whites.

The first section of the chapter grounds its contributions to studying the Civil War and its aftermath in disability studies and especially in the work of the historian Douglas Baynton. Baynton's scholarship provides a guide to how various forms of oppression connect, and helps us to under

---

2 James Baldwin, *The Fire Next Time* (New York: Vintage, 1993 [1963]), 96.

3 For Marx, see International Workingmen's Association, "Address to the National Labor Union" (May 12, 1866), available at marxists.org.

4 David R. Roediger, *The Wages of Whiteness: Race and the Making of the American Working Class* (London and New York: Verso, 1991), 173.

stand the specific role of ability and disability in shaping post–Civil War discourses regarding equality. The second section offers a brief history of the glorious coming of emancipation as an alternative vision to the bleak realities of wartime destruction. The self-active seeking of freedom by slaves and nominally free Blacks saturated US culture during and just after the war. Combined with the destruction of the war, such motion made possible a brief emancipation from whiteness.

WHITENESS, ABILITY, CARNAGE

For researchers in the critical history of whiteness in the United States, Baynton's recent "Disability and the Justification of Inequality in American History" represents the most exciting text since Cheryl Harris's mid-1990s publications of "Whiteness as Property" and "Finding Sojourner's Truth." Baynton wrote this article not as a scholar in the critical study of whiteness but as an historian of disability. However, his article reinforced Harris's conclusions regarding the assumptions, even among those whites having the most meager property or privilege, that in the natural order of things whiteness ought to lead to political and economic independence. Baynton began not with the white male's presumed fitness for freedom but with the situation in which such presumptions confined the victims of white male power. He showed that, in order to battle for equal rights, African Americans, women, and immigrants have had to argue that they were not disabled. If their rights were to be respected, the "normality" of Blacks had to be established against claims that they as a group were lacking in intelligence and reason, subject to physical deformities, and/or "prone to become disabled" if free. To vote, to control property, and to enjoy other civil rights, women needed to show that they were not irrational, hysterical, or weak and to demonstrate that moving outside traditional realms did not make them "monstrous." Immigrants needed to prove that they were not feeble-minded, sources of disease, or outside a standard of sanity defined by, among other things, heterosexuality.[5]

Exempt from having to make such defensive arguments were white men. Indeed the nation's republican experiment predicated itself on the independence not only of the new nation but also of its white male citizens. Increasingly the enfranchised came to include even property-less white men, so that race and gender grounded rights explicitly—"whiteness as property" was usually enough to enable full political citizenship even in the absence of ownership of wealth. White men constituted the able: able to productively "husband" the land, thus justifying settler colonial dispossession of Indians; able to own and supposedly control their own labor, able to own property; able to rule households; able to master slaves; and able to vote. Such ideology elided, as many scholars have noted, differences of class among whites. Baynton's insights underline that it further elided the presence of what is now called disability among all sectors of the population, including white men.[6]

Any cursory readings of antebellum literature at its most grand or its most popular would belie the notion that disability followed racial lines. Herman Melville's greatest works, from "Bartleby," to *Benito Cereno*, to *Moby Dick*, to *The Confidence Man*, all decisively turned on white disability, and the best-selling urban noir writings of George Lippard and others were peopled by characters embodying and causing disabilities. But the lawyer-narrator of Melville's "Bartleby," who presided over an office in which every adult worker suffered from work-related disabilities, alter-

---

5 Douglas Baynton, "Disability and the Justification of Inequality in American History," in *The New Disability History: American Perspectives*, eds. Paul K. Longmore and Lauri Umansky (New York: New York University Press, 2001), 33–57. Cf. Cheryl Harris, "Whiteness as Property," *Harvard Law Review* 106, no. 7 (1993): 1709–91, and Harris, "Finding Sojourner's Truth: Race, Gender, and the Institution of Property," *Cardozo Law Review* 18, no. 2 (1996): 309–409.

6 Ibid. For a superb study of US slavery and disability, see Jenifer L. Barclay, "Cripples All! Or, The Mark of Slavery: Disability and Race in Antebellum America, 1820–1860" (PhD diss., Michigan State University, 2011); on race, slavery, and disability, see Dea H. Boster, *African-American Slavery and Disability: Bodies, Property, and Power in the Antebellum South, 1800–1860* (New York: Routledge, 2013), 17–33 and 121–4.

nately processed the title character's work-related mental illness as utterly idiosyncratic and as a condition of "humanity." Disability was present but did not lead the narrator to question the links between whiteness, fitness, and rights in a nation fabricated on the ideal of white male independence. To mount such a challenge required going over the top in terms of both plot and symbolism, as in Edgar Allan Poe's 1839 short story "The Man That Was Used Up." In the latter, the white military hero referred to in the title was assembled and reassembled from prostheses regularly by an African-American servant, having lost all limbs.[7]

Powerful discourses typically mitigated and effaced tensions between white male disability and independence. Mary Klages's *Woeful Afflictions: Disability and Sentimentality in Victorian America* shows that reformers could selectively call on a substantial moral philosophy tradition making empathy, rather than rationality and productivity, the keys to social citizenship. They could shift debate in the antebellum years from whether those with limited hearing, sight, and/or mobility were "normal" to consideration of whether the disabled were "normalizable." But, in doing so, they often stressed economic independence, training disabled workers in the very crafts that industrialization was elbowing aside. When more feelings-based solutions were tried—emphasizing that the disabled had capacities to feel and the desirability of feeling for them was central to "True Womanhood" and "True Manhood"—normalizing seemed a mostly domestic matter, divorced from public realms and republican, manly claims to rights. As Klages writes, "In rejecting disability as a sign of inhuman difference . . . reformers had to embrace disability as a sign of

---

7 See esp. Melville, "Bartleby the Scrivener" (New York: Melville House, 2010) and Lippard, *The Quaker City, Or, The Monks of Monk-Hall* (Philadelphia: by the author, 1847). See also Cynthia Hall, "'Colossal Vices' and 'Terrible Deformities' in George Lippard's Gothic Nightmare" in *Demons of the Body and Mind: Essays on Disability in Gothic Literature*, ed. Ruth Beinstock Anolik (Jefferson, NC: McFarland & Company, 2010). For Poe, see eapoe.org and the discussion in Susan-Mary Grant, "Reconstructing the National Body: Masculinity, Disability, and Race in the American Civil War," *Proceedings of the British Academy* 154 (2008), 285–6.

weakness, suffering, and pathos."[8] This set of significations sat uneasily
alongside constitutional presumptions of ability and independence among
white men.

Thus, there was no solution to the problem of where to place the
population of not fully normalizable white males when the Civil War
swelled their ranks to unprecedented proportions. In the North alone,
about 282,000 soldiers survived wounds. With victims of what would
now be called post-traumatic stress disorder added in and given that
about three-fifths of the 364,000 killed in the war died of disease and
other non-combat causes (often after living with illness for a time), disability surpassed death as a consequence of combat for the over two
million soldiers and sailors serving the Union. Overwhelmingly young
or middle-aged, white, and formerly "able," these disabled veterans were
intimately associated with the very essence of republican patriotic sacrifice. But that sacrifice often left them unable to provide for families.
The Confederacy suffered wholesale wounding of soldiers, reaching
perhaps 15 percent of all participants on that side, though also lower
survival rates, leaving the South with about 137,000 survivors of wounds.
The historian Lisa Long puts the total number of casualties not resulting
in death at half a million, totaling losses on both sides. Sixty thousand
amputations resulted from the war. Three quarters of the Civil War
amputees survived. While the dead could be memorialized in a way
consigning the "republic of suffering" to the past, the disabled presented
greater challenges. As the leading historian of the war and disability,
Susan-Mary Grant has written that a pattern of "scholarly and public
preference for the sacrificial dead over the living veteran" quickly took
hold and continues to shape the Civil War memories we preserve. She
argues that Southern disabled veterans were "lost boys," invisible in a
society premised on "white masculine selfhood that stressed individual

---

8 Mary Klages, *Woeful Afflictions: Disability and Sentimentality in Victorian America* (Philadelphia:
University of Pennsylvania Press, 1999), 17–21, and 34–43.

agency and independence." Much the same could be said of the North's forgotten wounded.[9]

During the war and after, care of the wounded overwhelmingly fell to women. Female caregivers' courage in the face of danger and their presence around horrific injury meant that the caring labor of women was on display alongside the wholesale disabling of hundreds of thousands of mostly white men. Such a juxtaposition interrupted equations of white manhood and fitness for citizenship. Displays of feminine heroism were often strikingly public, but they were more often intimate. Perhaps the most telling representation of the new realities of gender and disability was Winslow Homer's August 26, 1865, *Harper's Weekly* wood engraving *The Empty Sleeve*. In it, a man and woman inhabited the semi-public space of a plush carriage moving along a beach. Her face was earnest, able, and as somber as that of her passenger, whose disability gives the sketch its title and her role of driver of the carriage. "The Empty Sleeve at Newport; Or, Why Edna Ackland Learned to Drive," the short fiction accompanying the image, was far more upbeat in its love-conquers-all ending but reflected the ideological work necessary to make optimism possible. The amputee in the story, Captain Harry Ash, had returned from war and was ordered to seek the healing sea breezes at Newport to recover. He spied Edna Ackland driving a carriage on the beach, a Black male servant sitting behind her. Ash had hoped Ackland would be waiting for him after the war, but his disability compounded their class differences in ways that made this seem impossible. She was of the "Uppertendom" and he distinctly was not. Now the war had left him with "his left sleeve pinned

9   Table 2-23, "Principal Wars in which the US Participated: US Military Personnel Serving and Casualties" prepared by Washington Headquarters Services, Directorate for Information Operations and Reports, US Department of Defense Records, as reprinted by United States Civil War Center at web.archive.org/web/20070711050249/http://www.cwc.lsu.edu/other/stats/warcost.htm; Grant, "Reconstructing the National Body," 281 ("preference") and 289–90; Lisa Long, *Rehabilitating Bodies: Health, History, and the American Civil War* (Philadelphia: University of Pennsylvania Press, 2004), 67; Grant, "The Lost Boys: Citizen-Soldiers, Disabled Veterans, and Confederate Nationalism in the Age of People's War," *Journal of the Civil War Era* 2 (June 2012), 233 ("selfhood") and 234–59; Drew Gilpin Faust, *This Republic of Suffering: Death and the American Civil War* (New York: Vintage, 2008).

empty to his breast, and his whole frame as feeble as that of any child."
Feeling she could not love a broken man "shut off from manly sports for
life . . . an invalid to be nursed and tended," Ash wished for his own death.
He made the carefree image of her driving the locus of his displaced rage.
"I grieve," he told her bitterly, "to see a woman unwomanly." Only when
she revealed that she learned to drive in anticipation of his needs as a
disabled veteran, and confessed her love, did Ash melt, asking at once for
her forgiveness, pity, and love. Coupled, they restore his manhood and
her femininity. In the very strained closing lines, he is said to guide her
driving, "so that in reality, she is only his left hand, and he, the husband,
drives."[10]

Winslow Homer, *Our Watering-Places—The Empty Sleeve at Newport*

---

10 Unsigned, "The Empty Sleeve at Newport; Or, Why Edna Ackland Learned to Drive," *Harper's Weekly* (August 26, 1865), 534. See also Jalynn Olsen Padilla, "Army of 'Cripples': Northern Civil War Amputees, Disability, and Manhood in Victorian America" (PhD diss.: University of Delaware, 2007), 165–6 and passim.

Both Union and Rebel armies formed an "Invalid Corps," attempting to make use of the wounded and diseased in lighter duty and to facilitate return of the disabled to combat. The Union's efforts in this regard enrolled 60,000 troops, far outdistancing the numbers in the entire army before the war. The name of the forces eventually changed to the Veterans Reserve Corps, but Cripples Brigade, Cripple Brigade, and Infidel Corps—the last tugging at broad social anxieties connecting disability and allegedly dissolute habits—were also heard. The war effort likewise renewed the issue of disability in the extent to which prospective enlistees and draftees were declared unfit for service. The popular war song "The Invalid Corps" actually focused on those judged unable to serve. Its lyrics suggested the ways in which war exacerbated the distance between able masculine social citizenship and disability:

> Some had "cork legs" and some "one eye"
> With backs deformed and crooked.
> I'll bet you'd laugh'd till you had cried
> To see how "cute" they looked.

In another example of musical identification of Invalid Corpsmen as unfit to serve from the start, rather than hurt in battle, a surgeon dismissed a recruit with

> Your lungs are much affected,
> And likewise both your eyes are cock'd
> And otherwise defected.

The alternative slur held that the Invalids were fit, and that the Corps set up "asylums for shirkers and cowards." As one officer observed, wounded men "frequently begged" to be sent back to combat rather than to stay in conditions more conducive to recovery. They wanted to avoid wearing the sky blue Invalid Corps uniform that troops saw as degrading and to avoid paying "the price of being called invalid." One injured soldier reckoned "purgatory" preferable to Invalid Corps service.[11]

The sustained and consequential policy response of the federal government to wartime disability recapitulated the problem of squaring white images of manly independence with the ravages of war. The massive Civil War pension program, begun in 1862, inaugurated important aspects of a modern welfare state, as the historian and political scientist Theda Skocpol has shown. In doing so, the program originally targeted the disabled (and families of those killed) for aid, awarding benefits to those maimed or made chronically ill in service of the Union. Only later, after 1890, did it more approximate an across-the-board benefit for surviving Union veterans as a group. Historians of disability and race Larry Logue and Peter Blanck point out that claiming a military pension was a risky way for veterans to "reaffirm their manly devotion" to the nation. Such pensions honored those who, as the *New York Times* phrased it, "sacrificed health [and] competence" to the nation's cause.[12]

The pension program grew to be massive, serving about three quarters of a million military veterans and families at one moment in the 1890s and many more than that overall. From 1880 until 1910, about a fourth of total federal government revenues went to such pension payments, and in some years the figure approached 50 percent. Wisconsin's Robert M. La Follette estimated in his autobiography that as much as a third of his time in Congress between 1885 and 1891 went to making inquiries

---

11   Charles F. Johnson and Fred Pelka, *The Civil War Letters of Colonel Charles F. Johnson, Invalid Corps* (Amherst, MA: University of Massachusetts Press, 2004), 14 ("shirkers," "defected," and "begged"), 133 ("Infidel"), and 1–39; "The Invalid Corps," reprinted at The Civil War Zone at civilwarzone.com ("cork"). Pelka's excellent introduction connects anxiety and disability compellingly. For "purgatory," see "Henry C. Gilbert to Hattie Gilbert" (November 22, 1863) in Henry C. Gilbert Letters at Clements Library at University of Michigan; for "Cripple Brigade," see "Thomas D. Willis to Brother Seth" (February 2, 1864) in Thomas D. Willis Letters at Clements Library at University of Michigan.

12   Theda Skocpol, *Protecting Soldiers and Mothers: The Political Origins of Social Policy in the United States* (Cambridge, MA: Harvard University Press, 1992), 102–51; Larry M. Logue and Peter Blanck, *Race, Ethnicity, and Disability: Veterans and Benefits in Post-Civil War America* (Cambridge, UK: Cambridge University Press, 2010), 3.

regarding military pensions. Indeed the preservation of records necessitated by the pension system so strained the architecture of one depository, the historic Ford's Theatre where Lincoln had been shot, that two floors collapsed in 1893, killing twenty-two. Pensions were a white entitlement but with important complications. Because whites served more frequently in the Union ranks without the period of exclusion suffered by African Americans, because their service was better documented, because their dependents and spouses were more readily identifiable, because they had more access to political power to influence decisions, and because they were favored by the pension boards over Black applicants, even when physicians recommended awarding the pension to the latter group, the dominant race dominated the pension rolls. The greatest freedom fighter associated with the Civil War military, the ex-slave and Underground Railroad activist Harriet Tubman, led many hundreds of slaves to freedom during the war, but she fought unsuccessfully for decades to gain her own pension before belatedly gaining one as a widow. Slaves emancipated during the war who became soldiers fared most poorly in the pension bureaucracy. However, Black disabled veterans did join Northern whites in drawing federal pensions, and Confederate veterans generally did not, settling for relatively meager state pensions. Such a pattern interrupted any firm connections between being a deserving citizen and being white. Indeed, the pension system served as a model for late-nineteenth-century African-American efforts to secure reparations for slavery.[13]

Heroism and neediness made the disabled veteran an apt symbol of republican sacrifice but not necessarily of republican manhood. According to a leading history of the Civil War, race, and disability, to collect the

---

13 Faust, *This Republic of Suffering*, 255–6; Catherine Clinton, *Harriet Tubman: The Road to Freedom* (New York: Little and Brown, 2004), 193–205; Skocpol, *Protecting Soldiers and Mothers*, 113–14, 121–2, and 139–40; Logue and Blanck, *Race, Ethnicity, and Disability*, 57 and 41–82; Mary Frances Berry, *My Face Is Black It Is True: Callie House and the Ex-Slave Reparations Movement* (New York: Vintage, 2006), esp. xiv, 34–5, and 48; Jim Downs, *Sick from Freedom: African-American Illness and Suffering during the Civil War and Reconstruction* (New York: Oxford University Press, 2012), 146–61.

pension, applicants had "to make public presentation of potentially stigmatizing disabilities." Though the pension process screened out those with
"vicious habits," helping to certify the pensioners as deserving, recipients
were also avowedly, or perhaps confessedly, dependent. Bearing what some
participants in a penmanship contest for disabled veterans thought of as
"honorable scars," a veteran also had to admit at times to being "a permanent cripple for life," as one contestant in the same competition lamented.
Revisions of pension law in 1866 recognized those needing "constant
personal aid and attention" in one category alongside those considered
"incapacitated for performing any manual labor." Beneficiaries thus certi-
fiably lacked independence and free labor, the cornerstones defining white
republican manhood.[14]

Disability was at once celebrated for its connection to heroism and
hidden for its connection to weakness. The featuring of the disabled in
memorial celebrations of the war and the record of some politicians
emphasizing their war-related disabilities in campaigns join the dignified
images of amputees produced by artists to show that wounds could sometimes be borne as honorable. Disability scholar Frances Clarke shows that
the Northern disabled veterans could personify a lost limb as itself a heroic
soldier "sacrificed to maintain the integrity of home and nation." They
mourned its loss and moved on, sometimes professing certainty that after
death they would again be whole. They often did not conceal injury with
prosthetic devices. But the refusal of prosthetic devices could also be read
as reflecting a desire to be apart from the benevolent societies making the
provision of limbs a key to rehabilitating and debilitating charity. During
and just after the war, participation rates of Union veterans in the pension
program remained startlingly small. The bureaucracy busied itself producing guidelines for compensating disabilities (one arm lost at the

---

14 Logue and Blanck, *Race, Ethnicity, and Disability*, 3 ("stigmatizing" and "permanent cripple"),
19 ("constant" and "manual"), 32 ("vicious habits"), 1–40; George Fredrickson, *The Inner Civil War:
Northern Intellectuals and the Crisis of the Union* (Urbana, IL: University of Illinois Press, 1993 [1965]),
79–112.

shoulder yielded eighteen dollars a month but if lost at the elbow, a sixth less). But in 1865, less than 2 percent of Civil War veterans in "civil life" had enrolled as pensioners. Even in 1875, only one survivor in sixteen was on the rolls. As Skocpol observes, twice that proportion of Union soldiers had suffered wounds and would have had a good case for pensions, but many refrained from making claims. Such abstention is perhaps unsurprising in light of the attitudes reflected in the words of United States Sanitary Commission head Henry Whitney Bellows, who branded the injured veteran as potentially not only "physically but morally disabled." When participation rates grew, the pension program became associated with charges of wholesale fraud, again interrupting connections of the state to the deserving veteran.[15]

Gender and race persistently inflected the complex connections of war-caused disability with being fit for citizenship but eligible for pensions. Disability connected injured veterans to women at the level of policy. During the war, Confederate practice for a time granted draft exemptions ensuring that, if a plantation were owned by a "feme sole" or an "unsound" man, exemption could be provided. Union policies of specifically preferring employment of "able-bodied" African-American men as contraband and then as troops also connected gender, race, and disability. After the war, Union pensions went to widows and disabled men. The freed slave and disabled veteran, both recently heroic and durably suspect, appeared in tandem again and again. The veteran in the penmanship contest who bemoaned having to identify as a "cripple" added that to do so was to lose "our place in society," making him think that he "might as well be black." The pairings sometimes told a story of discrimination, as in the singling

---

15 Frances Clarke, "'Honorable Scars': Northern Amputees and the Meaning of Civil War Injuries," in *Union Soldiers and the Home Front: Wartime Experiences, Postwar Adjustments*, eds. Paul Cimbala and Randall Miller (New York: Fordham University Press, 2002), 389–90 ("integrity"), 393, and 361–94; Padilla, "Army of 'Cripples,'" 149–54; Grant, "Reconstructing the National Body," 302 (Bellows) and 296–317; Laurann Figg and Jane Farrell-Beck, "Amputation in the Civil War: Physical and Social Dimensions," *The Journal of the History of Medicine and Allied Sciences* 48 (October 1993), 468; Skocpol, *Protecting Soldiers and Mothers*, 106–9 and, on fraud, 143–6 and 275–6.

out late in the war of Black and "invalid" troops as the only ones ineligible for reenlistment bonuses, a brutality that the officer writing one official report branded as based on "inequality and injustice."[16]

There were promising glimmers of solidarity, as in the exalted places the Invalid Corps and African Americans were accorded in early celebrations and in their roles in early Memorial Days, an African-American-initiated and, for a time, racially diverse site of memory of an emancipatory war rather than the vehicle for the celebration of white reconciliation across sectional lines that the day became. Nonetheless, the sense that each group was under scrutiny as to its fitness for rights made mobilization around disability issues difficult to broach. The decision to move many white Invalid Corps officers into positions of power in the Freedman's Bureau suggests the ways that connections could coexist with assumptions about hierarchy. The best documented career spanning both organizations, that of Colonel Charles E. Johnson, demonstrates tremendous political growth from deep wartime racism to a steady commitment to defending the lives and interests of freedpeople. Fred Pelka, who gathered Johnson's letters for publication, charts these dynamics and their "limits" meticulously, showing the transformations possible around issues of disability and race before Johnson's death in 1867. Over time, as Grant shows, retreating from Reconstruction also entailed turning away from such potential transformations and from celebrating both the disabled veteran and African-American heroism in favor of reconciliationist politics uniting whites.[17]

Perhaps the most fascinating linkage of race and disability in popular culture during the Civil War and Reconstruction lay in the connection of

16 Thavolia Glymph, *Out of the House of Bondage: The Transformation of the Plantation Household* (Cambridge, UK: Cambridge University Press, 2008), 121 ("unsound"); Logue and Blanck, *Race, Ethnicity, and Disability*, 3 ("our place" and "might as well").

17 Johnson and Pelka, *The Civil War Letters of Colonel Charles F. Johnson*, 33 ("limits") and 31–7, 300–1 ("distinction"), 304–17; David W. Blight, "The First Decoration Day" at davidwblight.com and *Race and Reunion: The Civil War in American Memory* (Cambridge, MA: Harvard University Press, 2001), esp. 64–90; Jim Downs, *Sick from Freedom: African-American Illness and Suffering during the Civil War and Reconstruction* (New York: Oxford University Press, 2012), 126; Grant, "Reconstructing the National Body," 273–318.

both to greenback currency. As the cultural historian Michael O'Malley has shown, conservative commitments to "sound" money backed by gold, or failing that, silver, were rocked by a war partly funded by the Union's printing of "greenback" currency. The basis of so much of the nation's supply of bank notes in the surety of slave ownership likewise unraveled quickly. The campaigns against Radical Reconstruction traded on the "unnatural" advantages of Northern "carpetbaggers" who moved south after the war, their flimsy luggage allegedly stuffed with unsound or counterfeit paper money. The white supremacist goal of the "redemption" of the South gestured toward not only theology but also to debt and currency. The human analogue of "queer" money was the emancipated slave, living in violation of the allegedly natural order of things. Popular culture paired paper money, seen during and after the war as a "people's" currency, expanding opportunities for those rising in the world with the prospect of arming the slaves as keys to speedy Union victory. Thus the wartime song, "How Are You Green-Backs" featured

> We're coming, Father Abram, nine hundred thousand strong,
> With nine hundred thousand darkies, sure the traitors can't last
> long.

Opponents of emancipation reversed the same connection, derogating worthless currency in an 1862 song and then asking

> What next I wonder? Nigger troops
> Or some such abomination.

The derogatory term for the greenback, "shinplaster," made the tie to disability, implying a note so worthless it could better serve as a bandage for the wounded than as money. In the wake of the war, comparisons of the greenback to the disabled veteran proliferated. A campaign poem from 1878 included

> O, Greenback, veteran of the years!
> Thou crippled soldier of the war!
> Baptized with blood and wet with tears.[18]

The figure of the Black veteran amputee, so tellingly used by Thomas Nast in an 1865 *Harper's Weekly* cartoon arguing for African-American voting rights and painted with such dignity by Thomas Waterman Wood, in particular challenged the separation of the rights of disabled veterans from those of freedpeople. Nast even paired his portrait of the Black amputee without the franchise with a drawing of "Pardon," featuring prominent forgiven Confederates.[19]

Ubiquitous encounters with unthinkable suffering demonstrated how fragile and how ordinary white male ability was. Just before the war, the white supremacist New York writer Dr. John H. Van Evrie had argued that all whites "naturally" excelled all Africans. He had to allow that the "idiotic, insane, or otherwise incapable" whites were exceptions. Combat put Black capability on display. It also swelled the ranks of disabled whites dramatically. Moreover, the fratricidal carnage proved a poor setting in which to exalt the rationality of white male citizenship. In the moment when the dependency of increasing numbers of white men became apparent, women showed unimagined capacities for independence. Women's nursing of the wartime wounded was perhaps the most dramatic example of how disability mattered in reshaping other axes of inequality. But more generally, women's contributions to patriotism in the North and

---

18   Michael O'Malley, *Face Value: The Entwined Histories of Money & Race in America* (Chicago: University of Chicago Press, 2012), 97 ("Abram"), 98 ("abomination"), 96 ("crippled"), and 83–123. On the greenback as a "people's money," see also David Montgomery, *Beyond Equality: Labor and the Radical Republicans, 1862–1872* (New York: Knopf, 1967), 425–47. On shinplasters, see John Russell Bartlett, *Dictionary of Americanisms: A Glossary of Words and Phrases Usually Regarded as Peculiar to the United States* (Boston: Little, Brown and Company, 1860), 402.

19   Grant, "Reconstructing the National Body," 307–8, reproduces the Wood paintings. Nast's "Pardon and Franchise" appeared in *Harper's Weekly* (August 5, 1865), 488–9.

Thomas Waterman Wood, *A Bit of War History: The Veteran*

Thomas Nast, *Pardon and Franchise*

treason in the South highlighted their abilities both to carry on household
economic activities independently and to attempt to rebuild male bodies
and spirits in the wake of male disability through caring labor. LeeAnn
Whites has written that the Southern soldier "had to recognize, if only
unconsciously, the extent to which his manhood and independence was
relational . . . built upon the foundations of women's service and love."[20]
Such was still more pointedly true for the disabled veteran, as Baynton
discusses regarding the pervasiveness of disability as a category in its own

20   Fredrickson, *The Inner Civil War*, 79 and 98. LeeAnn Whites, *Gender Matters: Civil War, Recon-
struction, and the Making of the New South* (New York: Palgrave, 2005), 21; see also Whites, *The Civil
War as a Crisis in Gender: Augusta, Georgia, 1860–1890* (Athens, GA: University of Georgia Press,
1995), 48, 112–14, 137–48, 200–1, and 223; Laura Edwards, *Gendered Strife and Confusion: The
Political Culture of Reconstruction* (Urbana, IL: University of Illinois Press, 1997), 107 and 113–14.
Van Evrie as quoted in Baynton, "Disability and the Justification of Inequality in American History,"
38. See also Susan-Mary Grant, "To Bind Up the Nation's Wounds: Women and the American Civil
War," in *The Practice of U.S. Women's History: Narratives, Intersections, and Dialogues*, eds. Susan Klein-
berg, Eileen Boris, and Vicky Ruiz (New Brunswick, NJ: Rutgers University Press, 2007), 106–125.

right and as one helping to constitute other axes of inequality. White men's claims to a unique fitness for independence faced challenges not only from disability in their own ranks but also from changing relations with African Americans and white women. Undoubtedly the most dramatic such change, one witnessed by all, was the seemingly impossible self-emancipation of four million slaves.

WITNESSING JUBILEE

The presence of those desiring freedom provoked divided responses among white troops, but as the war became bloodier and more uncertain, many wished that danger could be shared and hardship alleviated through use of slave labor in the Union war effort. The reasoning could be eminently practical. As Charles Graham Halpine's popular 1862 song "Sambo's Right to Be Kilt" put it

> Some tell me 'tis a burnin' shame
> To make the naygers fight,
> And that the trade of bein' kilt
> Belongs but to the white.
> But as for me, upon my soul!
> So lib'ral are we here,
> I'll let Sambo be shot instead of myself
> On ev'ry day in the year.[21]

Other soldiers reflected on the need for service work that fugitive women could provide. As historian Leslie Schwalm's account of emancipation in the upper Midwest shows, formerly enslaved women made

---

21 Irwin Silber, ed., *Songs of the Civil War* (New York: Columbia University Press, 1960), 308–9 and 328–30.

decisive contributions to the war effort by "cooking, sewing, washing, caring for horses, and nursing the sick and wounded." But dithering on the question of accepting their presence and using their skills characterized the early war. In July 1862, an Iowan stationed in Mississippi connected his own miseries regarding lack of food to the refusal to allow slaves to cross Union lines. Dismissal from the army, he complained, threatened troops caught employing a slave cook.[22]

Reactions to contrabands were never simple. In spring 1862, Commodore John Rodgers Goldsborough, commanding an encampment of contrabands at Fernandina Island, Florida, waited nearly three weeks to be able to mail a letter to his wife. The letter grew and grew, reaching about fifty pages of often vivid descriptions and conflicted feelings. Goldsborough reported that he threatened African Americans on the island with return to slavery if they did not obey perfectly. He fretted that the recalcitrance of men in particular would undermine his plans to make the island self-sufficient. But he also very quickly began to gain knowledge of slavery that made him think and listen. "Their tales of cruelty" by masters, he wrote of the slaves, "are too awful to relate and their manner of escape in several instances is truly wonderful." Goldsborough witnessed couples separated by masters joyously reuniting on the island and saw the importance parents attached to literacy for the young. Indeed he found that the "grown-up Negroes" were likewise "eager to go to school and learn" after a day's work. The women, "more industrious," made "excellent washers and ironers." Deep into the letter, he still worried that African Americans might eventually move north in great numbers. However, when Rebels tried to re-enslave or murder African Americans on Union-held St. Simon's Island, he described their raid as "diabolical."[23]

22 Leslie A. Schwalm, *Emancipation's Diaspora: Race and Reconstruction in the Upper Midwest* (Chapel Hill, NC: University of North Carolina Press, 2009), 60 and 280n43.
23 "Commodore John Rodgers Goldsborough to Mary Pennington Goldsborough" (April 21–May 8, 1862), Hargrett Rare Books and Manuscript Library, University of Georgia. Thanks to Bao Bui for research assistance on this reference. On the Rebels' desire to recapture slaves from the island, see also Du Bois, *Black Reconstruction in America* (1998), 61. Cf. Hiram M. Cash, 5th ME Volunteer Regiment,

William Ball of the 5th Wisconsin Battery offered an especially com-
prehensive view of the reasons that Union troops saw benefits in embracing
aid from escaped slaves in a series of letters from early in the war. "No
wonder," he wrote, "soldiers become abolitionists as they go south if they
were not before." For Ball, the war brought a series of object lessons in the
cruelty of masters, including cruelty to slaves whom he saw as phenotyp-
ically white. Ball reported that fleeing slaves often brought horses and
mules with them, as well as knowledge of Confederate troop movements.
He found those who came, men and women, to be "very useful as cooks
or washerman or hostlers." He praised their intelligence, heroism, and
bearing. According to Ball, "They bear the privations of camp life cheer-
fully, living with the hope that at the close of the war" they would "find a
home where the crack of the cruel driver's lash, or the bay of the fierce
bloodhound is not heard." He thought as early as May 1862, that valued
contrabands were "virtually free" and hoped that they would remain so.[24]

Flight to freedom by slaves, and the Confederate brutality it occa-
sioned, recruited white soldiers to abolitionism. They frequently saw
the work of contrabands as critical and noted how passionately African
Americans labored for the Union cause. Connecting the zeal to serve
the Union cause as laborers with a desire for freedom, whites often
argued that African Americans were superior to northern whites as war
workers. One superintendent of contraband labor reported that "the
lowest estimate is . . . that one negro is worth three soldiers." Other
lessons held more drama. Two slaves presenting themselves to a Union
officer in Baton Rouge in the summer of 1862 found little sympathy.

---

to his parents April 7/8, 1862; Warington Junction, VA, in Hiram M. Cash letters (University of
Virginia, Special Collections Library).

24 Ball's letters are in the US Army Military History Institute in Carlisle, Pennsylvania. For the
quotes, see "Ball to his brother Quigley" (March 28, 1862); "Ball to his brother D. Smith"(March 29,
1862); and "Ball to his brother Quig" (June 10, 1862); see also "Ball to his brother Quig" (May 30,
1862); Ball to his sister Lib" (August 13, 1862); and "Ball to his brother Smith" (September 8, 1862).
Also reporting particular horror at treatment of a white and blue-eyed slave, a master's son, was "George
W. Landrum, US Signal Corps, to his sister Amanda" (April 15, 1862) in George W. Landrum letters;
VFM 4704, Ohio Historical Society, Columbus, Ohio.

Returned to their master, they then showed up again, wounds gaping from beatings and each wearing a "horrid three-pronged iron collar." On reentering Union lines, they found sanctuary. Troops cheered their commander who refused to return the fugitives, suffering disciplinary action for his stance. Although we generally think of fugitives as coming before an officer who decided their fate, they would most often have first encountered enlisted men, the first-responders to their plight. The resulting direct-action abolitionism—receiving a fugitive on human terms—meant that familiarity with the need for manpower and later bearing witness to the valor of Black troops were not the only factors conditioning the often favorable opinions white troops held toward enlisting African Americans. Indeed, one recent account suggests that General John C. Frémont's efforts to free Missouri slaves early in the war stemmed in part from his imitating the direct actions of white troops who first refused to return runaway slaves; another notes that later in the war, white rank-and-file troops at times encouraged immediate enlistment by ex-slaves, without the intervention of an officer.[25]

There were also numerous stories of African Americans still enslaved using knowledge of local terrain in hiding and otherwise aiding Union troops in danger of being seized by Confederates. Slaves connected, in the view of some historians, those white Union troops evading capture with the Underground Railroad networks that had taken so many African Americans to freedom. The Union troops, some of them escapees from

---

25 Ira Berlin et al, eds., *Freedom: A Documentary History of Emancipation, 1861–1867*, Series 1, Volume 3, *The Wartime Genesis of Free Labor: The Lower South* (Cambridge, UK: Cambridge University Press, 1990), 20 ("estimate"); Schwalm, *Emancipation's Diaspora* 58; Donald Martin Jacobs, "A History of the Boston Negro from the Revolution to the Civil War" (PhD diss.: Boston University, 1968), 362–70; Chandra Manning, *What This Cruel War Was Over: Soldiers, Slavery and the Civil War* (New York: Vintage, 2008), esp. 13, 44–51, 76–8, 94–6, and 189–204. For reservations about the patterns of egalitarianism that Manning carefully lays out, see Gary Gallagher, *The Union War* (Cambridge, MA: Harvard University Press, 2011), 79–82. On rank-and-file German Americans' increasing sympathy with slaves' suffering in wartime Missouri, see Alison Clark Efford, *German Immigrants, Race, and Citizenship in the Civil War Era* (New York: Cambridge University Press, 2013), 93–4; see also Rebecca J. Scott, *Degrees of Freedom: Louisiana and Cuba after Slavery* (Cambridge, MA: Harvard University Press, 2005), 35.

Confederate custody, faced the bloodhounds and other harrowing experiences of hiding out that fugitive slaves had long known. Representations of their escapes called on tropes familiar in the narratives of those who had fled slavery. Frederick Douglass grounded postwar appeals for Black rights partly on just such heroism by slaves defending fleeing Union troops. He told white Republicans in 1879, "We were your friends in the South when you had no other friends there. The soldier boys knew we were their friends when they were escaping from Andersonville, and Libby, and Castle Thunder. They didn't like to see white men at that time." Instead, he continued, "Uncle Tom, and Uncle Jim, and Caesar . . . would feed them when hungry, show them the way when lost, and shelter them when they were shelterless."[26]

Conversely, white soldiers aided slaves in recovering property from their former households. In 1862, long before the Emancipation Proclamation and African-American troops, General William Tecumseh Sherman felt compelled to inveigh against such premature seeking of justice by white soldiers and contraband slaves. Sherman insisted that "The Clothing & effects of the negro are the property of the master & mistress." The general strike of the slaves confronted many white soldiers with the real choice that Huck Finn faced in fiction: to return an enslaved person to slavery or to abet his or her self-liberation. Quite apart from ideology, they decided whether to send slaves back to brutality. Even as a desire to be

---

26 Evan Kutzler, "Crossing Tracks in the Confederate South: The Underground Railroad, Race, and Union Prisoners of War" (Unpublished paper, University of South Carolina, Department of History, 2013); John C. Inscoe, "'Moving through Deserter Country': Fugitive Accounts of the Inner Civil War in Southern Appalachia," in *The Civil War in Appalachia*, eds. Kenneth W. Noe and Shannon H. Wilson (Knoxville, TN: University of Tennessee Press, 1997), 158–86; William B. Hesseltine, "The Underground Railroad from Confederate Prisons to East Tennessee," *The East Tennessee Historical Society's Publications* 2 (1930), 60 and 66. The Douglass quotation is from Frederick Douglass, "Alonzo B. Cornell and the Republican Party: An Address Delivered in Utica, New York, on 30 October 1879," in *The Frederick Douglass Papers, Series One: Speeches, Debates, and Interviews, Volume 4: 1864–80*, edited by John W. Blassingame and John R. McKivigan (New Haven, CT: Yale University Press, 1977), 541 and 533–42. In the same volume see also Frederick Douglass, "We Are Here And Want the Ballot Box: An Address Delivered in Philadelphia, Pennsylvania, on 4 September 1866," 127 and 132–3. Thanks to Evan Kutzler for material in this paragraph.

done with the war by winning it convinced many rank-and-file Union troops to support the end of slavery and to unevenly support Black enlistment, practical relations with contrabands began the process that ended in many white soldiers glorying in the passage of the emancipationist Thirteenth Amendment.[27]

Nor did the impression made by contrabands and Black soldiers confine itself to military heroism and the desire for freedom. Thomas Wentworth Higginson described the poetry of the music of those serving under him, focusing on language, not only rhythm. He found one song that he transcribed, "I Know Moonrise," to be a "flower of poetry" growing in "dark soil." Lingering over a line from it

I'll lie in de grave and stretch out my arms

Higginson decided that "Never . . . since man first lived and suffered, was his infinite longing for peace uttered more plaintively."[28]

In accounting for how freedpeople's activity and dignity transformed understandings of them, of the war, and of what was possible, a look at how emancipation's drama registered in US art provides a useful point of entry. During the war, the radical Pennsylvania Republican William Kelley predicted that future poets would single out the Black soldier as the figure about whom they would "sing in the highest strains." Artists reflected such a profound attraction almost immediately. The wartime market for "patriotic envelopes" produced commercially as both memorabilia and to ship mail, leading to an astounding 15,000 varieties of design from nearly 300 different companies. Images mostly reflected support for the Union. From very early in the war, these envelopes included arresting depictions of slaves as contraband. These contained a fair amount of hilarity and stereotype—

27 Glymph, *Out of the House of Bondage*, 207 (on Sherman); for Frémont, see Mark A. Lause, *Race and Radicalism in the Union Army* (Urbana, IL: University of Illinois Press, 2009), 51.
28 Thomas Wentworth Higginson, *Army Life in a Black Regiment* (Boston: Houghton, Mifflin and Company, 1900), 283–4.

punning on "contra-band" for example to connect refugees with minstrel music. But they also, from the earliest months of the war, made the drama of the slave fleeing to freedom central to the imagery of the war, capturing a sense of possibility for the Union and vulnerability for the Confederacy. A single drawing could combine parody of Black speech with an awareness that flight to freedom continued long traditions of slaves using the North Star as a guide to escape. Such resistance drained the South of the very "currency" on which the Confederacy's existence depended.[29]

"Southern Currency," Civil War envelope, c. 1863

The intersection of the slave's motion with the fate of the Union and Confederacy recurred consistently on the modest little envelopes. In "Contraband Barricade," Rebels are invited to "Come and

29   The image is found in the digital American Memory collection of the Library of Congress, in the section reproducing "Civil War Treasures from the New York Historical Society" at memory.loc.gov. In the same digital collection see especially "Bress de Lor, We Am Contraband" and "Music by the Contra-Band" as minstrel-inflected racist imagery. For further images showing the importance of the threat posed to masters by the flight of contrabands and the purposeful nature of their actions, see "Slave Escaping at Fort Monroe" and "Contraband of War; or Volunteer Sappers and Miners."

get your property." However to do so they will have to face not just
the guns of Yankee troops but the opposition of African Americans
armed with tools, supporting the war effort from the front of the
Union lines.

"Contraband Barricade," Civil War envelope, c. 1862

In another envelope image, probably from 1861, the flight to
freedom of a slave woman is labeled her "secession." As Steven R. Boyd,
a leading student of these envelopes, observes about that particular
image, "Thus two years before the Emancipation Proclamation [it]
raised the specter of the abolition of slavery . . . a freedom secured in
part by African Americans' willingness to take an active role in their
own liberation."[30]

The high art works of Henry Louis Stephens, Elihu Vedder, and above

---

30 "Contraband Barricade" is at the American Memory digital collection at memory.loc.gov. See
also Steven R. Boyd, *Patriotic Envelopes of the Civil War: The Iconography of Union and Confederate
Covers* (Baton Rouge, LA: Louisiana State University Press, 2010), 3, 72, Figure 4:31 and 69–77.
Schwalm, *Emancipation's Diaspora*, 87–9.

all Winslow Homer show similar hesitancies but also great transformations by late in the war, producing a powerful image of dignified ex-slaves as integral to the drama of the age. Stephens, a popular illustrator, would after the war contribute significantly to a small but compelling body of art exploring surgery, amputation, disability, and the nation. In the early 1860s, he reflected provocatively on shadows and race in ways the art historian Sarah Burns links with Herman Melville's earlier novella of slave revolt, *Benito Cereno*.[31]

Nevertheless, few caricaturists, North or South, drew more vicious anti-Black stereotypes than Stephens did prior to and early in the war. His 1860 *Vanity Fair* drawing *Substance and Shadow* foregrounds the fading white supremacist politician Stephen A. Douglas, midair in a minstrel dance pose. Douglas, popularly called the "Little Giant," looks babyish and dissipated simultaneously. The African-American shadow behind him, drawn in accordance with racial stereotypes, utterly overwhelms the politician. In May 1862, the Stephens sketch *The New Frankenstein* featured a cheering-enough image as a hulking Black figure prepared to toss Jefferson Davis off of a cliff and to his "fate," but the avenging slave is monstrous. Like others of Stephens's drawings commenting on the early war, *The New Frankenstein* laid out a powerful vision placing African Americans at the center of national events, but as shadows and as monsters complete with horns, not human actors. In *The Monotonous Minstrel*, Stephens portrayed Horace Greeley's abolitionism as a boring and repetitive tune that Lincoln rightly ignored. The slave population and Black abolitionists became the monkey that dances along to Greeley's tired act. Indeed, many *Vanity Fair* cartoons lacked any subtlety. In portraying abolition and African Americans, they traded on anti-abolitionist and racist stereotypes, especially those connecting slaves to monkeys and apes, and appealed to images of

---

31 Wood, *Black Scare*, 45, for Kelley; Sarah Burns, *Painting the Dark Side: Art and the Gothic Imagination in Nineteenth-Century America* (Berkeley, CA: University of California Press, 2004), 141 144, and 195–6.

monstrosity that raised specters of disability menacing republican freedom.[32]

The Monotonous Minstrel.

President Lincoln, (to H. G.)—"Go away, you tiresome vagrant! It's always the same old croaking tune, 'Abolition, Abolition, Marching On!'"

Henry Louis Stephens, *The Monotonous Minstrel*

---

32   Burns, *Painting the Dark Side*, 114–16 and 142–6 with several *Vanity Fair* illustrations reproduced therein. In Volume 5 of that magazine, see esp. (March 15, 1862) 129; (March 22, 1862) 139; (June 14, 1862) 286 (invoking the North Star as a symbol of flight to emancipation); in Volume 6, see (July 6, 1862) 11; (August 2, 1862) 60; (August 30, 1862) 102; (September 6, 1862) 119; (September 13, 1862) 123; (October 25, 1862) 204.

The slaves' motion changed things. None of the *Vanity Fair* drawings anticipated the quiet human dignity of the untitled Stephens watercolor commemorating the Emancipation Proclamation, probably completed in 1863.

Henry Louis Stephens, *Black Man Reading Newspaper*

Stephens portrays a figure learning of freedom reading by candlelight, much as Lincoln, author of the proclamation, legendarily had read in his youth. Neither caricatured nor fearsome, the old man at the work's center appears dignified and cerebral; indeed he is literally enlightened and is poised for citizenship, dressed beautifully and unobtrusively in red, white, and blue. As one recent account suggests, "The Emancipation Proclamation compelled Stephens to reconsider his previously virulently anti-abolitionist propaganda." *Vanity Fair* greeted the taking effect of the proclamation with a cartoon showing a promising new door opening.[33]

Stephens collaborated in 1863 with the Philadelphia lithographer James Fuller Queen in a series of twelve chromolithographs depicting the evolution of its subject from a slave to a Union soldier. The key image, *Blow for Blow*, shows the hero fighting back against whipping by the master, an assertion of desire for freedom directly echoing Frederick Douglass's account of the turning point in his own life.[34]

The painter Elihu Vedder, at that time making his mark as an interpreter of the "dark side" of human consciousness, at first pictured the slave's plight as mysterious and ominous, if art historians are right in arguing that his large 1863 *The Questioner of the Sphinx* would have been presumed by viewers to be about slavery. With a small, Black figure huddled against a sphinx, the painting joined a body of works of art showing the slave, and/or the nation, searching for signs, sounds, or visions as to the future of African Americans. But it is enigmatic in the extreme and could as easily be considered part of a body of Vedder paintings from this time in which the artist drew subject matter from his own drug use.[35]

---

33 See the Library of Congress press release "Mazie Harris to Discuss Civil War Era Chromolithographs by Henry Louis Stephens at Library of Congress" (November 17, 2008) at loc.gov; "The New Place," *Vanity Fair*, 6 (December 27, 1862), 307.

34 For Douglass, see his *Narrative of the Life of Frederick Douglass* (Boston: The Anti-Slavery Office, 1845), 60–74. The lithograph and description are housed in the digital collections of the Library Company of Philadelphia at lcpdams.librarycompany.org.

35 Burns, *Painting the Dark Side*, 170–1, and, on drugs, 166–70; see also Hugh Honour, *The Image of the Black in Western Art*, Volume 4, Part 1, *From the American Revolution to World War I* (Houston, TX: Menil Foundation, 1989), 229.

Henry Louis Stephens, *Blow for Blow*

Elihu Vedder, *The Questioner of the Sphinx*

Two years later, Vedder would produce the straightforwardly lovely
Jane Jackson, Formerly a Slave, giving a name to his subject in a way rare
when Black Americans were pictured.

Elihu Vedder, *Jane Jackson, Formerly a Slave*

Melville's volume of Civil War poetry, *Battle-Pieces*, which generally
abjured commenting on the meaning of emancipation for slaves, did offer
a tribute to Jane Jackson. Titled *Formerly a Slave*, the verses were written
after seeing his friend Vedder's painting:

> Her children's children they shall know
> The good withheld from her;
> And so her reverie takes prophetic cheer—
> In spirit she sees the stir.
>
> Far down the depth of thousand years,
> And marks the revel shine;
> Her dusky face is lit with sober light,
> Sibylline, yet benign.[36]

---

36 Herman Melville, *Battle-Pieces and Aspects of the War* (New York: Harper & Brothers, 1866),
154.

The composed and dignified (about-to-be) emancipated female slave emerged nowhere in art more gloriously than in Winslow Homer's small painting from the end of the Civil War, *Near Andersonville*. The power of the work lies in its capturing of the extent to which Douglass was right that slaves would bring about not only their own emancipation but also the defeat of the South. The growth in Homer's portrayal of African Americans during the war was striking. Traveling with the Army of the Potomac, Homer sketched the contributions of contrabands early in the war, producing an especially arresting 1862 drawing and watercolor, *Study of a Negro Teamster*. But what the historian and Homer expert Peter Wood calls the "condescending outlook, so prevalent among Northern whites especially early in the war" did not fail to touch Homer's sketches, as for example in *Our Jolly Cook* from 1863.[37]

Near Andersonville could hardly be more different. If Homer's *The Empty Sleeve* is arguably the finest portrayal of disability in Civil War art, *Near Andersonville* is surely the finest portrait of the drama of emancipation. Done at almost the same time, the two works invite comparison. Considering them together highlights the simultaneity of new representations of white male disability and of both female and African-American ability after 1863.

The subject of a fascinating recent short book by Wood, *Near Andersonville* re-narrates the Civil War in a way that was briefly possible when memories of the conflict were fresh. The title refers to the infamous Confederate prisoner-of-war camp in Georgia. The tiny image in the upper left of the painting barely shows Union troops captured by Rebels and presumably headed for Andersonville, the site of about a twentieth of all deaths of Northern troops during the war, though open for only the last fourteen months of the fighting. This in-the-corner drama—martial and

<hr>

37 Peter H. Wood and Karen C.C. Dalton, *Winslow Homer's Images of Blacks: The Civil War and Reconstruction Years* (Austin, TX: University of Texas Press, 1988), 34 and 33–7, including the illustrations discussed; Homer also illustrated disability caused by the war. See Burns, *Painting the Dark Side*, 196, and the discussion of *The Empty Sleeve* earlier in this chapter.

Winslow Homer, *Campaign Sketches: Our Jolly Cook*

Winslow Homer, *Near Andersonville*

white—is minimized, marginalized, and almost smudged. The center of attention and light is a slave woman—her composed countenance reflecting contemplation of opportunities the war presented for her as a Black woman and modern actor in history. Her African head-wrapping, Wood observes, also gestures toward the "liberty cap" so present in the iconography of revolutionary art at the time. Her shirt, he adds, suggested the "Garibaldi blouse" that was a fashion rage in the 1860s, modeling itself after the wardrobe of Italian revolutionary Giuseppe Garibaldi.[38] Long a part of the revolutionary Atlantic world, the African American appeared in *Near Andersonville* pictured as such.

Neither perspiring nor dirty, the woman in the painting appears not to be working much even during daylight. She may instead have been thinking about whether abetting the escape of the Union prisoners was possible. She stood as one of the numberless participants who joined in the general strike of the slaves without leaving the plantations. Her lack of labor contested the authority of mistresses and the depleted ranks of overseers on increasingly unmanageable plantations. She stands then as an apt illustration of Du Bois's observation that the general strike not only reflected "the desire to stop work" but also was conducted "on a wide basis against the conditions of work." The challenges that such slaves presented, as Armstead Robinson's and Thavolia Glymph's scholarship demonstrate, deepened the internal gender and class tensions that wrote the South's epitaph. Homer's subject was a part of the slave ranks who "moved silently," in Du Bois words—"listening, hoping, hesitating"—but whose motion and thought had made the impossible happen and minds change.[39]

---

38 Peter H. Wood, *Near Andersonville: Winslow Homer's Civil War* (Cambridge, MA: Harvard University Press, 2010), esp. 58, 59, and 74–7; see also Don H. Doyle, "Bully for Garibaldi," *New York Times* (September 26, 2011).

39 Du Bois, *Black Reconstruction in America* (1998), 67; Wood, *Near Andersonville*, 59 (quoting Du Bois); Armstead L. Robinson, *Bitter Fruits of Bondage: The Demise of Slavery and the Collapse of the Confederacy, 1861–1865* (Charlottesville, VA: University of Virginia Press, 2005), esp. 134, 181, and 283; Glymph, *Out of the House of Bondage*, esp. 68–71. Change in popular comic images of Blacks was significant but far more uneven; see Nickels, *Civil War Humor*, 115–50.

The slave woman in Homer's classic painting stands by herself, as do self-emancipators in most such artistic representations. The most spectacular counterexample representing collectivity is official photographer of the Army of the Potomac Timothy O'Sullivan's 1862 untitled photograph showing more than a hundred of the about-to-be emancipated slaves on the South Carolina coast. Some moved during the shot, creating blurring. Issues of exposure made the color of the subject sometimes seem to change.

Timothy O'Sullivan, Slaves, *J.J. Smith's Plantation, South Carolina*

Their posture, as the scholar of "counterhistories of visuality" Nicholas Mirzoeff observes, is that of people "aware of the historical significance of the moment." Mirzoeff names that moment as the "general strike of the slaves."[40]

---

40   Nicholas Mirzoeff, *The Right to Look: A Counterhistory of Visuality* (Durham, NC: Duke University Press, 2011), 44, for the image, and 100 and 101 (for quotations).

Chapter 3

After the Impossible:
Eight Hours, Black Labor,
Women's Suffrage, and Freedom
for All

We will . . . make strange combinations out of common things.
Percy Bysshe Shelley (1820)

The slave who freed himself or herself and then fought to free others was a particular symbol of possibility, the very embodiment of Lord Byron's 1812 injunction that those "who would be free, themselves must strike the blow." Abolitionists had made Byron's verse their own. When Frederick Douglass used the line, a favorite of his, it was so familiar to listeners as to not require attribution. Indeed, as early as 1843, the great African-American militant Henry Highland Garnet had glossed Byron's words as an "old and true saying." However, until the war, the struggles of the slave rebels Garnet associated with Byron's words had ended tragically. When Douglass used the line in an 1863 broadside to recruit African-American troops, he addressed rebels who would win. By then, other groups of Americans had begun to contemplate how to strike blows for freedom on their own behalf but in awareness of each other and of the example of the slave's emancipation. Having taken seriously Byron's, and Karl Marx's, injunction that all emancipation is at bottom self-emancipation, they also took up Shelley's call to "make strange combinations out of common things."[1]

This chapter will focus on the rise of labor mobilizations, especially those seeking the eight-hour day as the worker's Jubilee, and on the growth of a vigorous movement for women's suffrage. Those movements intersected with the emancipation of slaves by drawing on both its powerful "moral impetus" and its practical example.[2] They tried for a heady time to build alliances among people who shared experiences of oppression and perceptions of themselves as being in motion. Before considering those movements, it is worth placing them among the broad emancipationist trends that followed on the general strike of the slaves.

As slaves acted to change things for themselves, horizons broadened for almost everyone. Most spectacular, if least able to prevail, were the openings for new Native-American freedom struggles in the context of Jubilee and Civil War. The same mostly Kansas-based forces that opposed return of runaway slaves in Missouri, many of whom had roots in early antislavery armed struggles in Kansas and Nebraska, found Osage and other allies among Indians on the Plains. The five Southern tribes removed to Oklahoma three decades before were split between traditionalist opponents of accommodation and of slavery and pragmatic, often slaveholding, elites gravitating toward support for the Confederacy. Direct action by "Black Indian" slaves finding their ways to freedom helped to galvanize opposition to pro-Confederate alliances. The general strike of the slaves extended into Indian country as

---

1 George Gordon Noel Byron, Lord Byron, *Childe Harold's Pilgrimage,* Canto ii, stanza 76 (1812) at gutenberg.org. For Douglass, see Philip S. Foner, ed., (as adapted and abridged by Yuval Taylor) *Frederick Douglass: Selected Writings and Speeches* (Chicago: Chicago Review Press, 1999), 366 and 675 and the full reproduction of the "Men of Color to Arms" broadside at lib.rochester.edu. For Garnet, see Sterling Stuckey, ed., *The Ideological Origins of Black Nationalism* (Boston: Beacon Press, 1972), 169. The epigraph is from Shelley's 1820 lyrical drama, *Prometheus Unbound,* Scene 3, 3: 32–3. For Marx on self-emancipation, see Hal Draper, "The Principle of Self-Emancipation in Marx and Engels" (1971), available at marxists.org.

2 For "moral impetus" see Karl Marx's words in International Workingmen's Association, "Address to the National Labor Union" (May 12, 1866) at marxists.org.

African slaves of Native Americans escaped. Runaways and their supporters made Kansas a destination, and joint forces of African Americans, American Indians, and whites, the last group sometimes recruited from Southern non-slaveholders, emerged to win important military and moral victories.[3]

Episodically supported by federal authorities nonetheless eager in other moments to reign in egalitarian impulses, such experiments remained fragile. They sharply conflicted with the general connections of Republicans to accelerated settlement and to brutal suppression of any real or imagined Indian resistance. Nonetheless, the Kansas developments had echoes elsewhere, particularly among some of the Lumbee in North Carolina, who resisted conscripted labor demanded by the Confederacy during the war and fought the Ku Klux Klan after it. Abolitionists took up the cause of Indian rights after emancipation, sometimes in ways plagued with paternalist assumptions but not without some remarkable interventions. Wendell Phillips expressed solidarity in 1869 with Indian attacks on the building of the Transcontinental Railroad.[4] By 1869, Frederick Douglass had also spoken against the tendency of too many Americans to "assent to the dying out of the Indians." The abolitionist Lydia Maria Child likewise wrote in 1867 that US relations with Indians constituted an "almost unvaried history of violence and fraud." Child's 1867 "Appeal for the Indians" expressed the urgency of adding to the "vigilant watch over the rights of black men" a new campaign supporting

---

3 Mark A. Lause, *Race and Radicalism in the Union Army* (Urbana, IL: University of Illinois Press, 2009), esp. 47–107; David Chang, *The Color of the Land: Race, Nation, and the Politics of Landownership in Oklahoma, 1832–1929* (Chapel Hill, NJ: University of North Carolina Press, 2010), 19–26.
4 William McKee Evans, *To Die Game: The Lowry Band, Indian Guerrillas of Reconstruction* (Syracuse, NY: Syracuse University Press, 1995), 6 and passim; Alexander Saxton, *The Rise and Fall of the White Republic: Class Politics and Mass Culture in Nineteenth-Century America* (New York: Verso, 2003, [1990]), 247–92; Roy W. Meyer, *History of the Santee Sioux: United States Indian Policy on Trial* (Lincoln, NE: University of Nebraska Press, 1993), 109–32. On Phillips, see Angela F. Murphy, "Wendell Phillips on the Transcontinental Railroad," available at universalemancipation.wordpress.com; Irving H. Bartlett, *Wendell Phillips: Brahmin Radical* (Boston: Beacon Press, 1961), 380–1; James Brewer Stewart, *Wendell Phillips: Liberty's Hero* (Baton Rouge, LA: Louisiana State University Press, 1986), 292–3.

those of "red men." Her appeal, as the magnificent biography of Child by
Carolyn Karcher observes, "marked a high point in nineteenth-century
analysis of the 'Indian problem,'" although it also at times reflexively urged
assimilationist strategies incorporating Indians into an existing order of
"civilization."[5]

For Irish-American soldiers on the Union side, the war brought an
opportunity to fight for their adopted nation and to learn skills that
they hoped would soon be useful in liberating Ireland from Britain.
"Volunteering for Ireland and America," as one recent account has it,
they marched under green banners while fighting for the red, white, and
blue US flag. Irish Americans often lost enthusiasm for the carnage and
particularly for conscription and for a system of class-based exemptions
saving the rich from having to serve in a war in which Irish units took
especially terrible losses. At times, they fretted that African-American
freedom would come at Irish expense. Fenians, as militant Irish nationalists were called, worried in the latter stages of the conflict that the
revolutionary and military knowledge hard won in combat would be
lost in the bloodshed. Nevertheless, much such expertise survived. The
most committed nationalists, some of them veterans of Irish revolutionary risings of 1848, led invasions of Canada after the war, acting with
an adventurist spirit consonant with the experience of revolutionary
time in the United States. That these initiatives failed did not keep the
United States from becoming the world's hub of Irish nationalism after
the Civil War. Much more broadly, Irish-American citizenship became

---

5 John Blassingame and John McKivigan, eds., *The Frederick Douglass Papers, Series One: Speeches,
Debates, and Interviews, Volume 4, 1864–1880* (New Haven, CT: Yale University Press, 1991), 599.
Lydia Maria Child, *An Appeal for the Indians* (New York: William P. Tomlinson, 1868) 1, 13–15;
Linda Kerber, "The Abolitionist Perception of the Indian," *Journal of American History* 62 (September
1975), 287, quoting Child on "fraud." See also Carolyn L. Karchner, *The First Woman of the Republic:
A Cultural Biography of Lydia Maria Child* (Durham, NC: Duke University Press, 1994), 555 and
553–60. See also Francis Paul Prucha, *American-Indian Policy in Crisis: Christian Reformers and the
Indian, 1865–1900* (Norman, OK: University of Oklahoma Press, 1976), esp. 26–8, and, for a pro-
vocative recent account, Steven Hahn, "Slave Emancipation, Indian Peoples, and the Projects of a New
American Nation-State," *The Journal of the Civil War Era* 3 (September 2013), 307–30.

more secure, making bold nationalist and Catholic self-expression more possible.[6]

Irish nationalism proved decisive for the labor reform movement, one focus of this chapter. As the Marxist historian David Montgomery put it, "The battering ram that first breached the walls of ethnic isolation . . . was not labor reform, but the Irish nationalist movement." That it brought immigrants "into conflict with their Church and Party leaders" created space in which they could become "contributors, rather than obstacles, to the Radical and labor reform traditions." In Chicago, to take one well-studied example, Irish nationalism quickly and enduringly wove itself into the fabric of trade unionism and labor politics. At its most impressive, the coincidence of Irish nationalism, immigrant rights, and Black freedom gave the nation a figure like Terence Powderly, reared by an abolitionist mother, who became at once an advocate of Irish freedom, leader of the nation's most important and egalitarian labor organization in the 1880s, and one of the first Irish-American Catholic mayors of an important US city. The connections to abolition were more direct in the case of Patrick Ford, the influential Irish nationalist labor and land reformer and editor of the postwar *Irish World and Industrial Liberator*.[7] Before the war, Ford had served as printer's devil at William Lloyd Garrison's abolitionist organ *The Liberator*. The direction of motion ran on several tracks. Irish nationalism fractured immigrant loyalties, making room for prewar radicals to

6 Gary Gallagher, *The Union War* (Cambridge, MA: Harvard University Press, 2011), 5, 24–9, and 93; Thomas Brown, *Irish-American Nationalism, 1870–1890* (Philadelphia: Lippincott, 1966), 36–7 and 56–7; Susannah Ural Bruce, *The Harp and the Eagle: Irish-American Volunteers and the Union Army, 1861–1865* (New York: New York University Press, 2000), 2, 21, 42 ("volunteering") 81, 112, 193, and 236–43; Kevin Kenny, *Making Sense of the Molly Maguires* (New York: Oxford University Press, 1998), 87–90; on Irish Americans, the Civil War, and race, see Iver Bernstein, *The New York City Draft Riots: Their Significance for American Society and Politics in the Age of the Civil War* (New York: Oxford University Press, 1990).

7 David Montgomery, *Beyond Equality: Labor and the Radical Republicans, 1862–1872* (New York: Knopf, 1967), 127 and 126–34; Richard Oestreicher, "Terence V. Powderly, the Knights of Labor, and Artisanal Republicanism" in *Labor Leaders in America*, eds. Melvyn Dubofsky and Warren Van Tine (Urbana, IL and Chicago: University of Illinois Press, 1987), 30–61. See also A. Flaherty, "The Mollies Were (Also) Labor" (April 14, 2013), available at mythofmollymaguires.blogspot.com.

have broader roles. At the same time, the freedom fighter Wendell Phillips, more likely to be mobbed than heard by Irish-American opponents of abolition and equality before the war, became an eloquent ally of Irish nationalists after emancipation. In 1869, Phillips advanced the freedpeople's call for forty acres of land in the Irish context, casting it as a demand central to liberation there and in the US South.[8] More shockingly still, in 1871 the Irish nationalist leader O'Donovan Rossa invited African-American militiamen to join a parade welcoming Irish leaders to New York City. Despite trepidation on both sides, the invitation was accepted and marked in music and toasting after the event. One toast proclaimed: "Ireland will now be free, for the Irish and the nagurs can whip the whole world." Within months that display of internationalism was followed by African-American soldiers prominently joining the International Workingmen's Association's New York march in honor of the martyrs of the Paris Commune.[9]

The Irish-Americans' experience of intensifying commitment to nationalism in their homeland, to US nationalism, and to internationalism unfolded in a different way for immigrant German Americans, and particularly for radical immigrant veterans of the 1848 revolutions in the German states. The war opened new space for such German Americans to participate in freedom struggles in the United States, nurturing their interventions in initiatives for immigrant rights and especially their sup-

---

8 On Ford, see Eric Foner, "Class, Ethnicity, and Radicalism in the Gilded Age: The Land League and Irish America," *Politics and Ideology in the Age of the Civil War* (New York: Oxford University Press, 1980), 157–200 with also the material on Phillips and "forty acres" at 181; for Ford and Garrison, see Christian G. Samito, *Becoming American under Fire: Irish Americans, African Americans and the Politics of Citizenship during the Civil War Era* (Ithaca, NY: Cornell University Press, 2009), 224; for further on Phillips, see his introduction to Patrick J. Flatley, *Ireland and the Land League* (Boston: O'Loughlin and Co., 1881), iii–ix, and Angela F. Murphy, *American Slavery, Irish Freedom: Abolition, Immigrant Citizenship, and the Transatlantic Movement for Irish Repeal* (Baton Rouge, LA: Louisiana State University Press, 2010), 24. On Chicago, see John B. Jentz and Richard Schneirov, *Chicago in the Age of Capital: Class, Politics, and Democracy during the Civil War and Reconstruction* (Urbana, IL: University of Illinois Press, 2012), 58–78.

9 Timothy Messer-Kruse, *The Yankee International: Marxism and the American Reform Tradition, 1848–1876* (Chapel Hill, NC: University of North Carolina Press, 1998), 198 (toast), and 199–202.

port for abolition. Military experience and ethnically based recruitment ensured that German-American revolutionaries of various stripes rose to command German-American forces. While Irish regiments often received lectures in Irish nationalism in army camps in the United States, some German-American soldiers regularly heard lectures on Marxism.[10]

More broadly, the Civil War raised popular consciousness of oppression beyond US borders and of the importance of international solidarity. The Union hoped mightily, for example, that the Italian freedom fighter Giuseppe Garibaldi might contribute manpower and moral stature to its cause. Garibaldi pressured the United States early in the conflict by pointing out that the war did not promise freedom for slaves, and would be far easier to support if it did so. After the Emancipation Proclamation, Garibaldi praised Lincoln as the "heir to the aspirations of John Brown." He aptly predicted in an 1863 letter to Lincoln that "posterity will call you the great emancipator."[11] Similarly, the British labor movement, active in efforts to prevent mobilization of British support for the Confederacy, made it clear that hesitancy on emancipation made solidarity more difficult. The complex ways in which struggles spread become still more striking when we realize that anti-Confederate working-class activism played a role in creating the confidence, organization, and ability to think beyond national boundaries that underwrote the organization of the International Workingmen's Association (IWA), the first important transnational organization of radical labor.[12]

10 Alison Clark Efford, *German Immigrants, Race, and Citizenship in the Civil War Era* (New York: Cambridge University Press, 2013), 53–142; Montgomery, *Beyond Equality*, 94–6.
11 Don H. Doyle, "Bully for Garibaldi," *New York Times* (September 26, 2011); Denis Mack Smith, *Garibaldi* (Englewood Cliffs, NJ: Prentice Hall, 1969), 72 ("Brown" and "great emancipator"). See also 69.
12 Philip S. Foner, *American Socialism and Black Americans: From the Age of Jackson to World War II* (Westport, CT: Greenwood, 1977), 37–44; Royden Harrison, *Before the Socialists: Studies in Labour and Politics, 1861–1881* (London: Routledge and Kegan Paul, 1965), 46–69, esp. 54; Karl Obermann, *Joseph Weydemeyer: Pioneer of American Socialism* (New York: International Publishers, 1947), 128–31.

THE INSPIRED BIRTH OF ONE NEW WORKING-CLASS MOVEMENT

Shortly after the war ended, Karl Marx hailed a new day for all workers in the United States. Writing on behalf of the IWA, he drew heavily on the language of slavery and emancipation, as well as that of ability and disability:

> Every independent movement for the workers was paralyzed so long as slavery disfigured a part of the Republic. Labor cannot emancipate itself in the white skin where in the black it is branded. But out of the death of slavery a new life at once arose. The first fruit of the Civil War was the eight hours' agitation that ran with the seven-leagued boots of the locomotive from the Atlantic to the Pacific, from New England to California.

Marx's associate Joseph Weydemeyer, a German immigrant veteran of the 1848 revolution, an abolitionist, a Union army officer, and (as both Republican and revolutionary) county auditor in St. Louis, reinforced this point. He wrote in 1865 that the eight-hour movement signaled the arrival of "the modern labor question—the question of hired labor, which is better known under the euphemistic name of 'free labor' . . . before the social forum." Free labor, no longer judged so in comparison to the lot of four million slaves, "strips off the secondary character which heretofore adhered to it on this continent [and] raises itself to a social question." That is, by no longer having such easy recourse to the ideology that their race uniquely fit them for freedom, white workers had new room and new necessity to think, imagine, and act regarding their own oppression. Shortly before his death in 1865, Weydemeyer proclaimed in a series of articles on the hours of labor that a "real workingmen's party" was emerging, unfettered by "prejudices of birth and color." Shortly thereafter, demonstrating both the extent to which the eight-hour demand was and was not able to work such magic, Chinese workers building the Transcontinental Railroad struck for eight hours. They had caught the mood of impossible freedom but received anything but solidarity from organized white labor. Management broke the strike partly by threatening to replace the Chinese with African Americans.[13]

The eight-hour day carried its own aura of glorious impossibility. The ten-hour day demand had been the watchword of antebellum labor struggles, and it was by no means in place as a standard in the early 1860s. Labor from "sunup to sundown" drained the lives of many workers. In northernmost cities, nearly two thirds of the day elapsed between arrival at work and the end of the shift on hot, pretty, and long late spring and summer days. The eight-hour demand was first prominently made in 1810 by the British utopian socialist Robert Owen. It remained a utopian demand in Europe in 1860 and not a demand at all in the United States. The French rising of 1848 had achieved only a twelve-hour day. The IWA initiated the first broad eight-hour campaign in Europe in 1866, after workers in the United States and Australia (where some urban building trades workers won the reform in 1856) had advanced the demand.[14]

In the United States, the ten-hour day struggles from the 1830s to the 1850s raised the slogan "From six to six" with two hours for breaks. Thus, the ten-hour demand divided the day in half, split between working time

13 Karl Marx, *Capital: A Critique of Political Economy*, Volume 1 (New York: International Publishers, 1967 [1867]), 301; Weydemeyer, "The Eight-Hour Movement," *St. Louis Daily Press* (August 8, 1866); Obermann, *Joseph Weydemeyer*, esp. 120–40; Alison Clark Efford, *German Immigrants, Race, and Citizenship in the Civil War Era* (New York: Cambridge University Press, 2013), 128–9; Manu Vimalassery, "Skew Tracks: Racial Capitalism and the First Transcontinental Railroad" (PhD diss., New York University, 2010), 98–9.

14 David R. Roediger and Philip S. Foner, *Our Own Time: A History of American Labor and the Working Day* (New York: Verso, 1989), 19–100; Philip S. Foner, *May Day: A Short History of the International Workers' Holiday* (New York: International Publishers, 1986), 11–12; Andrea Panacionne, *The Memory of May Day: An Iconographic History of the Origins and Implanting of a Workers' Holiday* (Venice: Marsilio Editori, 1989), 16 and 753; Frederick Chamier, *A Review of the French Revolution of 1848*, Volume 2 (London: Reeve, Benham and Reeve, 1849), 206–7. On Owen, see Eugene V. Debs, "The Eight-Hour Work Day," *International Socialist Review* 12 (August 1911), available at marxists.org.

and the worker's time. The eight-hour demand carved working days into thirds, with only one third controlled by the boss. Its remarkable slogan became, "Eight hours for work. Eight hours for rest. Eight hours for what we will." Almost overnight, in the emancipated United States, the demand for time to repose, recreate, love, and learn swept the North and Midwest. Unuttered in 1860, eight hours had become the legal working day by 1868 in New York, Pennsylvania, Illinois, California, Connecticut, Wisconsin, and Missouri as well as among federal employees. Although these laws featured loopholes preventing effective enforcement, the social movements that caused their passage had transformed labor. The Eight-Hour Leagues catalyzed massive petition campaigns, demonstrations, and, especially after the laws went unenforced, strikes. The impressive new national workers' organization, the National Labor Union (NLU), launched itself with the eight-hour day as a centerpiece in 1866.[15]

Such spectacular change connected at every turn to the experience of war and specifically to that of witnessing emancipation. In terms of the eight-hour movement's origins, personnel, rhetoric, vision, and even logic, such was the case. Unions, weak at the war's start, suffered decimation as members enlisted, sometimes as a group. Later, the draft cost locals members. However, the fighting also deepened class consciousness around grievances regarding wages, prices, and the ability of those with resources to avoid military service by paying for a substitute. Combined with labor shortages placing workers in a favorable bargaining position, such grievances brought uneven revival to unions later in the war. By then, workers also sought meaning for their tremendous sacrifices of life and limb in a time of Jubilee. Eight hours promised revitalization.[16]

The military encampment represented a site of political education for workers. The army was in significant measure both immigrant and working

15 Roediger and Foner, *Our Own Time*, 87 and 81–91; Montgomery, *Beyond Equality*, 302 and 296–334.
16 John R. Commons et al., *History of Labour in the United States*, Volume 4 (New York: Macmillan, 1918–1935), 2: 14–15; Roediger and Foner, *Our Own Time*, 83.

class. Its camps and battlefields were the largest workplaces of the time and brought together the largest crowds many workers had ever seen. In this highly charged, life-and-death atmosphere, soldiers debated the meaning of their service for their working lives after the war. It was after the revolutionary developments ratifying and encouraging the self-emancipation of slaves in the second half of 1862 that the eight-hour cry gained a hearing. The nation's leading labor newspaper, *Fincher's Trades' Review* in Philadelphia, began to append "Eight Hours: A Legal Day's Work for Freemen" to its masthead in 1863, casting the change as the "Nation's gift to workingmen in the army." Its editorials encouraged the spread of eight-hour agitation among troops and even suggested gaining the "cooperation of the army" as key to the movement's success. To the eight-hour leader Ira Steward, the new demand was part of a redistribution of happiness owed workers who had earned it "by their manhood on many a bloody field of battle."[17] Nevertheless, much more than calculation regarding patriotic sacrifice informed the new demand for the unthinkable. Those making the demand had seen with the slave's unfolding emancipation that the impossible could be made real. They had watched the government make revolutionary changes in response to heroism and sacrifice by the oppressed. The language of freedom, so central to eight-hour agitation, ripened in a situation in which speakers could no longer assume that being "freemen" was facilely defined by being free white male citizens.[18]

If the rank-and-file of the Eight-Hour Leagues breathed the air of the emancipation, shorter-hours leaders often had direct antislavery connections. Some, like Steward, the great theorist of the movement, as well as George McNeill, Edward Rogers, and Weydemeyer, had fought against slavery in the 1850s. Steward did so in support of John Brown's

---

17 *Fincher's Trades Review* (June 17, 1863 and May 20, 1865); John R. Commons et al., *A Documentary History of American Industrial Society*, Volume 10 (New York: Russell & Russell, 1958 [1909]), 9: 279–80 and 305; Montgomery, *Beyond Equality*, 93–101, 199, and 249.

18 Weydemeyer, "The Eight-Hour Movement"; David Roediger, "Ira Steward and the Anti-Slavery Origins of American Eight-Hour Theory," *Labor History* 27 (Summer 1986), 421.

forces in the fierce Kansas battles against the expansion of the slave system.[19]

Others who had prioritized abolition before the war and had hesitated to muddy its moral claims by loosely discussing "wage slavery" among white workers were freed by emancipation to jump into the eight-hour struggle. Such abolitionist luminaries as Karl Heinzen, Josiah Abbott, Elizabeth Cady Stanton, Susan B. Anthony, William Lloyd Garrison, and Gerrit Smith made this transition. The most compelling such figure, Wendell Phillips, wrote in 1865 that "the next great question . . . is the rights of the laboring class" with the eight-hour day as the "first rule" for securing those rights. Phillips expressed his support in the *Boston Daily Evening Voice*, the labor publication most advanced on questions of race and class. Garrison, in a letter directed to Ira Steward, proclaimed his backing for shorter hours on "the same principle which had led [him] to abhor and oppose the unequalled oppression of the black laborers of the South." Like Phillips, the *Voice* supported redistribution of planters' lands to freedpeople, reprinting the arguments of Thaddeus Stevens and Charles Sumner favoring such a course.[20]

The *St. Louis Daily Press*, like the *Voice*, founded by striking printers, embraced the Radical positions on race for part of its short existence. Another variant of the links between the radicalism of the slave's Jubilee and that of eight hours came from New Orleans, where freedpeople brought the length of labor before the Freedmen's Bureau as a policy

---

19 Roediger, "Ira Steward and the Anti-Slavery Origins of American Eight-Hour Theory," 422; Philip S. Foner, "A Labor Voice for Black Equality: The *Boston Daily Evening Voice*," *Science and Society*, 38 (1974), 325–41; *Boston Daily Evening Voice* (November 3, 1865). Significant biographical material on Steward, especially as regards Kansas, appears in Thomas Edie Hill, *Hill's Album of Biography and Art* (Chicago, Danks & Co, 1891), 362–3. On Steward and the abolitionist heritage in Boston, see David A. Zonderman, *Uneasy Allies: Working for Labor Reform in Nineteenth-Century Boston* (Amherst, MA: University of Massachusetts Press, 2011), 76–178.

20 *Boston Daily Evening Voice* (October 12 and November 3, 1865); Roediger and Foner, *Our Own Time*, 95–6; Foner, "A Labor Voice for Black Equality," 318–20; Walter M. Merrill, ed., *Let the Oppressed Go Free, 1861–1867, Volume Five, The Letters of William Lloyd Garrison* (Cambridge, MA: Belknap Press, 1979), 401 and 402–3; Philip S. Foner, *Women and the American Labor Movement from Colonial Times to the Eve of World War One* (New York: Free Press, 1979), 130–1.

issue. The Radical-Republican and African-American *New Orleans Tribune* tried to build an interracial alliance inclusive of the city's huge shorter-working-day movement by adopting the eight-hour demand as it had been phrased on the masthead of *Fincher's Trades' Review*.[21]

For Steward, the abolitionist critique that the slaveocracy was brittle and backward because it could not generate a strong internal market or innovate technologically informed a political economy justifying eight hours. More leisure, Steward argued, would generate ever-increasing consumer demand, higher wages, and greater investment in technology. "If laborers ought to consume as little as possible," he held, "tyrants and slaveholders have always been right," and William Lloyd Garrison would have therefore been wrong. The leading historical account of labor and Reconstruction is surely apt in terming Steward the "intellectual child of radicalism" where racial justice was concerned.[22] Cross-fertilizations did not end there, as Phillips, a co-laborer with Steward in the Boston labor movement, developed ideas regarding a well-funded program of emancipation that appealed to the idea of the development of consumption as the key to reconstruction of the South.[23]

The language and logic of the eight-hour movement likewise mirrored that of the slave's freedom. Detroit's leading eight-hour activist declared, "We are about to be emancipated." Eight-hour music sang of "Jubilee" and incorporated the tune and energies of "John Brown's Body."[24] Steward

---

21 Foner, "A Labor Voice for Black Equality," 315 (quoting Phillips); David Roediger, "Racism, Reconstruction, and the Labor Press: The Rise and Fall of the *St. Louis Daily Press*, 1864–1866," *Science and Society* 42 (Summer 1978), 156–77; *New Orleans Tribune* (August 30, September 2, and November 1, 1866); Philip S. Foner, *Organized Labor and the Black Worker* (New York: International Publishers, 1982), 17–19; Roger W. Shugg, *Origins of the Class Struggle in Louisiana* (Baton Rouge, LA: Louisiana State University Press, 1972), 184–8; Montgomery, *Beyond Equality*, 114–15.

22 *Chicago Socialist* (July 12, 1879); Roediger, "Ira Steward and the Anti-Slavery Origins of American Eight-Hour Theory," 410–26; see also Lawrence Glickman, "Workers of the World, Consume: Ira Steward and the Origins of Labor Consumerism," *International Labor and Working-Class History* 52 (September 1997), 82–96. On "child of radicalism," see Montgomery, *Beyond Equality*, 251.

23 Gerald David Jaynes, *Branches without Roots: Genesis of the Black Working Class in the American South, 1862–1882* (New York: Oxford University Press, 1986), 43.

24 Trevellick as quoted in Albert Blum and Dan Georgakas, *Michigan Labor and the Civil War* (East

spoke of the eight-hour demand as a "first step" in reforming virtually everything. Even the idea of a "first step" came by way of analogy. Steward likened eight hours to the "first step" of "the emancipation of the slave," which for him was to be fully meaningful only after "the ballot" and a triumph over poverty secured African-American gains. In the long list of next steps he imagined following the shortening of the working day, the eight-hour system meant "anti-pauperism . . . anti-monopoly, anti-prostitution [and] an end to waste, idleness, Woman's endless drudgery and War." Seeing free time for women as especially vital, the *Daily Evening Voice* maintained that "The laboring classes will never be elevated without the elevation of women." Central to the list of all such reforms was "anti-slavery." Steward reckoned that workers knew as much: "The laborer instinctively feels that something of slavery still remains, or that something of freedom is yet to come."[25]

The inspiration of the slave's self-emancipation and the attendant eight-hour ferment that followed influenced the course of Marxism itself. As the socialist-humanist philosopher Raya Dunayevskaya argues, the most concrete chapter in Marx's *Capital*, that on the working day, probably owed its inclusion to the great dynamism of US movements for shorter hours after 1863. More fundamentally still, when Marx and others launched the First International in 1864, the first clause of the first rule of the new organization proposed a universal and liberating claim very much hearkening to the particular moral impetus and language provided by the situation of US slaves: "CONSIDERING, That the emancipation of the working classes must be conquered by the working classes themselves." If abolitionists made Lord Byron's "who would be free, themselves

Lansing, MI: Michigan Civil War Centennial Observation Commission, 1964), 24; Philip S. Foner, ed., "Songs of the Eight-Hour Movement," *Labor History* 13 (Fall 1972), 571 and 574–80; Roediger, "Ira Steward and the Anti-Slavery Origins of American Eight-Hour Theory," 420–1. For the suffusing of shorter-hours appeals with the language of revolution and emancipation, see Zonderman, *Uneasy Allies*, 101.
25   Ira Steward, *Poverty* (Boston: Boston Eight-Hour League, 1873), preface and 4; Commons et al., *A Documentary History of American Industrial Society*, 9: 279–83 and 288–9; *Voice* as quoted in Foner, "A Labor Voice for Black Equality," 309.

must strike the blow" their own, socialists took inspiration and language from the Jubilee of slaves.[26]

ANOTHER NEW WORKING-CLASS MOVEMENT

Less than fully noticed by the white labor movement in the late 1860s but also impossible to completely ignore was the incredible rise of a working-class movement among freedpeople. When the Marxist historians Theodore Allen and Noel Ignatin, following Du Bois, spoke of white workers' "white blindspot," they meant not only a lack of appreciation for how the interests of workers crossed the color line but also an inability to even apprehend consistently the militancy and example of African-American labor.[27] This was dramatically the case during Jubilee, when ongoing Black self-activity could hardly have been missed altogether but was not seen as pivotal in new struggles against wage slavery. The blow-by-blow story of how national unions did and mostly did not embrace inter racialism is in the next chapter on how Jubilees fell apart, together and separately. Here, the emphasis remains on the extent of new social motion, which, despite sharp limits, was infinitely greater in terms of possibilities for Black-white unity than anything on offer in the pre-emancipation years. The line best

---

26 Raya Dunayevskaya, *Marxism and Freedom: From 1776 until Today* (Amherst, NY: Humanity Books, 2000 [1958]), 53 and 85–91. Marx, *Provisional Rules of the Association*, in The General Council of the First International; *Minutes, 1864–66* as quoted in Hal Draper, "The Principle of Self-Emancipation in Marx and Engels" (1971), available at marxists.org. Draper regards self-emancipation as a "new principle," but, amid much mention of other kinds of "slavery," among whites does not connect it to the close following and championing of the slave's self-emancipation by Marx. Robin Blackburn, ed., *An Unfinished Revolution: Karl Marx and Abraham Lincoln* (New York: Verso, 2011), 66, reads this matter very differently, seeming to argue that Marx regarded slaves, but not wage workers, as needing emancipators.

27 Noel Ignatin, "White Blindspot," in *Understanding and Fighting White Supremacy*, eds. Noel Ignatin and Ted Allen, 1967, at sojournertruth.net/whiteblindspot.html; this work also built directly on Du Bois's insights in *Black Reconstruction*. See David Roediger, "Accounting for the Wages of Whiteness: U.S. Marxism and the Critical History of Race," in *The Wages of Whiteness and Racist Symbolic Capital*, eds. Wulf Hund, David Roediger, and Jeremy Krikler (Berlin: LIT, 2011), 9–36.

illustrating the possibility comes from the Baltimore ship caulkers' leader Isaac Myers when he broke color barriers by addressing the 1869 convention of the NLU. Myers came not as a supplicant but as a liberator: "Slavery, or slave labor, the main cause of the degradation of white labor, is no more. And it is the proud boast of my life that the slave himself had a large share in the work of striking off the fetters that bound him by the ankle, while the other end bound you by the neck." The white blindspot had to suppress this memory, but such forgetting could not happen overnight.[28]

The alternative to Myers's view was more pedestrian, even when it included the call for a "second emancipation proclamation" for wage workers but not land for the ex-slave. William Sylvis, the key figure in the NLU, suggested issuing such a proclamation. Sylvis's soaring rhetoric connected the freedom of ex-slaves with that of white workers who had been "slaves" before the war and remained so. He noticed the militant strikes of Black workers in Mobile, Baltimore, Charleston, Philadelphia, and other urban settings and condemned the "fanatical bigotry" of hate strikes against employment of African Americans, but there was no hint that he remembered the self-emancipation of chattel slaves. Nor was there a sense of the power of Jubilee for freedpeople, who had merely "transferred . . . from one condition of slavery to another." Such differences are elaborated in the next chapter's discussion of what Du Bois calls the "price of disaster." But introducing the idea of a "white blindspot" here guards against our reproducing it as historians. Supposing that labor struggles were mainly forwarded by white workers makes us fail to discern fully how Jubilee was, again according to Du Bois, "part of our labor movement."[29]

---

28 Myers's "Address of the Colored Delegate" is reprinted from the *New York Times* (August 19, 1869) in *Black Workers: A Documentary History from Colonial Times to the Present*, eds. Philip Foner and Ronald Lewis (Philadelphia: Temple University Press, 1989), 154–7, with the quotation at 155.
29 James C. Sylvis, *The Life, Speeches, Labors, and Essays of William H. Sylvis* (Philadelphia: Claxton, Remsen and Haffelfinger, 1872), 220–1 and 232–3; Du Bois, *Black Reconstruction in America* (1992), 325 ("disaster") and 727 ("part"); Philip S. Foner, *Women and the American Labor Movement from Colonial Times to the Eve of World War One*, 135 ("fanatical bigotry").

Whites arguing for inclusion of African Americans in (often segregated) unions held that the labor movement should include Black workers in some way so that they could not be used as strikebreakers or to reduce wage rates. Powerful as these appeals occasionally were, they avowedly proceeded from self-interest in incorporating Black workers into what was seen as an existing (white) labor movement in need of defense against possible African-American threats. The problems were twofold. First, there was no existing stable labor movement with social weight until emancipation. It was precisely during Jubilee that the eight-hour ideal took hold, that city central labor unions became the most important locus of labor protest, that the membership of labor unions grew wildly, and that a viable national labor movement was organized. The working-class movement included many organizations not organized on trade union lines. Eight-Hour Leagues, mutual aid societies, land reformers, cooperatives, political initiatives, secret orders, nationalist formations, and organizations of working farmers were all at times considered labor organizations in the postbellum period. At the original whites-only conference of the NLU in 1866, for example, distribution of public land excited much more attention than strike support. That is, there was no labor movement that was not under construction and reconstruction, maturing in large measure in organizational spaces opened by the self-emancipation of slaves.[30]

The greater problem with the argument that African-American labor needed to be encouraged and brought to organization so as not to endanger the existing labor movement was that such a stance risked missing the existence of tremendous working-class Black self-activity already present in the South. Such militancy remained obscured for Northern white workers' organizations. Many of the most impressive and creative responses occurred within white Southern households where ex-slave women worked as domestic labor. Such settings were, as Thavolia

---

30 Montgomery, *Beyond Equality*, 134–41; David Roediger, "What Was the Labor Movement? Organization and the St. Louis General Strike of 1877," *Mid-America* 67 (January 1985), 37–51. On the 1866 convention, see *Baltimore Sun* (August 23–25, 1866).

Glymph shows, not private places distinct from the public realm. Protests regularly went beyond the household, as women workers left, often carrying stories and the property of planters with them. Freedpeople burned planters' homes, especially during periods of concerted efforts to prevent masters from moving back in and seizing land ex-slaves farmed provisionally. At a more daily level, halfway patterns emerged among domestic workers, with work in white households continuing but with employers "compelled to bargain and haggle" as freedwomen asserted the right to quit and frequently opted for part-time waged household work in order to devote more time to labor serving their own families. One small but telling assertion was to refuse to labor outside one's craft. Cooks who might be able to accomplish a day's work in three hours attempted to avoid filling the rest of the day with cleaning, for example. Jubilee encouraged the revolutionary notion that "Every cook can govern" and the practical one that, for her employer, she should only be required to cook. The "guiding assumption" of freedpeople, historian Tera Hunter writes, was that "wage labor should not emulate slavery—especially in arbitrariness of time and tasks."[31] No Northern-based national labor organization could appreciate the daily struggles to make this so.

The many "plantation strikes" of agricultural workers in the postbellum South could also seem disconnected from what Northern workers thought of as organized labor. Contemporary observers found freedpeople on the land to be "constantly striking for higher wages." But the forms of protest remained so connected to legacies of slavery and to land that urban Northerners would have had to strain to find comparisons with their own experiences. Mostly confined to individual

---

31 Tera Hunter, *To 'Joy My Freedom: Southern Black Women's Lives and Labors after the Civil War* (Cambridge, UK: Cambridge University Press, 1997), 27; Thavolia Glymph, *Out of the House of Bondage: The Transformation of the Plantation Household* (Cambridge, UK: Cambridge University Press, 2008), 97, 100–36, and 149–62 and esp. 172 ("haggle" at 149), and on arson esp. 105 and 111 and passim; Jim Downs, *Sick from Freedom: African-American Illness and Suffering during the Civil War and Reconstruction* (New York: Oxford University Press, 2012), 131. For "Every cook can govern," see Noel Ignatiev, ed., *A New Notion: Two Works by C.L.R. James* (Oakland, CA: PM Press, 2010), 129.

farms or plantations, such strikes were often brief affairs, designed to take advantage of a short-lived advantage in the cycle of agricultural labor or to respond to particular abuses. As the economic historian Gerald David Jaynes notes, such forms of protest ought to be thought of as a "logical extension of the work stoppages and protests under slavery" as modified by the experience of the general strike of the slaves and by new opportunities to organize after emancipation. In time, they reached beyond single workplaces, arguably amounting to an "incipient labor movement," but they retained distinct local peculiarities. One of the postbellum plantation strikes turned on unpaid wages but also on a demand for each worker to receive a one-acre plot of land from their Louisiana employer.[32]

The most fascinating missed connection between freedpeople's militancy and Northern labor lay in the hours of labor. "Control over time," Jaynes wrote, "was exactly what planters did not want freedpeople to have." Such control therefore emerged as a central goal of the emancipated just as the movement for a shorter working day matured in the Midwest, New England, and New York. At times, as in the case of the eight-hour demand championed by the *New Orleans Tribune* after Black workers had helped militantly lead the working-class movement on the city's waterfront, the demand of freedpeople mirrored the most popular slogan of workers outside the South. Occasionally, Reconstruction governments and agencies instituted or debated a ten-hour (or even, in winter, nine-hour) working day for agricultural labor. But most struggles over time were intensely local. In occupied South Carolina as early as 1863, a federal official reported being plagued by "a serious [*sic*, and fascinatingly so, as the apparent intent was to write "series"] of daily Experiments to test the minimum of labor which would be accepted as a day's work." A planter in the Tennessee Valley reported in 1866 that,

32 Jaynes, *Branches without Roots*, 116 ("constantly"), 117 ("stoppages"), and 118–20; Foner and Lewis, eds., *Black Workers*, 139–40; Leon F. Litwack, *Been in the Storm So Long: The Aftermath of Slavery* (New York: Vintage, 1980), esp. 435–6.

in addition to refusing to care for his mules, workers tested the timing of breaks and of the start of work.[33]

Hours as well as pace were at issue. In some Union-controlled areas, early attempts were made during the war to enforce sunup-to-sundown labor as it had presumably applied in slavery. Black plantation workers objected that this hardly seemed like emancipation and that it ignored provisions of free time, especially on Saturdays, long conceded by masters. In Mississippi, Louisiana, and elsewhere, the ten-hour day became the summertime standard for wartime plantation labor in Union-held areas, cutting the working day by a third or more in some sugar-producing areas. The period after the war, in which planter interests implemented the repressive Black Codes, saw a return to sunup to sundown as the legal working day in some but not all states.[34]

Local practices were still more varied, especially regarding Saturday labor, on which employers often had to make concessions. An old Black woman could briefly be as powerful as a legislature, a Freedmen's Bureau official, a planter, or a general. In 1866 on Johns Island near Charleston, South Carolina, such a woman claimed to have had a vision in which God forbade work on Friday or Saturday, with Sunday already not a working day. The social movement supporting her vision partially prevailed, though only after federal authorities threatened to drive freedpeople from the

33 Jaynes, *Branches without Roots*, 115; Steven Hahn et al., eds., *Freedom: A Documentary History of Emancipation, 1861–1867*, Series 3, Volume 1, *Land and Labor, 1865* (Cambridge, UK: Cambridge University Press, 2008), 594; Ira Berlin et al., eds., *Freedom: A Documentary History of Emancipation, 1861–1867*, Series 1, Volume 3, *The Wartime Genesis of Free Labor: The Lower South* (Cambridge, UK: Cambridge University Press, 1990), 257 ("Experiments"), 367, and 645; Michael W. Fitzgerald, *The Union League Movement in the Deep South: Politics and Agricultural Change During Reconstruction* (Baton Rouge, LA: Louisiana State University Press, 1989), 138 and 167; Roediger and Foner, *Our Own Time*, 87–8.
34 Ira Berlin et al., eds., *Freedom: A Documentary History of Emancipation, 1861–1867*, Series 1, Volume 2, *The Wartime Genesis of Free Labor: The Upper South* (Cambridge, UK: Cambridge University Press, 1993), 50–1; Berlin et al., eds., *Freedom: A Documentary History of Emancipation, 1861-1867*, Series 1, Volume 3, 105, 183, 367, 385, 513, 524, 804, 857; Hahn et al., eds., *Freedom: A Documentary History of Emancipation, 1861–1867*, Series 3, Volume 1, 56–7; Du Bois, *Black Reconstruction in America*, 168.

island. A compromise granted the workers a Saturday half-holiday. Some workers, mainly women with household responsibilities, got all of Saturday off. Such Saturday leisure was a demand that would await the twentieth century for unionized Northern workers, but the ways it was gained hardly mapped onto the programs of the Eight-Hour Leagues. In 1866, when many Black South Carolinians accepted the "two-day compromise"—trading two days a week labor in rice fields for tenancy on a plot of land under their own control—their action would not have been legible to the mainstream labor movement as a victory for either the movement for shorter working time or for land reform.[35]

Indeed the land question in the South, so vital for freedpeople and so fundamentally a class demand, seldom received mention in a US labor press with a long history of linking labor reform and land reform for whites. Here too, there were mitigating factors accounting for what white labor leaders could and could not discern. The 160-acre homesteads for whites who went west seemed to promise market-oriented economic independence while the forty-acre plots desired by freedpeople promised to nurture a peasantry on a model seen as already having failed in Haiti. However, the US South had a large working class and a significant service sector in which freedwomen asserted rights, not infrequently by leaving waged jobs to work in fields when they could not get terms of labor that they desired. Militant African-American workers particularly worried employers and the Freedmen's Bureau by opposing long-term contracts, preferring to bargain seasonally. With the means of subsistence established, such workers would have gained leverage in dealing with employers. The bargaining power that would have accrued to workers whose families controlled land did not feature in the rare appeals for land redistribution by the white labor movement. Instead, the logic remained on grounds of self-interest: Land would secure freedpeople in the Southern countryside,

---

35 Litwack, *Been in the Storm So Long*, 410 and 434; Roediger and Foner, *Our Own Time*, 185, 187, 215, 228, 237, and 242; Leslie Schwalm, *A Hard Fight for We: Women's Transition from Slavery to Freedom in South Carolina* (Urbana, IL: University of Illinois Press, 1997), 226–31.

keeping them from becoming competitors of whites within urban labor markets.[36]

The fullest appreciation of just how deeply land reform challenged control over Black labor would come in the early 1870s from freedpeople's enemies. Conservative Democrats and liberal Republicans connected Black South Carolinians' efforts to gain land through political agitation and direct action with the workers' radicalism of the Paris Commune. At times, as the historian Heather Cox Richardson remarks, accounts of the "riotous" and "communist" campaigns of organized labor in the North and the clashes in the South literally ran in abutting columns in the mainstream press. The borders between such columns were too often all that white organized labor could discern where questions of land and politics were concerned. Even the *Boston Daily Evening Voice* declared Reconstruction over shortly after the war, even as critical struggles over land continued.[37]

Many of the great labor successes of African-American workers combined political pressure with direct action. Myers spoke of the Republican Party as a "friend of labor" out of personal experience. His very successful Baltimore shipyards cooperative of caulkers formed out of the need to employ Black workers after whites on the waterfront engaged in "hate strikes" to drive them from jobs. Such terror was part of a broader pattern he later lamented as the tendency of white artisans to organize "for the extermination of colored labor." His experiment benefitted from a government contract and grew to include hundreds of workers, some of them white. It is small wonder that Myers professed to believe that the Fifteenth

---

36 Fitzgerald, *The Union League Movement in the Deep South*, 170–237; Eric Foner, *Nothing But Freedom: Emancipation and Its Legacy* (Baton Rouge, LA: Louisiana State University Press, 1984), 11–13 and 40–3 on the ubiquitous lens that Haiti provided for thinking about Reconstruction; George C. Rable, *But There Was No Peace: The Role of Violence in the Politics of Reconstruction* (Athens, GA: University of Georgia Press, 1984), 16–32; Philip Foner, "A Labor Voice for Black Equality," 318–19.
37 Heather Cox Richardson, *The Death of Reconstruction: Race, Labor, and Politics in the Post-Civil War North, 1865–1901* (Cambridge, MA: Harvard University Press, 2001), 64, 85–7, 96–7; Jaynes, *Branches without Roots*, 101; Foner, "A Labor Voice for Black Equality," 321–2.

Amendment enfranchising African-American men would inexorably lead to integrated workplaces.[38] In Atlanta, Black workers mounted campaigns to gain access to more and better railroad jobs by petitioning the Union army. In 1866 in Jackson, Mississippi, washerwomen mounted what Philip Foner and Ronald Lewis's excellent documentary history of Black workers called, perhaps forgetting slave resistance, the "first collective action of Black women workers." The washerwomen's effort to enforce a scale of prices by levying fines "regulated by the class" on those who undercut those rates gave rise to a petition to the city's mayor. In Florida, organized Black labor could at times use direct action threats to keep white (and African American) strikebreakers from taking their jobs because Reconstruction governments were hesitant to intervene and because Black workers served on juries when charges were filed. Prosecution of arson directed against planter or company interests was likewise more difficult where freedpeople had political power.[39] Even ten years after the Civil War, South Carolina strikers on rice plantations could count on aid, or at least the absence of attacks, from Black militias. The historian Eric Foner describes the rice workers as drawing on the knowledge that "Republican political power, after all, had helped create the context within which successful collective action was possible." Equally, Black workers' earlier collective actions in

---

38 On Myers and the cooperative, in which Frederick Douglass, who had worked on the Baltimore waterfront as a slave, held a share, see Philip Foner and Ronald Lewis, eds., *The Black Workers: A Documentary History from Colonial Times to the Present, Volume Two, The Black Worker during the Era of the National Labor Union* (Philadelphia: Temple University Press, 1978), 416 ("friend of labor"), 418 and 424; Foner, *Organized Labor and the Black Worker*, 21, 35 ("extermination"), and 39; Peter Rachleff, *Black Labor in Richmond, 1865–1890* (Urbana, IL: University of Illinois Press, 1989 [1984]), 61; see also, on the connection of the franchise and jobs, Ena Farley, *The Underside of Reconstruction New York: The Struggle over the Issue of Black Equality* (New York and London: Garland, 1993), 79.

39 Jonathan W. McLeod, *Workers and Workplace Dynamics in Reconstruction-Era Atlanta: A Case Study* (Los Angeles: UCLA Center for Afro-American Studies and Center for Industrial Relations, 1991), 34; Foner and Lewis, eds., *Black Workers*, 142 ("regulated"); Jerrell Shofner, "Militant Negro Laborers in Reconstruction Florida," *Journal of Southern History* 39 (August 1973), 403–5; Shofner, "Negro Laborers and the Forest Industries in Reconstruction Florida," *Journal of Forest History* 19 (October 1975), 188–90.

the general strike of the slaves had made Republican political power possible.[40]

When freedom came, urban Black Southerners built a dense web of working-class institutions, as excellent scholarship on Richmond, Mobile, the state of Florida, and elsewhere shows. These institutions included the secret societies that Peter Rachleff has described as the "circulatory system" of African-American life, including churches, associations providing sick and death benefits, cooperatives, and trade-based organizations. The initiatives overlapped and the same individuals typically participated in several different kinds of institution-building. Some of the organizations based on work resembled modern trade unions and attempted to bargain with employers. Others more resembled modern workers' centers for immigrants, providing mutual support and a variety of social services.[41] The ones behaving on trade union lines in non-plantation settings—those struggles that should have been fully legible to white labor—often interrupted the script of Black workers needing to be tutored in the art of collective action so as not to break strikes by whites. Not only did they frequently mount strikes of their own, but Black workers also seem to have been more likely in the twenty-five years after emancipation to have to face down white strikebreakers in the South than to themselves scab on white workers who were on strike.[42]

---

40 Foner, *Nothing but Freedom,* 91–106 and at 103 for "Republican political power."

41 Rachleff, *Black Labor in Richmond,* 13–33; Michael W. Fitzgerald, *Urban Emancipation: Popular Politics in Reconstruction Mobile, 1860–1890* (Baton Rouge, LA: Louisiana State University Press, 2002), 49–131; Paul Ortiz. *Emancipation Betrayed: The Hidden History of Black Organizing and White Violence from Reconstruction to the Bloody Election of 1920* (Berkeley, CA: University of California Press, 2005), 9–32.

42 David Roediger, "What If Labor Were Not White and Male? Recentering Working-Class History and Reconstructing Debates on Race and the Unions," *International Labor and Working-Class History* 51 (Spring 1997), 88–9; Jerrell Shofner, "The Labor League of Jacksonville: A Negro Union and White Strikebreakers," *Florida Historical Quarterly* 50 (January 1972), 278–82; Foner and Lewis, eds., *The Black Workers,* 339–357; Rachleff, *Black Labor in Richmond,* 45, 73, 146, and 160; Richardson, *The Death of Reconstruction,* 84 and 100; Foner, *Organized Labor and the Black Worker,* 21.

FROM THE EMANCIPATION OF SLAVES TO THE
EMANCIPATION OF WOMEN

If any antebellum political demand rivaled that of immediate emancipation of slaves for sheer impossibility, it was that of women's suffrage. When
300 women and a few feminist men met in a pioneering women's rights
convention at Seneca Falls, New York, in 1848, even they seemed ready
to vacillate on the issue. Douglass editorialized that the "rights of animals"
might have been more easily discussed in the United States. Conference
organizer Lucretia Coffin Mott opposed resolving in favor of the right to
vote as a move that would "make us ridiculous." A variety of other apt
priorities, including emphases on Indian rights and social radicalism, made
many delegates not share Elizabeth Cady Stanton's view of suffrage as a
central issue. A stirring convention speech by Douglass, himself accustomed to demanding the impossible, endorsed suffrage and the resolution
was adopted over opposition. Douglass's fledgling newspaper *The North
Star* led off its masthead in 1848 with the motto "RIGHT HAS NO
SEX." Stanton's own husband, on the other hand, refused to attend the
conference, protesting her forwarding of the suffrage resolution.[43]

The women's rights meeting in Worcester, Massachusetts, in 1850, from
which the movement subsequently dated itself, generated a controversy
in which feminists debated how Lord Byron's verse on self-liberation
applied to them. The newspaper editor Jane Grey Swisshelm objected to

---

43 Frederick Douglass, "The Rights of Women," *The North Star* (July 28, 1848); Marjorie Spruill
Wheeler, ed., *One Woman, One Vote: Rediscovering the Women's Suffrage Movement* (Troutdale, OR:
New Sage Press, 1995), 9; William S. McFeely, *Frederick Douglass* (New York: W.W. Norton, 1991),
156; Nancy Isenberg, *Sex and Citizenship in Antebellum America* (Chapel Hill, NC: University of
North Carolina Press, 1998), ix, 2–4, 19, and passim; Nancy A. Hewitt, "Re-Rooting American Wom
en's Activism: Global Perspectives on 1848," in *Women's Rights as Human Rights*, eds. Patricia Grimshaw
et al. (New York: Palgrave, 2001), 123–37; Alexander Keyssar, *The Right to Vote: The Contested History
of Democracy in the United States* (New York: Basic, 1991), 140–3; Carrie Chapman Catt and Nettie
Rogers Shuler, *Woman Suffrage and Politics: The Inner Story of the Suffrage Movement* (Seattle: University of Washington Press, 1969 [1923]), 19–31. For the motto, see, for example, *The North Star* (June
2, 1848). On Douglass's feminism, see also Gary L. Lemons, *Womanist Forefathers: Frederick Douglass
and W.E.B. Du Bois* (Albany, NY: State University of New York Press, 2008), 23–52.

the convention's conjoining of abolitionism and women's freedom. Herself an outspoken abolitionist, Swisshelm nevertheless turned Byron against the conflation of feminism and African-American rights: "We are told that those who would be free themselves must strike the blow; but the action of this Convention adds an improvement, and now those who would be free must strike for themselves and everybody else in bonds." Hers was a minority position but it portended future debates on just how African Americans' and women's rights connected. At moments, Swisshelm urged that the long odds against abolition made it too large a burden for feminists to take on. At others, she suggested that the slave's cause was "already before the people" and independent agitation was necessary for women to catch up. Mostly, she registered the seeming impossibility of both reforms, in her phrasing a pair of "little boats," tempest-tossed, and unable to take on each other's cargoes.[44]

The 1850s saw small headway for the little boat of women's rights. An authorized history of women's suffrage would later point to favorable attention by two state legislatures as evidence of forward motion, but the very idea of women voting nationally—and their recognition as fully able, rational republican persons fit to vote—remained a dream.[45] As the movement unraveled financially, its prospects dimmed further, although at decade's end two gifts from benefactors promised some stability. The first, from the real estate broker Francis Jackson, gave $10,000 to fight slavery and half that to support women's rights. The second, from Boston merchant Charles Hovey, gave $50,000 to abolition and other causes "such as women's rights, non-resistance, free trade, and temperance." The Hovey funds prioritized attacking slavery but held that if abolition occurred, women's rights would be the "residual legatee." Uncontroversial at the time

---

44 Sylvia Hoffert, *Jane Grey Swisshelm: An Unconventional Life* (Chapel Hill, NC: University of North Carolina Press, 2004), 143–4 ("boats"); Faye Dudden, *Fighting Chance: The Struggle over Woman Suffrage and Black Suffrage in Reconstruction America* (New York: Oxford University Press, 2011), 21, and assumption.edu/WHW/old/NarrativeGuide.html for other Swisshelm quotes.
45 Lois Banner, *Elizabeth Cady Stanton, A Radical for Women's Rights* (Boston: Little, Brown and Company, 1980), 37; Catt and Shuler, *Woman Suffrage and Politics*, 19–31.

but very controversial over the next decade was the choice to place Wendell Phillips at the head of committees administering the funds' dispersals.[46]

By the last two years of the Civil War, Stanton and her co-thinkers could convene national conventions of up to 1,200 delegates and coordinate petition drives gathering hundreds of thousands of signatures. By the decade's end, although aware of mounting defeats, they could force debates over women's suffrage during the passage of the Fourteenth and Fifteenth Amendments, lead an impressive campaign on the issue in Kansas, and publish a hard-hitting newspaper aptly named *Revolution*. Congress would soon hear testimony favoring women's suffrage. The impossible—constitutional recognition of women's right to vote—would have to wait for another half century, but unthinkable growth of a social movement had occurred.[47]

For better and worse, during the triumphs and the stinging setbacks of women's suffrage in the 1860s, feminism matured in close relation to war and emancipation. More than in the case of the labor movement, women's rights leaders had longstanding, formative relationships to abolition and particularly to Black abolitionists. Douglass, at a particularly raw moment in postwar relations between the Republican Party, which he supported, and women's suffrage advocates, tried to humorously defuse matters by suggesting that the tension in his case could only run so deep. After all, he remarked, he "belonged" to abolitionist-feminists. They had long ago paid his master so that he was not exposed to being kidnapped and returned to slavery, and they had defended his public presence from mobs. While Douglass often raged against antebellum labor leaders who loosely compared chattel slavery and wage slavery, he tolerated metaphors describing

---

46 Catt and Shuler, *Woman Suffrage and Politics*, 28; Dudden, *Fighting Chance*, 22 and 23 (for both quotes).

47 Ellen DuBois, *Feminism and Suffrage: The Emergence of an Independent Women's Movement in America* (Ithaca, NY: Cornell University Press, 1978), 53–125; Alma Lutz, *Created Equal: A Biography of Elizabeth Cady Stanton, 1815–1902* (New York: Octagon Books, 1974), esp. 130–71.

gender oppression as "sex slavery."[48] Women gained skills organizing events, petitions, and boycotts as abolitionists. They defied conventions against women speaking publically in order to speak for the slave's freedom. Many first contested male privilege in abolitionist groups. The Douglass example at Seneca Falls and the uses to which Sojourner Truth's speech (that others) titled "Ar'n't I a Woman?" was put exemplify how ex-slaves played symbolic roles in contesting divisive issues within women's rights organizations. As Karen Sanchez-Eppler argues, even the painful and often suppressed issue of domestic violence by Northern husbands and fathers was allusively considered, though also evaded, by white women activists via their graphic and sympathetic discussion of slave women imperiled by masters.[49]

Women impressively and visibly supported the Union and Confederate war efforts from the conflict's inception. They continued and expanded the typically unpaid female work of production and of social reproduction done before the war but with far greater visibility. Much of this work remained private, keeping households, farms, and workshops running while men were in battle, raising children amid chaos, doing the emotional and physical labor of caring for family members and others disabled, and too often organizing funerals for those killed. But the labor was also frequently civic, and sometimes paid, including nursing in military hospitals and camps, sewing uniforms, and cooking and cleaning. Female "camp followers" did sex work, laundry, and more; not a few cross-dressing women soldiered as well. The plain heroism of nursing legend Clara Barton set a daunting standard as a role model for

---

48   Frederick Douglass, "Women's Rights Are Not Inconsistent with Negro Rights: An Address Delivered in Boston, Massachusetts on 19 November 1868" in *The Frederick Douglass Papers,* Volume 4, eds. Blassingame and McKivigan, 181–2; David Roediger, "Race, Labor, and Gender in the Languages of Antebellum Social Protest," in *The Terms of Labor: Slavery, Serfdom, and Free Labor,* ed. Stanley Engerman (Stanford, CA: Stanford University Press, 1999), 168–87.
49   Harris, "Finding Sojourner's Truth," passim, and Karen Sanchez-Eppler, *Touching Liberty: Abolition, Feminism, and the Politics of the Body* (Berkeley, CA: University of California Press, 1993), 97–8 and passim.

women facing danger and becoming public figures on the basis of their labor. But a host of other liberating models and possibilities were on offer. Women's suffrage consciously appealed to this heroism in arguing that voting rights were owed women.[50] The "patriotic envelopes" discussed as evidence of changing attitudes toward African Americans in the previous chapter likewise say much in their portrayals of women in that they were significantly designed to be consumed by females. Women figure on the envelopes as packing to go to the front and as doing laundry at home while dreaming that there might be a role for females in the military.[51]

At every turn, women's suffrage was inspired, organized, and challenged by the fact of the slave's Jubilee. Strong feminist organization of women's patriotism did not begin until May 1863—that is, after the Emancipation Proclamation. The resulting National Loyal Women's League (NLWL), led by Stanton and Susan B. Anthony, could support an emancipationist war with full vigor. As Anthony noted at the time, "If it can be true that loyal women are lukewarm, it is because [before emancipation] the objects of the war have been confused." The timing of the group's founding thus directly reflected the moral impetus attending emancipation and struggles for it. Lincoln's proclamation changed that. Indeed, just after the Emancipation Proclamation took effect, the abolitionist Theodore Tilton wrote Anthony to enthuse that the millennium was "on its way," offering "Three cheers for God!" Stanton in turn offered the view that still "higher ideas of liberty" were on the horizon, particularly those involving women's

---

50 Jeanne Attie, "Warwork and the Crisis of Domesticity in the North," in *Divided Houses: Gender and the Civil War*, eds. Catherine Clinton and Nina Silber (New York: Oxford University Press, 1992), 247–59; Thomas Power Lowry, *The Story the Soldiers Wouldn't Tell: Sex in the Civil War* (Mechanicsburg, PA: Stackpole Books, 1994); John D'Emilio and Estelle Freedman, *Intimate Matters: A History of Sexuality in America* (Chicago: University of Chicago Press, 1997), 124–34; Bonnie Tsui, *She Went to the Field: Women Soldiers of the Civil War* (Guilford, CT: TwoDot, 2006). On women's household labor and its devaluing before the Civil War, see the excellent Jeanne Boydston, *Home and Work: Housework, Wages, and the Ideology of Labor in the Early Republic* (New York: Oxford University Press, 1990).
51 Steven R. Boyd, *Patriotic Envelopes of the Civil War: The Iconography of Union and Confederate Covers* (Baton Rouge, LA: Louisiana State University Press, 2010), 84–5 and Figures 4:27 and 4:28.

suffrage. The acceptance of women speaking out increased, reflecting their roles in supporting the war effort and abolition.[52]

Cheers for God mixed with cheers for the self-emancipation of slaves. The badge that the NLWL produced and hoped every loyal woman would wear registered anew an awareness of Byron's wisdom on self-liberation. Stanton wrote to Elizabeth Smith Miller in September 1863 that "Our badge is done . . . It represents a negro, half-risen, breaking his own chains." New realities demanded new iconography, she added: "We have had the negro in every variety of posture—hopeless, imploring, crouching at the feet of the Goddess of Liberty. But now, in harmony with our day, *our* negro is striking the blow himself with his own right hand."[53]

The giant wartime petition drive that the NLWL coordinated focused on the slave's plight, not women's suffrage. Noting the limits of the scope of the Emancipation Proclamation, the group aimed to ensure permanent freedom for all slaves. Although many local organizations of loyal Northern and Border State women balked when support for the troops came to encompass causes they regarded as extraneous—that is, abolition and women's rights—the petitions gathered roughly 400,000 signatures. The message accompanying their delivery to Senator Charles Sumner reflected both a sense of the revolutionary time that they were experiencing and a sense of grievance: "Inasmuch as the 'right of petition' is the only political right woman has under the Constitution, it is the duty of her representatives to give prayer an earnest and serious consideration." Organizers asked that the petitions be placed in the "national archives, as part of the history of our second revolution."[54] Lincoln, against whose initial uncertainties

---

52 DuBois, *Feminism and Suffrage,* 53 (Stanton and Tilton), 51–8 and 73; Lutz, *Created Equal,* 143; Anthony as quoted in Nina Silber, *Gender and the Sectional Conflict* (Chapel Hill, NC: University of North Carolina Press, 2008), 64; Michael D. Pierson, *Free Hearts and Free Homes: Gender and American Antislavery Politics* (Chapel Hill, NC: University of North Carolina Press, 2003), 188–9.
53 Theodore Stanton and Harriot Stanton Blatch, eds., *Elizabeth Cady Stanton,* Volume 2 (New York: Arno, 1969), 95.
54 Stanton and Blatch, eds., *Elizabeth Cady Stanton,* 2: 97; James McPherson, *The Struggle for*

about the Thirteenth Amendment the petitions were partly aimed, later credited those signatures as a barometer of public support for the measure. The NLWL demonstrated the ability of women to intervene effectively on the most important moral and political issue of the day. But Anthony also regarded the NLWL as grander for its unique commitment to "universal emancipation and enfranchisement." By late 1865, campaigns for petitions for women's suffrage were being planned.[55]

The very emphasis on voting also suggested connections to African-American history. Women's rights, long a multifaceted movement, came to focus more insistently on the ballot. As the leading historian of women's suffrage in this period, Ellen DuBois, writes, Black suffrage "dominated reform politics," and this "helped to destroy whatever doubts remained among feminists that suffrage was the key issue for the legal position of women as well." She continues, "Indeed, almost without anyone noticing the change, 'women's rights' was replaced by 'woman suffrage' as the designation for the movement for equality for women."[56]

On the ground in the South, the work of Northern women with freedpeople underlined the same point. Carol Faulkner's excellent history of such work, *Women's Radical Reconstruction*, identifies "freedmen's aid" by women reformers as a critical site for the development of the racial and radical ideas of feminists, often in vexed ways, and for learning to struggle with the state. "Abolitionist-feminists understood freedmen's aid as a way to exert the moral influence of women in government and national policy," she writes, "while working for women's suffrage." Josephine Griffing, an

---

Equality: Abolitionists and the Negro in Civil War and Reconstruction (Princeton, NJ: Princeton University Press, 1964), 124–6; DuBois, *Feminism and Suffrage* 53, placed the petition signatures at 400,000. See also Dudden, *Fighting Chance*, 52–3.

55 LeeAnn Whites, *Gender Matters: Civil War, Reconstruction, and the Making of the New South* (New York: Palgrave Macmillan, 2005), 25–44, esp. 26–7; Catt and Shuler, *Woman Suffrage and Politics*, 34–5; DuBois, *Feminism and Suffrage*, 53–78; Banner, *Elizabeth Cady Stanton*, 93–5; Stanton and Harriot, eds., *Elizabeth Cady Stanton*, Volume 2: 97 and 103–7, especially the letters to Charles Sumner and to Wendell Phillips.

56 Ellen Carol DuBois, ed., *Elizabeth Cady Stanton, Susan B. Anthony: Correspondence, Writings, Speeches* (New York: Schocken Books, 1981), 88.

influential ally of Stanton and Anthony and the western agent of the NLWL, helped to initiate the Freedmen's Bureau. Stanton and Anthony's newspaper, *The Revolution*, supported Griffing's work. White women returning from work among freedpeople became important rank-and-file supporters of votes for women. Frances Harper, the great African-American activist and thinker, pushed decisively for direct aid to ex-slaves, civil rights for African Americans, and universal suffrage.[57]

As with white wage laborers, white women faced a challenging new relationship with African Americans, and a clearer confrontation with their own degradation, following the slave's freedom. The legal scholar Cheryl Harris has pointed out that for most of US history, white women could only give birth to free children and almost all Black women could only give birth to slaves. This social fact placed white women in a different material position than African-American men or women. It powerfully supported the ideology that educated white women held an "influence" complementary to male power because of their nurturing of children and moving men toward greater empathy and morality. Abolitionist activism gave rise to important challenges to such ideology, but not typically frontal challenges. Emancipation squarely challenged reflexive natalist connections of white women, social reproduction, and the nurturing of republican freedom.[58]

If Black men were to be citizens—perhaps voting ones—and Black women the mothers of freedom, the educated white woman conceivably had no special position. White women's support for universal suffrage broadened in such a context by positing a society formally without special privilege, including no privilege for white men, as the goal. However, when initiatives to expand civil rights and the franchise stopped with the African-American male, Stanton's forces reacted not only on gender but also on

---

57 Carol Faulkner, *Women's Radical Reconstruction: The Freedmen's Aid Movement* (Philadelphia: University of Pennsylvania Press, 2004), 70–8, 84, 91 ("while working for"), 150–1; DuBois, *Feminism and Suffrage*, 69–70.

58 Harris, "Finding Sojourner's Truth," 309–409; on "influence," see Ann Douglas, *The Feminization of American Culture* (New York: Farrar, Straus and Giroux, 1998), 46, 59, and passim.

race and class grounds. Rightly noting that the Fourteenth Amendment explicitly introduced "that word 'male'" as a criterion for constitutional rights, Stanton joined forces with those questioning the ability of "ignorant" Black men to intelligently vote. She registered pain at their (as well as Irish and Chinese immigrants') doing so while the "educated white woman" could not. Stanton began rehearsing such arguments just after the war, when voting by Black men was anything but assured—indeed it never was in the nineteenth century. She wrote that women were "the only class who stand outside the pale of political recognition" as early as late 1865, suggesting a need to confront an anxiety-producing possible reality that was far from established at that point.[59]

Reformers' processing of male sexual violence and abuse within households by projecting them onto the plight of slave women (and to a lesser extent onto the plantation mistress) before the war also became less plausible after it. Temperance discourses on alcohol and abuse provided one avenue for raising such issues with regard to Northern households, but frank discussion of the issue was difficult. When Stanton briefly raised it in 1860 as part of arguments for liberalized divorce as a feminist demand, Phillips and Horace Greeley moved to shut down debate with extraordinary overkill. It was this issue, not suffrage, that first led Stanton to pronounce that "with all his excellence and nobility, Wendell Phillips is a man." If Greeley and Phillips were the only problems, that would have been one thing. However, as the leading modern account observes, the contradictions also lay within the female rank-and-file of a feminist movement accustomed to claiming some authority by virtue of moral influence and sacrifice and ready to oppose divorce reform as "Christian women."[60]

59 McFeely, *Frederick Douglass*, 265–9; DuBois, *Feminism and Suffrage*, 176–88; Blassingame and McKivigan, eds., *The Frederick Douglass Papers*, 4: 213–17 and 146–8; 173–6 and 182–5; Philip S. Foner, ed., *The Life and Writings of Frederick Douglass*, Volume 4 (New York: International Publishers, 1952), 212–13. On "that word 'male,'" see "Elizabeth Cady Stanton, to Gerrit Smith" (January 1, 1866) in *The Selected Papers of Elizabeth Cady Stanton and Susan B. Anthony*, Volume 1, eds. Gordon et al., 566 and 569.
60 Bartlett, *Wendell Phillips*, 374–5 ("nobility"). See also DuBois, *Feminism and Suffrage*, 184 and

Similarly, the move to open advocacy of women's suffrage doubtless still seemed too self-interested to many women's rights reformers. The feminist campaign to petition for an emancipationist Thirteenth Amendment on behalf of ex-slaves garnered about ten times as many signatures as any petition that urged that the Fourteenth Amendment protect the rights of women. While some coolness toward the latter petitions may have been the product of their being seen as politically "most inopportune"—as Senator Charles Sumner ungraciously said in reluctantly presenting Lydia Maria Child's petition on the Fourteenth Amendment and women's rights—such an imbalance in the numbers of petition signatures also reflected the continued pull toward an altruism nurtured in fighting within and alongside abolitionism.[61]

By 1869, the surge of postwar activism that put Stanton and Anthony briefly in coalition with Douglass, and even at times Phillips, had receded. The initiative to keep the activist remnants of abolitionism alive, in pursuit of suffrage for African-American men and for all women, had fallen apart. This fact tempts us to read the entire history of women's suffrage and African-American rights backward from the bitter splits between the movements. The gloom that greeted the failure of these new initiatives to deliver votes for women, the attempts of some former abolitionists to limit discussion of women's suffrage, the similar attempts to persuade women's suffrage advocates to postpone their agitation because this was the "Negro's hour" to gain rights, and the subsequent turn of some feminists to alliances

---

192; Stacey M. Robertson, *Parker Pillsbury: Radical Abolitionist, Male Feminist* (Ithaca, NY: Cornell University Press, 2000), 58–63; Adam Tuchinsky, *Horace Greeley's New-York Tribune: Civil War-Era Socialism and the Crisis of Free Labor* (Ithaca, NY: Cornell University Press, 2009), 117–21; and Ellen Carol DuBois, "'The Pivot of the Marriage Relation': Stanton's Analysis of Women's Subordination in Marriage" in *Elizabeth Cady Stanton, Feminist as Thinker*, eds. Ellen Carol DuBois and Richard Cándida Smith (New York: New York University Press, 2007), 88–9. See also Dudden, *Fighting Chance*, 35–7.

61   For the numbers, see DuBois, *Feminism and Suffrage*, 61–2; Stanton and Blatch, eds., *Elizabeth Cady Stanton*, Volume 2: 108n1; Catt and Shuler, *Woman Suffrage and Politics*, 35 and 137 ("inopportune").

with anti-Black Democrats are well-rehearsed by historians.[62] However, because even the calculations of an increasingly beleaguered movement, in its attempts to unite differing visions of Jubilee, so reflected the slave's emancipation and organized labor's emergence, the high hopes of the period deserve emphasis here, before the dashing of those hopes are treated in the final chapter.

The pro-suffrage campaigns for women and for African-American men shared a sense that the slave's emancipation demonstrated that the nation had entered a period of "revolutionary time." This describes both the actual pace of events and the consciousness of that pace among participants. It attempts to capture the dizzying appreciation that events are compressed as the unaddressed horrors of prior decades surface and as decisions shaping the possibilities of decades to come are being made. As an early biographer of Stanton observed, "Never before had there been such an opportunity to demand the enfranchisement of women" as that of the postwar moment when "the nation was taking stock of the rights of citizens." Wendell Phillips, for a time a leading advocate of both Black male suffrage and women's rights, caught the mood: "These are no times for ordinary politics; these are formative hours. The national purpose and thought ripens in thirty days as much as ordinary years bring it forward." By the late 1860s, as Southern states were already scenes for successful Ku Klux Klan terror and as Republican support for women's suffrage and for labor reform proved hollow, such a perception of revolutionary time and its waning cut two ways. The case that African-American male suffrage had to be snatched from the last moments of revolutionary time was compelling, but so was the idea that, if missed now, women's freedom would be long in coming.[63] Both sides frequently

<hr />

62 See esp. DuBois, *Feminism and Suffrage*, 53–125; "Elizabeth Cady Stanton to *National Anti-Slavery Standard*" (December 26, 1856) in *The Selected Papers of Elizabeth Cady Stanton and Susan B. Anthony: In the School of Anti-Slavery, 1840 to 1866*, Volume 1, eds. Ann D. Gordon et al. (New Brunswick, NJ: Rutgers University Press, 1997), 564–5 on the "Negro's hour."
63 Lutz, *Created Equal*, 143; Phillips as quoted in Michael Les Benedict, *A Compromise of Principles: Congressional Republicans and Reconstruction, 1863–1869* (New York: W.W. Norton, 1974), 106.

phrased matters in terms of whose "hour" it was. Phillips's contention
as early as the end of the war that it was the "Negro's hour" reverberated
widely. He tried to confine the focus of revolutionary time gently and
optimistically, writing in May 1865 that he hoped soon to be "as bold
as [John] Stuart Mill and to add to the last clause [regarding rights]
'Sex'!! But this hour belongs to the negro." However, many in the wom-
en's rights movement answered that it was the hour for universal suffrage.
The pressured discussions left room for excommunications of those
disagreeing—such excommunications were hardly rare within the abolitionist tradition—but also for great exhilaration and increased political
independence by women activists.[64]

For a time, it looked as if exhilaration would be the dominant mode.
As 1864 drew to a close, Stanton wrote to Anthony, "I cannot tell you
how happy I am to find Douglass on the same platform with us. Keep him
. . . on the right track. Tell him in this revolution, he, Phillips, you and I
must hold the highest ground and truly represent the best type of the
white man, the black man and the woman." Her words not only presaged
a sidelining of Black women that feminism would long struggle to overcome, but they also demonstrated a perception of how important
Douglass would be symbolically. The unity of Stanton, Anthony, Phillips,
and, to an extent, Douglass had earlier found expression in their support
for John C. Frémont's 1864 left-of-Lincoln presidential candidacy. After
the war, all opposed Garrison when he moved to close the American Anti-
Slavery Society (AASS) by declaring its work over after emancipation.
Even though Stanton quickly staked out positions prioritizing white
middle-class women's claims to the ballot and Phillips championed the
idea of "the Negro's hour" by limiting debate on women's freedom and by

64 DuBois, *Feminism and Suffrage*, 59 quotes Phillips. See also Stanton and Blatch, eds., *Elizabeth
Cady Stanton*, Volume 2: 112–13; Dudden, *Fighting Chance*, 63; Gordon et al., eds., *The Selected Papers
of Elizabeth Cady Stanton and Susan B. Anthony*, Volume 1: 566; Ann D. Gordon et al., eds., *The
Selected Papers of Elizabeth Cady Stanton and Susan B. Anthony: Against an Aristocracy of Sex,
1866–1873*, Volume 2 (New Brunswick, NJ: Rutgers University Press, 1997), 63.

manipulating use of the Hovey funds, a united movement for suffrage persisted for at least three years.[65]

Douglass's most forceful ongoing contribution to the debate did not oppose women's suffrage but argued instead that white riots, hate strikes against Black workers, and attacks on schoolchildren had created a state of emergency requiring prioritization. In this view, Black male suffrage was an urgent form of self-defense for the entire community. Thus, in his speech to the American Equal Rights Association (AERA) at its inaugural 1866 meeting, Douglass allowed, "By every fact to which man can appeal with justification of his own right to a ballot, a woman can also appeal with equal force." But he warned simultaneously that "equal rights" must not become "merely women's rights." For African Americans, he reasoned, "disenfranchisement means New Orleans, it means Memphis [naming sites of anti-Black postwar violence], it means New York mobs, it means being driven from the workshops and schools." While such remarks underscored the great urgency of gaining votes for Black men, Douglass titled his speech "Let No One Be Excluded from the Ballot Box." Tilting decidedly away from Phillips, he became vice-president of the equal rights organization in New York, championing women's suffrage.[66]

The care with which Douglass tried to balance concerns was not unique to him. It ran, in different ways, through the contributions of Child, Lucretia Mott, Sojourner Truth, and above all Harper, all of whom sought viable middle ground that proved impossible to occupy only in the longer run. Indeed if not viewed through a bound-for-disaster prism, in the immediate postwar years the overlap between campaigns for enfranchising women and those for enfranchising Black men was an impressive testimonial to the possibilities unleashed by Jubilee and the desire for some semblance of unity even among those who made unity difficult. *The*

---

65 Stanton and Blatch, eds., *Elizabeth Cady Stanton*, Volume 2: 103–4 ("best type"); McFeely, *Frederick Douglass*, 234; Bartlett, *Wendell Phillips*, 376; Dudden, *Fighting Chance*, 65, 59, and 63.

66 The speech is reprinted in Blassingame and McKivigan, eds., *The Frederick Douglass Papers*, Volume 4: 146–8 with the quotation at 147. See also Dudden, *Fighting Chance*, 82.

Standard, the organ of the American Anti-Slavery Society, came under the editorship of Parker Pillsbury, the leading "male feminist" of his time and a firm adherent of the emphasis on joint progress toward suffrage unlimited by race or sex. Quarrels with Phillips led Pillsbury to resign, but the resignation was at first not accepted by the organization's leaders and Pillsbury continued editing until he was only later forced out.[67]

The breathing space for building common efforts, especially through the AERA, opened because neither the rights of freedpeople nor those of women were seen as adequately addressed by the Fourteenth Amendment. As Reconstruction under the conservative presidency of Andrew Johnson readmitted Southern states and former Confederates as voters, the cruel irony of the white South gaining political representation through its rebellion threatened. That is, when slaves had been held, each counted as three fifths of a person for purposes of representation, artificially inflating white Southern voting power. Emancipated but without the vote, Afro-Southerners would potentially now count 100 percent for apportionment, making the overrepresentation of the white South that much greater. Plantation districts would especially gain. This prospect was part of the practical crisis that Phillips had in mind when he argued that a specific political moment that enabled the success of African-American male suffrage but not women's suffrage had arrived. Enfranchisement of Black men seemed the cleanest way to prevent white conservative politicians from benefitting from emancipation. But when drafted, the Fourteenth Amendment took no such path and instead muddied the question insofar as it suggested that the rights of Blacks as citizens might be protected without their constitutionally becoming voters. It penalized states in terms of apportioning representatives if they disqualified male citizens from voting but did not mandate voting rights for African Americans. Despite

---

67 Karcher, *The First Woman of the Republic*, 540–2; Blassingame and McKivigan, eds., *The Frederick Douglass Papers*, Volume 4: 261n; Dudden, *Fighting Chance*, 162–3 and 96–101; for Harper, see also womenshistory.about.com; DuBois, *Feminism and Suffrage*, 70; Robertson, *Parker Pillsbury*, 138–43.

being written by Radical Republican icon Charles Sumner, who claimed
to have agonized over many drafts trying to find language that would
address women's rights concerns, the amendment initially alienated many
radicals on race as well as gender grounds.[68]

Ex-abolitionists prioritizing African-American male suffrage at first
opposed the amendment as strongly as Stanton and Anthony did. Phillips
so wished to halt the Fourteenth Amendment in late 1866 that he briefly
courted AERA support. Despite having blocked a vote in AASS on the
question of merging abolitionism with the women's rights movement—
AERA was thus formed as a mostly feminist-initiated united
front—Phillips briefly and carefully emphasized his points of agreement
with those seeking women's suffrage and Black suffrage together. In campaigning against New York state's ratification of the Fourteenth
Amendment, he sought AERA's organizing skills, funding their petition
campaign with $3,000 from the Hovey funds. Even in his more typical
oppositional moments, he sometimes adopted conciliatory language. At
one point, he reassured Stanton, "I'm fully willing to ask for women's vote
now, and will never so ask for negro voting as to put one single obstacle
in the way of getting it." Attempting to frame the issues of suffrage and
civil rights as ones still concerning abolition, he wrote that he would
become the most radical of women's suffragists when emancipation was
truly secured: "I am now engaged in abolishing slavery in a land where
abolition of slavery means conferring or recognizing citizenship, and
where citizenship supposes the ballot for all men. Whenever I begin to
labor on suffrage as such, be sure I will never stultify myself by claiming
it for only half the race." By 1867, Republicans in Congress had made
African-American male suffrage a part of military Reconstruction of the
South, and Phillips fell into line behind their support of the Fourteenth
Amendment, with a view to pressuring Republicans to support a Fifteenth

---

68 DuBois, *Feminism and Suffrage*, 53–78; Dudden, *Fighting Chance*, 67–101, esp. 94–5; see Lutz,
Created Equal, 133, on Sumner's drafts.

Amendment enshrining Black male suffrage constitutionally. In 1868, as prospects for Black male suffrage became more certain, Phillips and his followers supposed that the "women's hour" may be arriving, but they did not return to the AERA. Indeed, his behavior in keeping the Jackson and Hovey funds away from women's rights campaigners would have perhaps left him unwelcome had he returned.[69]

Nevertheless, the story of a women's suffrage movement tragically bereft of allies is a very partial truth. Sometimes it was a story Stanton and Anthony chose to tell—one of themselves arrayed against a hostile male reform establishment and against women too often unwilling to confront it. Seeing themselves in this way, they sometimes became proud sectarians, sure only that they were right, morally and strategically. For better and worse, like the "come-outers" in the Garrisonian abolitionist tradition, they stood willing to be marginalized in order to launch powerful critiques of injustice. But through 1866 and in some ways through 1869, they were not only that. They still lived in Jubilee, sustained first by Douglass, Harper, Truth, and other Black radicals who gave the most electric speeches at AERA events. As this initiative imploded, there came a new series of alliances with the eccentric, self-advertising financier, Fenian, and labor reformer George Francis Train and with the racism represented by the Democratic Party. The giddy hopes of some on the ground in Kansas that Train "was the special instrument of Providence to secure the Irish vote" came to little. Instead, the relationship with Train would help to lose them the support of Douglass, who nevertheless attended Stanton- and Anthony-organized meetings as late as 1869, coming knowing that he would be bitterly attacked and warmly applauded. Sojourner Truth likewise lost enthusiasm for AERA conventions only as the organization's alliances with Democrats flourished.

---

69 Dudden, *Fighting Chance*, 94–5, 105–7, and 162–3. On the sharp limitations and deep compromises marking the Fourteenth Amendment, see James D. Anderson, "Race-Conscious Educational Policies Versus a 'Color-Blind Constitution': A Historical Perspective," *Educational Researcher* 36 (2007), 249–57.

Nevertheless, as soon as the Fifteenth Amendment passed, Douglass proposed a Sixteenth Amendment enfranchising women.[70] In choosing Train over testing what kind of movement could be built in concert with radicals once the suffrage of Black men was constitutionally established, Stanton and Anthony positioned themselves to experience the tragic end of Jubilee from a particularly awful vantage.

However, in the late 1860s, advocates of women's suffrage could still see themselves as part of the unfolding of the impossible. In 1867, they strongly contested the suffrage referendum in Kansas with solid, though brief, funding from Train, and in 1869 the Wyoming legislature provided the "first victory" for the seemingly impossible where votes for women were concerned. By then, Stanton and Anthony's forces had a newspaper, *The Revolution*. Its mottoes, besides "educated suffrage" for all, included "equal pay to women for equal work, eight-hour labor [and] abolition of standing armies." The class demands reflected a growing attempt to ally with working women and to remake the NLU into a force for women's suffrage. For a time, the support of William Sylvis and other NLU leaders identified feminism and labor as another fresh alliance brought together by war and Jubilee. Ultimately, such forays were only a little less costly than the alliance with Train; like that alliance they belong mainly in the next chapter's description of how revolutionary time ended, sometimes before radicals knew that it had. However, even in their turn to what Ellen DuBois calls an "independent feminist movement" in establishing the National Woman Suffrage Association (NWSA) in 1869, Stanton and Anthony moved away from their abolitionist ties but not away from the heritage of Jubilee. At the 1870 NWSA

---

70 Patricia Holland, "George Francis Train and the Woman Suffrage Movement, 1867–70" from *Books at Iowa* 46 (April 1987) at lib.uiowa.edu; Dudden, *Fighting Chance*, 141, 185, and 103–67; Catt and Shuler, *Woman Suffrage and Politics*, 74–9; Willis Thornton, *The Nine Lives of Citizen Train* (New York: Greenberg Publishers, 1948), 180 ("Irish vote"). On Truth in AERA, see Nell Irvin Painter, *Sojourner Truth: A Life, A Symbol* (New York: Norton, 1996), 244–53. On the logic and force of "come-outerism," within abolition, see Aileen Kraditor, *Means and Ends in American Abolitionism: Garrison and His Critics on Strategy and Tactics, 1834–1850* (New York: Pantheon, 1968).

meeting, the chairwoman welcomed delegates with the reminder that
"They who would be free themselves must strike the blow," echoing the
line's usage in Anthony's 1868 speech to the NLU and a glorious Black
abolitionist tradition.[71]

71 The proceedings of the 1870 gathering are at the site of the Worcester Women's History Project
at wwhp.org ("blow"); DuBois, *Feminism and Suffrage*, 121 (Anthony "blow"), 202 ("independent"),
111–25 (labor), and 189–200. For the *Revolution* demands, see Lutz, *Created Equal*, 157. On the
important attempted alliances with the NLU and with working women, see also Montgomery, *Beyond
Equality*, 395–8 and the next chapter.

Chapter 4

Falling Apart:
The First Rainbow Coalition and the
Waning of Revolutionary Time

It was a tragedy that beggared the Greek.
W.E.B. Du Bois on the aftermath of Reconstruction (1935)

In remarking on Frederick Douglass's 1872 characterization of the Republicans as the "true workingmen's party," W.E.B. Du Bois allowed that such an assessment was puzzling, especially if the party's policies in the North at that time were under review. However, Du Bois found much to recommend in Douglass's view of the Republicans as pro-labor in the South. The idea of the Grand Old Party (GOP) as a labor party, so jarring to modern sensibilities, was "strange for the North but it was at the time true for the South."[1] Du Bois's mixed verdict signals how hard it is to determine when Jubilee ended and counterrevolution began. Not only does the region matter; the Republican Party varied dramatically in its relation to labor from state to state. Republicans ruled very briefly in most of the South, but in some areas they remained in office for almost a decade. Adding to the picture feminists, labor organizations, and others inspired by Jubilee scrambles matters of periodization further. Did Jubilee end when those

---

1 The epigraph is from W.E.B. Du Bois, *Black Reconstruction in America, 1860–1880* (1998), 727, and the discussion of Douglass is from 367 in the same study.

forces failed to coalesce into a broad Rainbow Coalition of causes, races, and genders and began to turn on each other?[2] Such was surely the case by the period from 1867 to 1869. Indeed, the previous chapter suggests that at least the seeds of disunity existed from 1865 forward, for example in the blindspot that caused white workers to not recognize freedpeople's class consciousness or in the early tension between Wendell Phillips and Elizabeth Cady Stanton. However, in 1869, Radical governments were still just taking hold in much of the South, promising to transform the region. Alternatively, perhaps Jubilee failed group-by-group, state-by-state, and even town-by-town. Focusing as it does on tragedy, this chapter adopts multiple chronologies of when and how things fell apart. It shows that by the late 1860s, alliances among the oppressed had fallen into disarray even as revolutionary time persisted briefly in the South before succumbing to a sustained and effective reign of political terror and to the clarification among Republicans that social justice was not to be the party's sustained concern in any state or region.

In describing the tragedy of social movements suffering defeats at the hands of their enemies and of each other, questions of tone are as important as those of timing. If our options are between the two categories of tragedy that the Marxist cultural critic Raymond Williams laid out, there is little difficulty in choosing: The end of Jubilee was a "social tragedy" in which racialized and gendered class formations and the political system did not permit revolutionary time to continue. It was not in the main the result of terrible or malicious decisions made by tragically flawed individuals.[3] But, within that social tragedy, individuals and movements also made destructive decisions, deepening conflicts in ways costly to them and

---

2   I take "Rainbow Coalition" from the martyred Chicago revolutionary Fred Hampton and the transformative interracial solidarity politics he used it to promote, though in popular usage it is now more associated with the work of Reverend Jesse Jackson, Sr. See Amy Sonnie and James Tracy, *Hillbilly Nationalists, Urban Race Rebels and Black Power: Community Organizing in Radical Times* (New York: Melville House Publishing, 2011), vi and 1–3.

3   Raymond Williams, *Modern Tragedy* (Peterborough, ON, Canada: Broadview Encore Editions, 2006), 149–68.

to us. They drew lines in ways that permitted little backpedaling from division and behaved without the political acumen of the white supremacist terrorists who defeated Jubilee in the South or the Republican leaders who managed to retain national power while retreating from the cause of freedom for the ex-slave. By 1870, the women's movement was bitterly divided and the National Labor Union was gone. By 1871, Tennessee, Virginia, North Carolina, and Georgia had all experienced "Redemption," as the restoration of white supremacist government was called by those coming to power. By 1875, only South Carolina, Louisiana, and Florida retained Republican governments. The compromise that decided the contested presidential election of 1876 doomed those holdouts by trading the removal of the last few federal troops protecting Black civil rights in the South for continued Republican control over the executive branch of government nationally.[4]

THE ENDS OF SOLIDARITY: WHEN JUBILEE DIVIDED

The glimmers of solidarity among supporters of the rights of freedpeople, Northern wage workers, and feminists dimmed by the decade's end as the groups fell out with each other. By far the most theatrically tragic of these fallings out involved the women's suffrage movement's historic leaders finding their ways out of the alliances with abolitionism that so shaped their development as dissenters and their sense of what was possible. The extreme rhetorical bitterness surrounding the split between former abolitionists supporting passage of the Fourteenth and Fifteenth Amendments and those insisting on immediate prioritization of women's suffrage conceals the rather straightforward reasons that the American Equal Rights

4 The narrative, if not the drama, of Reconstruction is best traced in Eric Foner, *Reconstruction: America's Unfinished Revolution* (New York: Harper Perennial, 2002 [1989]); on the compromises resulting from the 1876 election, see C. Vann Woodward, *Reunion and Reaction: The Compromise of 1877 and the End of Reconstruction* (New York: Oxford University Press, 1966).

Association (AERA) was almost bound to collapse. The organization formed to forward Black and women's suffrage together, but by 1867, only a minority in its ranks any longer committed themselves to doing so. The Kansas referenda campaign that year saw at best a half-hearted and episodic commitment by leading abolitionists to women's suffrage and mostly rhetorical support, compromised by racism, for Black male suffrage from women's suffrage speakers in the state. As the Fourteenth Amendment passed in 1868 and the Fifteenth prevailed two years later, the basis for the AERA no longer existed, and women's suffrage had emerged as a separate issue. It should hardly then be surprising that a new women's suffrage organization formed in 1869. But in fact two organizations formed. Neither the Stanton- and Anthony-led forces, furious at what they saw as betrayal by most male and some female abolitionist leaders, nor the more moderate suffragists led by Lucy Stone could command enough support to transform the AERA into an organization expressing their agenda. The former group formed the National Woman Suffrage Association (NWSA) at the time of the AERA's 1869 convention. The latter formed the American Woman Suffrage Association (AWSA) weeks later. The issues involved were largely retrospective, ratifying divisions already clear since 1867, but the NWSA was also more committed to a woman-led movement, without males, and to independence from the Republican Party.[5] The closing of the window of revolutionary time made for urgent claims and sharp debates.

The terrible logic of the mutual recrimination of the feminist and abolitionist movements is sometimes missed because we retrospectively know that Black male suffrage did prevail for a time, making it seem practical in ways the women's suffrage was not. We are apt to credit the wisdom of

---

5 Ellen DuBois, *Feminism and Suffrage: The Emergence of an Independent Women's Movement in America* (Ithaca, NY: Cornell University Press, 1978), 79–202; Philip Foner and Ronald Lewis, eds., *Black Workers: A Documentary History from Colonial Times to the Present, Volume Two, The Black Worker during the Era of the National Labor Union* (Philadelphia: Temple University Press, 1978), 411.

Sumner, Phillips, and others that women's suffrage could not possibly have prevailed. The idea that the nation was ready for Black male suffrage but not for women's suffrage underpinned the insistence of many former abolitionists and Republican strategists that it was the "Negro's hour" to gain the ballot after the war, though women activists also claimed the "hour" for themselves in 1865. Historians have generally agreed that only suffrage for Black men had enough support to prevail.[6] Such waters deserve to be troubled somewhat. In the immediate way that legislative debates unfolded, African-American male suffrage certainly had greater support than women's suffrage, but both demands had seemed impossible in 1864, and women's right activists could point to astonishing transformations that made the whole idea of "impossible" demands seem questionable. The possibility of Black men voting certainly registered the enormity of changes following the self-emancipation of slaves. But whether what was popular mattered much in the process remains another question.

The most directly democratic way to gauge support was in statewide referenda, in which only those already enfranchised—that is, white men—could vote. In Kansas in 1867, for example, women's suffrage lost such a vote among white men by more than a two-to-one margin. But the referendum on Black male suffrage in the same state at the same time was defeated almost as badly, indeed securing only 400 more positive votes, of nearly 30,000 cast, than did women's suffrage. (Tragically, Anthony, who had emphasized at times that the Kansas campaign was for both Black and women's suffrage, exulted privately on seeing early returns that the women's suffrage vote was in places "vastly ahead of [the] negro.") Voters rejected Black male suffrage in Minnesota, Pennsylvania, and Ohio the same year before a spirited campaign secured its approval in Iowa a year

---

6   Foner, *Reconstruction*, 255–6; Ann D. Gordon et al., eds., *The Selected Papers of Elizabeth Cady Stanton and Susan B. Anthony: In the School of Anti-Slavery, 1840 to 1866*, Volume 1 (New Brunswick, NJ: Rutgers University Press, 1997), 566. This reference to the woman's "hour" comes in regard to what is commonly regarded as the first woman's suffrage petition, dated December 26, 1865, in an appeal made by Stanton, Anthony, and Lucy Stone and signed as "National W.R. Com."

later. In Wyoming in 1869, the pioneering victory for women's suffrage did not come by referendum but through the action of the small territorial legislature.[7] Republicans wisely offered no referenda among white men in the South to decide on extending the franchise across the color line, addressing the matter instead at the federal level. Many white Republicans supported votes for African-American men as a tactical measure to produce Republican electoral victories, but they were nothing like a majority anywhere. The national GOP's desire for electability further conditioned its championing of the Fifteenth Amendment, with Black male voters thought to constitute a far more reliable base of Republican support than women. There was, given the need to respond to the Black Codes and to terror in the South, strong reason to campaign for enfranchising African-American men, but the relative popularity of the demand did not drive its passage. Indeed, what popularity it did enjoy often flowed from a Southern electoral strategy that the Republicans would abandon within a decade.[8]

The split between the NWSA and the AWSA lasted for over two decades, but worse still was the fact that white supremacy and anti-immigrant racism found a place in some quarters of the women's movement. In her 1869 address to the NWSA convention, Elizabeth Cady Stanton asked her audience to "Think of Patrick and Sambo and Hans and Yung Tung" exercising the right to vote. Such voters, she alleged, "do not know the difference between a monarchy and a republic." None could "read the Declaration of Independence" or even "Webster's spelling book." Nonetheless, she cautioned, they would be making laws for Lucretia Mott,

---

7 Dudden, *Fighting Chance*, 123, 125, 130–2, and 189; DuBois, *Feminism and Suffrage*, 96–7. See also Patricia Holland, "George Francis Train and the Woman Suffrage Movement, 1867–70" from *Books at Iowa* 46 (April 1987) at lib.uiowa.edu for Anthony's reaction to the returns.

8 Michael W. Fitzgerald, *The Union League Movement in the Deep South: Politics and Agricultural Change During Reconstruction* (Baton Rouge, LA: Louisiana State University Press, 1989), 22–3 and 43; see John Blassingame and John McKivigan, eds., *The Frederick Douglass Papers, Series One: Speeches, Debates, and Interviews, Volume 4, 1864–80* (New Haven, CT: Yale University Press, 1991), 146–8 for Douglass on terror and suffrage.

Ernestine I. Rose, and Anna E. Dickinson, naming three leading white feminists as among the offended. The excellence of the aggrieved and rightless native-born white woman became a recurring theme for Stanton. Sometimes the actress Fanny Kemble made her list of those invidiously compared to Irish and German male immigrants and to men of color.[9] Her performance was theatrical but ham-handed politically. It pretended that Chinese men were being enfranchised when they were not, pandering not only to racism against the Chinese but to paranoia. It left out Black women, who, the historian Christine Stansell has aptly pointed out, often functioned as little more than a "cipher" for Stanton, as well as disappearing the huge numbers of immigrant women.[10] Her proposals for an "educated suffrage" played also to class bias at just the moment when Stanton's forces were attempting to make alliances with working-class organizations and tragically predicted just the way that the many Black men, and not a few working-class whites, would soon be disenfranchised through literacy tests.

The excesses involved in the justification for a split among feminists reflected the power of white supremacist ideas to recreate themselves in changed circumstances. They did so by functioning not only as an ideology about the present but also as a "theory of history."[11] Anthony's speech to a Black section of the Union League in New York City in June 1868 was symptomatic of how memories of Black self-emancipation were discarded. In the revised history of emancipation that she offered there, "The black

9 Stanton, "Address to the National Woman Suffrage Convention" delivered in Washington, DC, on January 19, 1869, reprinted in *The Concise History of Woman Suffrage: Selections from the Classic Work of Stanton, Anthony, Gage, and Harper,* eds. Mari Jo Buhle and Paul Buhle (Urbana, IL: University of Illinois Press, 1978), 254; Ann D. Gordon et al., eds., *The Selected Papers of Elizabeth Cady Stanton and Susan B. Anthony: Against an Aristocracy of Sex, 1866 to 1873,* Volume 2 (New Brunswick, NJ: Rutgers University Press, 1997), 196 (Kemble). Louise Michele Newman, *White Women's Rights: The Racial Origins of Feminism in the United States* (New York: Oxford University Press, 1999), 5.
10 Christine Stansell, "Missed Connections: Abolitionist Feminism in the Nineteenth Century" in *Elizabeth Cady Stanton, Feminist as Thinker,* eds. Ellen Carol DuBois and Richard Cándida Smith (New York: New York University Press, 2007), 41.
11 Alexander Saxton, *The Rise and Fall of the White Republic: Class Politics and Mass Culture in Nineteenth-Century America* (New York: Verso, 2003 [1990]), 390.

man was rescued from slavery." And white women did the rescuing.[12] The feminists' ally and financial backer George Francis Train united bad politics, bad history, and bad poetry in attempting to render Anthony's point in a couplet:

> Woman votes the black to save,
> The black he votes to make the woman slave.[13]

Stanton revisited the history of abolition in order to intervene in the present. White Northern women, she said, were defenders of Black women before the war but now had to defend them against Black men rather than against slave-masters. Making but misusing the critical point that half the African-American population was female, she added, "If the two millions of southern black women are not to be secured in their rights . . . then their emancipation is but another form of slavery." As Stanton implausibly continued, "In fact, it is better to be the slave of an educated white man, than of a degraded ignorant black one."[14]

Such an argument lost track of real enemies, and it missed the fact that freedwomen at times decisively intervened in Black community meetings in the emancipated South, setting priorities, voting, and instructing male lawmakers on how to vote. At the very moment Stanton had the most reason to be angry at what she viewed as betrayal by native-born white men, often highly educated, she managed to conjure up the threat of unlettered Black and immigrant men voting.[15]

Her remarks, and those of others in the debates, often hinted at an acute

---

12 Gordon and others, eds., *The Selected Papers of Elizabeth Cady Stanton and Susan B. Anthony*, Volume 2, 144.

13 Train as quoted in DuBois, *Feminism and Suffrage*, 94.

14 "Elizabeth Cady Stanton to Martha C. Wright" (December 20, 1865), in *Elizabeth Cady Stanton*, eds. Theodore Stanton and Harriot Stanton Blatch (New York: Arno, 1969), Volume 2, 109–10.

15 Elsa Barkley Brown, "Negotiating and Transforming the Public Sphere: African-American Political Life in the Transition from Slavery to Freedom," *Public Culture* 7 (1994), 107–46; Steven Hahn, *A Nation under Our Feet: Black Political Struggles in the Rural South from Slavery to the Great Migration* (Cambridge, MA: Harvard University Press, 2003), 175–6 and 214.

worry that women were being consigned to disability in the eyes of the public and the state while Black men gained acceptance as normal and able. In 1867, the Greeley Committee recommendation on suffrage in New York state drew just such a line: "Adult rational manhood" qualified voters while the disfranchised—including children and "idiots, lunatics [and] felons"—were characterized by "dependence on others." Women were in the disqualified group. Stanton once tellingly said that she would sooner "cut off her right hand" than advance suffrage rights for Black men without providing the same for women. She complained after the defeats of 1867 that women "still stand with idiots, lunatics, minors, criminals [and] paupers."[16]

Male supremacy, like white supremacy shaken by the Civil War and Jubilee, also remained to deepen fractures between potential allies. Republicans campaigning in Kansas attacked Stanton and Anthony with all manner of misogynist weapons. After one of the former's eloquent speeches, the GOP paper in Fort Scott described her as a "jolly looking woman, fat and probably forty." Sexual innuendo regarding "free love," compounded by the travels of the leading feminist women with Train, coexisted with syrupy Republican encouragement that feminists desist because women already allegedly occupied a "nobler position than she could possibly acquire as a voter." Perhaps the oddest contribution came from Horace Greeley as part of a weak and belated Radical and ex-abolitionist response to attacks on women's suffrage leaders in Kansas. Greeley's grounds for supporting the suffrage measure in Kansas emphasized the need to pass it in order to expose its preposterous and malignant features.

---

16 Barbara Goldsmith, *Other Powers: The Age of Suffrage, Spiritualism, and the Scandalous Victoria Woodhull* (New York: Harper Perennial, 1999), 116 ("cut off"); Vivian Gornick, *The Solitude of Self: Thinking about Elizabeth Cady Stanton* (New York: Farrar, Straus and Giroux, 2005), 49–50; Victoria Woodhull, "A Lecture on Constitutional Inequality" (New York: Journeymen Printers' Co-operative Association, 1871), 22; David Quigley, *Second Founding: New York City, Reconstruction, and the Making of American Democracy* (New York: Hill and Wang, 2004), 56 (Greeley Committee); Dudden, *Fighting Chance*, 131 ("lunatics"). See also Buhle and Buhle, eds., *The Concise History of Woman Suffrage*, 273.

He wrote of regarding the measure "with mistrust" but was willing to "see it pioneered by Kansas" so that citizens would come to see it in practice as "a plague rather than a profit."[17]

Amid such fevered and bad-faith appeals on both sides, a noteworthy reservoir of good will and good judgment persisted. Figures like Henry Wright, Lucretia Mott, and Lydia Maria Child weighed competing claims with great care. Child apparently left the ranks of the Stanton and Anthony forces, but not feminism, precisely over the "rotten timbers" introduced to the movement by racism.[18] Black abolitionists, such as Sojourner Truth, Frances Harper, and Douglass, carefully avoided final breaks and sometimes absented themselves at moments when such breaks seemed likely to occur. They offered a defense of freedmen against increasingly extravagant charges by some white feminists. Truth observed tellingly that she would have been a victim of the "reading qualifications" that Stanton supported. Truth was literate, as she put it, in reading "men and nations" rather than "such small stuff as letters."[19]

Though arguments for an "education-" and therefore class- and race-based entitlement to rights, as well as racist rhetoric regarding Sambo, had been a sad part of Stanton's repertoire almost since the end of the war, by the end of the 1860s, she and her associates had left behind the rich associations with movements against white supremacy that checked those impulses. The betrayal, for someone like Frederick Douglass, mainly lay not in their racial attitudes but in the severing of ties with

---

17 Dudden, *Fighting Chance*, 126 for quoted passages and 117–34; William S. McFeely, *Frederick Douglass* (New York: W.W. Norton, 1991), 266–7; see also James McPherson, *The Struggle for Equality: Abolitionists and the Negro in Civil War and Reconstruction* (Princeton, NJ: Princeton University Press, 1964), 377 (on Greeley and women's suffrage in 1867); DuBois, *Feminism and Suffrage*, 94 notes that Train himself was the source of some of the sexual innuendo.

18 Carolyn L. Karchner, *The First Woman of the Republic: A Cultural Biography of Lydia Maria Child* (Durham, NC: Duke University Press, 1994), 541–2 ("rotten timbers"); Gordon et al., eds., *The Selected Papers of Elizabeth Cady Stanton and Susan B. Anthony*, Volume 2, 66; McFeely, *Frederick Douglass*, 266–8; Blassingame and McKivigan, eds., *The Frederick Douglass Papers*, Volume 4, 261n.

19 McFeely, *Frederick Douglass*, 366–7; Dudden, *Fighting Chance*, 142, 185–6; Buhle and Buhle, eds., *The Concise History of Woman Suffrage*, 270–1 (for the best of Harper); Nell Irvin Painter, *Sojourner Truth: A Life, A Symbol* (New York: Norton, 1996), 252 (quotes on reading) and 244–53.

old allies in favor of new ones with the Democratic Party and anti-Black racism. Douglass had, after all, cooperated with Stanton long after her earlier references to Sambo.[20] He expressed for a time an unwillingness to be "driven away" from Stanton even after she toured Kansas in 1867 in alliance with Train, a wealthy, charismatic, and white supremacist Democrat.[21]

Thus Jubilee was not without its forces of resilience, but neither was it insulated from racism, sexism, and the waning of revolutionary time. By 1869, when the last convention of the AERA met, the ratification of the Fifteenth Amendment seemed assured. Indiana Republican Congressman George Julian had already proposed a Sixteenth Amendment enfranchising women, an initiative Douglass strongly supported and one that attracted interest from Anthony. Douglass and his critics sparred with some rancor but also some humor as an era ended at the last AERA meeting. At the same gathering, Lucy Stone, who would be central in the AWSA and in keeping feuds alive, not only struck a position favoring equal emphasis on Black male and women's suffrage but also began an incisive answer to the contention that women did not face terror.[22] Douglass offered a series of resolutions trying to commit the organization to expressing some joy about Black male suffrage while deploring any Constitution without universal suffrage as "defective, unworthy [and]

20 See Ann D. Gordon, "Stanton and the Right to Vote: On Account of Race or Sex," 121 and 122–5, and Michele Mitchell, "'Lower Orders,' Racial Hierarchies, and Rights Rhetoric: Evolutionary Echoes in Elizabeth Cady Stanton's Thought During the Late 1860s," esp. 135 on how Stanton's opposition to "universal *manhood* suffrage" came to question both "universal" and "manhood." Both are in DuBois and Cándida Smith, eds., *Elizabeth Cady Stanton*. See also Gordon et al., eds., *The Selected Papers of Elizabeth Cady Stanton and Susan B. Anthony*, Volume 1, 566, and Stacey M. Robertson, *Parker Pillsbury: Radical Abolitionist, Male Feminist* (Ithaca, NY: Cornell University Press, 2000), 140–1 on earlier Stanton formulations regarding "intelligence" and "Sambo."
21 Dudden, *Fighting Chance*, 142 ("driven away"); McFeely, *Frederick Douglass*, 265–9.
22 Elizabeth Cady Stanton, Susan B. Anthony, and Matilda Joslyn Gage, eds., *History of Woman Suffrage*, Volume 2 (New York: Fowler and Wells, 1882), 333, 482, and 801; Buhle and Buhle, eds., *The Concise History of Woman Suffrage*, 259–60 for Stone at the 1869 AERA meeting. The best account of the 1869 meeting is Rosalyn Terborg-Penn, *African-American Women in the Struggle for the Vote, 1850–1920* (Bloomington, IN: Indiana University Press, 1998), esp. 32–4.

oppressive." Harper attempted one last compromise, but with Stanton's reiteration of her opposition to "allowing ignorant negroes and ignorant and debased Chinamen to make laws for her to obey," the organization not only died but did so in such a way as to trouble any unified push for a Sixteenth Amendment.[23]

The divisions of African Americans and of women from the labor movement broke up relationships that were far less longstanding than those between abolitionists and feminists. However, in the late 1860s in the warm afterglow of Jubilee, high hopes for broad unity through the labor movement had grown. They were tragically and consequentially dashed by the decade's end. It has been tempting for historians to cite the "ignorance of trade union principles" of reformers from outside the labor movement as central to why things fell apart.[24] The truth in such a view coexists with great complications. The trade union movement was itself in the 1860s far from the only form of working-class organization. Other bodies, often accepting of "middle class" members and even leaders, made it possible to imagine a labor–African American–feminist alliance not centered on trade union practice. More importantly, for all of the positive changes wrought by the war and the self-emancipation of slaves, exclusion of Black and women workers remained itself an important trade union principle in many craft-based organizations. In that sense, the breaches of "trade union fundamentals" by the excluded reflected not just ignorance of how unions operated but also knowledge of their practices.[25]

Such dynamics shaped in particular the failed embrace of African Americans and the National Labor Union (NLU). A bricklayers' strike in New

23 Blassingame and McKivigan, eds., *The Frederick Douglass Papers*, Volume 4, 218 ("'unworthy"), 219 ("Chinamen"), and 213–19 passim; Buhle and Buhle, eds., *The Concise History of Woman Suffrage*, 257–73; McFeely, *Frederick Douglass*, 269.
24 DuBois, *Feminism and Suffrage*, 155, and David Montgomery, *Beyond Equality: Labor and the Radical Republicans, 1862–1872* (New York: Knopf, 1967), 399, converge on exactly the same language in this regard; DuBois's discussion of the full dynamics of the competing claims at 158 is superb.
25 David Roediger, "What Was the Labor Movement?: Organization and the St. Louis General Strike of 1877," *Mid-America* 67 (January 1985), 37–51; Montgomery, *Beyond Equality*, 399 ("fundamentals").

Orleans in 1865 prefigured much of what was to come. White bricklayers sought their own Jubilee in the form of an eight-hour working day. Black workers, not accepted into union organization, continued to work during the strike. White unionists realized that in the new world of emancipation some cooperation across the color line would be required for practical reasons, but they wished to control its limits. They approached Black bricklayers with a call for unity but still envisioned an all-white union. When the African-American bricklayers insisted on joint organization as a condition for fully supporting the struggle, the whites chose segregation over victory. In 1866 in the same city, an all-white Eight-Hour League arose, putting labor's grandest demand and worst habit together. When the mixed-race, Black-owned *New Orleans Tribune*, the only strong supporter of eight hours among the city's newspapers, challenged the League's insistence on segregation, the organized white workers rejected overtures toward common effort. The *Tribune* described the white workers' self-destructive position as "Do justice to me; but, above all, do not do justice to my neighbor." Its castigation of the "strange blindness" animating such a stance was reported in the Northern pro-labor press, especially in contrast to more successful biracial struggles in St. Louis, contributing to a national discussion of emancipated labor and the labor movement.[26]

The most important venue for discussions of such questions was the NLU, where stirring examples of change could not supplant the same "strange blindness" found in New Orleans. Two logics appeared from white NLU leaders, one vastly more humane than the other but neither able to build an integrated labor movement nor even to challenge practices of exclusion of Black workers from unions and jobs. The appreciation of a new world anchored the first logic. As the Chicago labor editor A.C. Cameron wrote of freedpeople before the NLU met in 1867: "They number four million strong, and a greater proportion of them labor with

---

26 Foner and Lewis, eds., *The Black Worker*, Volume 1, 397–8 (quoted passages); Philip S. Foner, *Organized Labor and the Black Worker* (New York: International Publishers, 1982), 17–18.

their hands than . . . among any other people on earth." The NLU needed this new force, Cameron argued, for both "their moral influence, and their strength at the ballot-box." To "make them enemies" would harm the working-class movement more than any "efforts of capital" could accomplish. William Sylvis, the most charismatic NLU leader, likewise referred to the ballot-box in his prediction that failure to cooperate with Black workers would be the death of the labor movement.[27]

This insistence on the centrality of the issue of race coexisted in the first three NLU conventions with a total absence of Black workers. Debates among the all-white attendees, even at their best, centered on self-interest. W.E.B. Du Bois's compelling brief account of these matters paraphrases Cameron and Sylvis's case for unity, often rightly but incompletely read as a great advance, with a caution. "Here was the first halting note," Du Bois wrote, "Negroes were to be welcomed to the labor movement, not because they were laborers but because they might be competitors in the market, and the logical conclusion was either to organize them or to guard against their actual competition by other means." Those two strategies—a pragmatism based on white interests and exclusion—scripted the very limited progress of the NLU in coming to grips with race. At the 1866 convention, discussion yielded no action among divided delegates. In 1867, a Committee on Negro Labor reported but found the issue "involved in so much mystery" that action remained "inexpedient." One delegate worried that white unionists were being asked to "carry [Blacks] on their shoulders." In 1868, convention delegates applauded the end of slavery but ignored the issues following on emancipation yet again.[28]

Conservative positions on race, the opposing views to those articulated by Cameron and Sylvis, enjoyed great advantages because of the full-throated way that they responded to shoring up white supremacy under new conditions of emancipation. They especially thrived at the level of

27 Foner, *Organized Labor and the Black Worker*, 20 (quoting Cameron) and 21 for Sylvis.
28 Du Bois, *Black Reconstruction in America*, 354–5 ("halting" and "shoulders"); Foner, *Organized Labor and the Black Worker*, 20–2.

individual national craft unions and their locals. As Frederick Douglass emphasized, emancipation produced a period of backward motion where Blacks' abilities to use their craft skills were concerned.[29] Even as high-minded rhetoric sometimes graced NLU debates, unions such as the bricklayers and carpenters offered aggressive new color bars reflecting the supposed threats to their trades after freedom. The carpenters in 1869 combined noble words and exclusion: "Resolved that we are ever willing to extend the hand of fellowship to every laboring man . . . the prejudices of our members against the colored people are of such a nature that it is not expedient . . . to admit them as members." When one house carpenter objected to a color bar resolution as unnecessary, since members were admitted as individuals and no Black individual would be approved, he was told of the intent to make exclusion "doubly sure."[30] Hate strikes against the employment of skilled African Americans so successfully supplemented bars to membership that the *New York Times* reported in 1869 that New York City almost totally lacked opportunities for Black artisans to work. Sylvis inveighed against the "fanatical bigotry" inherent in such practices but also opposed equality in social relations, and even questioned Blacks serving on juries, undercutting much of his own position. A powerful tendency to, as one New York City cooper put it, let the "men most interested" decide whether Black workers belonged in their workplaces and unions dovetailed with opposition to social intimacy across the color line to reinforce the very color bars Sylvis decried.[31]

In the summer of 1869, two dramas conspired to show how much and how little white labor had learned and to underline the importance of

29 Blassingame and McKivigan, eds., *The Frederick Douglass Papers,* Volume, 4, 232; Foner and Lewis, eds., *The Black Worker,* Volume 1, 389.

30 Foner and Lewis, eds., *The Black Worker,* Volume 1, 384–5; Foner, *Organized Labor and the Black Worker,* 28 and 29 ("doubly sure").

31 Foner and Lewis, eds., *The Black Worker,* Volume 1, 371 ("men most interested") and 335–6 (Sylvis); Foner, *Organized Labor and the Black Worker,* 23 ("fanatical bigotry") and 23–9. On masculinity, unionism, and the importance of social equality, see David Roediger, *Towards the Abolition of Whiteness: Essays on Race, Class and Politics* (London and New York: Verso, 1994), 140–4.

local practice as well as national debate. In the first, Frederick Douglass's son Lewis became the center of a controversy inside—though he was made to stay outside—the International Typographical Union (ITU). Douglass, a Civil War soldier disabled in combat, had then worked for a time as a printer in Denver, where union membership was not open to him. When he moved to Washington, DC, and a job at the Government Printing Office, Douglass applied for his union card, a requirement of the job. Union members divided at a stormy meeting focusing on the charge that he had worked as a "rat" (that is, nonunion) printer in Denver. His supporters at the meeting had a majority but not the super-majority required for his admission and were forced to move to adjourn the meeting amid chaos. A protracted battle involving also the admission of another of Douglass's sons, Frederick Jr., ensued. Frederick Douglass Sr. summarized his view in a remarkable commentary on one side of craft union principles: "Lewis is made a transgressor for working at a low rate of wages by the very men who prevented his getting a high rate. He is denounced for not being a member of the Printers' Union by the very men who would not permit him to join." The *Printers' Circular* offered the union's view. Deferring to "deep-seated prejudices" held by members (a majority of whom in this case had favored Douglass's admission), the journal held, "surely no one who has the welfare of the craft at heart will seriously contend that the union [of] tens of thousands of white printers should be destroyed for the purpose of granting a barren honor of membership to few Negroes."[32]

In summer 1869, the NLU met, mourning Sylvis's death and welcoming the first African Americans ever to attend its convention. Isaac Myers's eulogy of Sylvis and speech on race and labor made him a towering figure at the conference. His words, recorded by the *New York Times* as the "Address of the Colored Delegate," excoriated color bars and hate strikes,

32 Blassingame and McKivigan, eds., *The Frederick Douglass Papers*, Volume 4, 232n19. Foner and Lewis, eds., *The Black Worker*, Volume 1, 379 ("transgressor" and "barren"), and 375–83; Foner, *Organized Labor and the Black Worker*, 27–9.

such as the one that had led him to build a very successful workers' cooperative on Baltimore's waterfront, even as he extolled the progress bringing
him to the gathering. He asked whether the local labor bodies "throughout
the country" would respond to the NLU's initiatives, but those initiatives
themselves remained incomplete. Though resolving that the NLU knew
"neither color nor sex," the convention abjured integration except at the
level of national conventions. When Myers returned to the national convention in 1870, his insistence that the Republican Party served workers'
interests provoked a groundswell of opposition. Myers's energies went to
trying to keep alive the Colored National Labor Union, founded in 1868
to build cooperatives and to combat color bars partly insisted on by white
workers. Important precedents notwithstanding—Sylvis's formulation
that "it is impossible to degrade one group of workers without degrading
all" approximated the famous watchwords under which the Knights of
Labor and the Industrial Workers of the World would later organize inter-
racially—the moment of Jubilee yielded little that was concrete in terms
of Black-white working-class solidarity.[33]

Women's suffragists found entry into the NLU in 1868. By the time
Black delegates were admitted a year later, Stanton and Anthony's forces
were on their way out. On arriving, despite all the bitterness over the
Kansas referendum and recent suffragist capitulations to racism in
attempting to gain support from the Democrats nationally, Stanton
lamented the lack of Black representation. She looked forward to African
Americans, women, and labor uniting in a radical third party in 1872.[34]

---

33 Foner and Lewis, eds., *The Black Worker*, Volume 1, 413 ("throughout") and 411–14 (reprinted
from *New York Times*, August 19, 1869); Peter Rachleff, *Black Labor in Richmond, 1865–1890*
(Urbana, IL: University of Illinois Press, 1989 [1984]), 64–5; Foner, *Organized Labor and the Black
Worker*, 23, ("degrading"), 26 ("nor sex"), and 27; Montgomery, *Beyond Equality*, 191–2; Paul Moreno,
Black Americans and Organized Labor: A New History (Baton Rouge, LA: Louisiana State University Press, 2006), 27–32. The Knights of Labor slogan would be: "An injury to one is the concern
of all." For the Industrial Workers of the World, the phrasing became: "An injury to one is an injury
to all."

34 DuBois, *Feminism and Suffrage*, 125; Dudden, *Fighting Chance*, 154; Lois Banner, *Elizabeth Cady
Stanton: A Radical for Women's Rights* (Boston: Little, Brown and Company, 1980), 103–5.

Stanton and Anthony shared with many NLU leaders a deep suspicion that the Republican Party would never address their issues. Some NLU leaders had participated in failed feminist overtures to the Democrats, who also rejected labor's demands. To some labor leaders, women offered a possible constituency for labor party initiatives leaders were projecting. Hopes soared among feminists who had just lost abolitionist allies and who sought new ones. Some within organized labor noted that *The Revolution* circulated fairly widely and supported all central working-class demands.[35]

The women who attended the 1868 convention as delegates all championed equal rights to the franchise. None worked for a wage, although three had credentials from recently formed associations including or purporting to represent interests of working women. The convention call had, after all, sought participation by all seeking "amelioration of the condition of those who work for a living." Only Stanton presented herself as a friend of labor simply by virtue of representing a suffrage organization. The initial challenge to her seating, on the grounds that she brought politics to the NLU and that her presence would leave the impression that the convention endorsed women's suffrage, failed to get even 30 percent of the vote. Sylvis, perhaps the best male supporter of women's rights in the labor movement, endorsed her presence as that of "one of the leading friends of working people." Nevertheless, delegates based in the building trades threatened to bolt from the gathering after the vote to admit her.[36] The compromise that followed left her credentials approved but added the caveat that such action implied no endorsement of her "ideas," particularly regarding votes for women. When the convention's Committee on Female Labor, chaired by Stanton, returned a report including women's

35 Philip S. Foner, *Women and the American Labor Movement from Colonial Times to the Eve of World War One* (New York: Free Press, 1979), 130–3; DuBois, *Feminism and Suffrage*, 108–25.
36 Israel Kugler, "The Trade Union Career of Susan B. Anthony," *Labor History* 2 (1961), 92 ("amelioration") and 90–3; Gordon et al., eds., *The Selected Papers of Elizabeth Cady Stanton and Susan B. Anthony*, Volume 2, 170 ("friends" and for the vote), 175n10, and 169–75; Foner, *Women and the American Labor Movement*, 132–3; DuBois, *Feminism and Suffrage*, 123–4.

suffrage as one way to empower women workers, the debate renewed. One bricklayers' delegate averred that, given the "very fertile imaginations" of women, inclusion of such language would be taken to put the NLU on record as pro-suffrage. Some male delegates affirmed that their opposition to Stanton reflected a deep hostility to women voting. Philadelphia's Jonathan Fincher, whose newspaper had so helped make the eight-hour day symbolize a Jubilee for workers, pledged that "the 'ism' of Woman's Suffrage will never be endorsed by the trades unions."[37] Nevertheless, the NLU elected a woman officer, Kate Mullany, a leader of Troy's collar workers, who had apparently foregone attending in the belief that it was impossible that women would be admitted. Feminists actually received a full hearing, and points of agreement on equal pay for equal work, eight hours, and even greenback currency were significant. Anthony left the convention eager to begin new organizing among women workers.[38]

Such organizing has at times been dismissed as an "opportunistic adventure" by "monomaniac" suffragists given to hectoring working-class women, but such dismissals describe poorly the flexibility of early initiatives toward forming a "Working Women's Association." In the run-up to the 1868 NLU convention, for example, delegates at the association's initial meetings, held in the offices of *The Revolution*, refused to endorse women's suffrage. Stanton and Anthony contested the workers' position but accepted their decision, leaving suffrage to be addressed later. The printer Augusta Lewis, a supporter of addressing the right to vote only after organizing "to get fairly paid," conducted an especially comradely debate with Anthony, specifically challenging the article of faith that electoral politics would always "elevate" voters. Association initiatives

---

37 Montgomery, *Beyond Equality*, 398; Kugler, "Trade Union Career," 93 ("ideas") and 94; DuBois, *Feminism and Suffrage*, 124 ("fertile" and "ism"). On Fincher and eight hours, see Chapter 3.

38 DuBois, *Feminism and Suffrage*, 122–3; Mullany's name is also variously spelled by historians as Mullaney and Mullhaney; Kugler, "Trade Union Career," 93–7; Foner, *Women and the American Labor Movement*, 133–5.

concentrated at first on building a base of women printers like Lewis. Anthony deftly helped to maneuver Alexander Troup, leader of the important Local 6 of the National Typographical Union (NTU) in New York City, into accepting on-the-spot initiation union fees for a few such women, who organized themselves into the Women's Typographical Union (WTU). When a firm in Galveston, Texas, requested printers from the WTU at below-union rates, Lewis, Anthony, and the membership applied trade union principles in rejecting the offer. Anthony herself participated in a variety of organizing drives, especially among sewing women.[39]

However, within a year, the possibility of a broad labor-centered alliance of the forces of Jubilee had largely vanished. Ironically, the successes of the WTU laid tensions bare. For years, and especially during the Civil War, women had gained fragile footholds in the least desirable jobs in printing partly by working below union rates and by strikebreaking. By the late 1860s, they may have accounted for one worker in five in the printing trades in New York City. They held both the worst jobs in the trade and some of the best jobs for working-class women at a time when Anthony estimated women's wages for the whole economy at only half or even a third of those of men. It was very much in their interest to secure union protections and union wages, but the NTU regarded women as competitors and rejected even ineffectual resolutions to include them as late as 1867. Feminist agitation made headway against such a position in part because a bitter, ten-month strike against the *New York World* had shown how vulnerable male unions could be to female strikebreaking. Indeed, Lewis herself worked at the *World* during the strike. When the Working Women's Association and the WTU began organizing, their attention was divided between the *World*, which would dismiss women printers and deride their skills when men returned to work, and the NTU. However,

---

39 Kugler, "Trade Union Career," 100 ("adventure" and "monomaniac"); Gordon et al., eds., *The Selected Papers of Elizabeth Cady Stanton and Susan B. Anthony*, Volume 2, 165 ("fairly" and "elevate").

as Troup more and more sought compromise, the NTU become only the second US craft union to accept women members and admitted the WTU as a chapter by 1869.[40] With success, the WTU attracted more of the energy of printers who had built the Working Women's Association. As attempts to incorporate other organizations and to recruit sewing women failed, the Association itself became more and more a body of what Ellen DuBois calls "middle-class working women" without wage-earners.[41]

When a strike began among job and book printers in New York in January 1869, women in the union energetically supported Local 6's efforts to prevent strikebreaking. Their solidarity led to their full recognition as a local by the union. Anthony, however, interpreted her mandate, and that of the Working Women's Association, as the expansion of opportunities for women to break into printing, an issue not part of Local 6's priorities. She met with employers—including the firm printing *The Revolution*—and offered to find women anxious to train during the strike. She knew that they would be unemployed once the strike ended but reckoned their experience and training would lead to future jobs. Local 6 denounced her effort as "an infamous measure," and the NLU's corresponding secretary noted her violation of "basic trade union principle." When the NLU met in convention in New York City in September 1869, Anthony's presence was sure to be so divisive that she was for a time persuaded not to go. However, the NTU still insisted on a vote on her credentials and she attended to answer charges, alternating between a tone of apology and the observation that her association was not a trade union but a body dedicated to expanding opportunities for working women. The vote went fifty-five to fifty-two in her favor, with over 42 percent of the trade union delegates enough persuaded by her position, or enough

---

40 Gordon et al., eds., *The Selected Papers of Elizabeth Cady Stanton and Susan B. Anthony*, Volume 2, 240 (Anthony on wage rates); DuBois, *Feminism and Suffrage*, 154; Foner, *Women and the American Labor Movement*, 143–51.

41 DuBois, *Feminism and Suffrage*, 160 ("middle class working women") and 144–53. More generally, see Ava Baron, "Women and the Making of the American Working Class: A Study of the Proletarianization of Printers," *Review of Radical Political Economics* 14 (Fall 1982), 23–42.

impressed by the value of alliance with feminists, to vote affirmatively. Local 6 then threatened to boycott the gathering. Anthony lost twenty-four supporters in the second vote, with twenty of her original trade union supporters changing their view. Although the fact that Lewis had been fired for union activities by the firm printing *The Revolution* counted heavily in the Local 6 case, more generally, the arguments for unseating Anthony included broad appeals to ratify male prerogatives as the natural order of things. Stanton's one-sided conclusion that workingmen were the worst enemies of women's suffrage actually came the week before the NLU met. Its proceedings reflected far less unmitigated hostility than her assessment allowed, but her suggestion that the forces of Jubilee based on women's suffrage and those based on eight hours could scarcely coexist bore out. By 1872, the great feminist orator Anna Dickinson was assailing not only unions but also the eight-hour day, to the astonishment of former allies. Adding to the gloom was the fact that the African-American delegates who broke the color line at the 1869 NLU convention all voted against Anthony's seating.[42]

As if to underline yet again the fact that groups oppressed in differing ways, who spectacularly came together under the inspirations of Jubilee, could quickly divide, the WTU members who acted on the trade union principle of solidarity during strikes soon ran afoul of the craft union dictum that one does not expand access to jobs in the trade. Lewis, who had strong reasons to support the NTU and who married Troup in 1874, complained at the typographical union convention that admission of "union girls" had left them with even less access to work than before. "We refuse to take the men's situations when they are on strike, and when there is no strike if we ask for work in union offices we are told by union foremen

---

42   DuBois, *Feminism and Suffrage*, 157 ("principle") and 155–61; Kugler, "Trade Union Career," 97–100; Foner, *Women and the American Labor Movement*, 151 ("infamous") and 149–52; Montgomery, *Beyond Equality*, 399; Giraud Chester, *Embattled Maiden: The Life of Anna Dickinson* (New York: G.P. Putnam's Sons, 1951), 146–7; for Stanton's view, see Philip S. Foner, *History of the Labor Movement in the United States*, Volume 1 (New York: International Publishers, 1997), 386.

'that there are no conveniences [restrooms] for us.'" Female compositors, she thought, held the opinion that they received more just treatment from employers and even from "rat" (nonunion) foremen than from union men. Lewis still believed that "the principle is right" with regard to supporting the union but added that "the disadvantages are so many that we cannot much longer hold together." By 1878 the WTU had disappeared.[43]

FACES OF TERROR

Impulses to solidarity growing out of Jubilee fell apart internally, but Southern opponents and Northern friends quickened their dissipation. As much as divisions among the oppressed hastened the end of Jubilee, and as much as the Republican Party would prove crucial to the disappearing of freedom dreams, the ability to combine terror and political acumen on the part of white supremacist Southerners also proved crucial in defeating meaningful emancipation. The odd syllables Ku Klux Klan, and the oddly titled Grand Cyclopses, Grand Wizards, and Grand Dragons providing leadership to that organization, capture the popular understanding of such terror. Picturesquely robed and hooded disguises completed a mystique that, as W.E.B. Du Bois wrote, gave "glamour" to terror.[44]

The Klan certainly was at the center of racial violence for a long and decisive moment when civil rights acts, constitutional change, and relatively strong military occupation of the region put the question of how

---

43 Foner, *Women and the American Labor Movement*, 160–1 (for the quoted material); see also DuBois, *Feminism and Suffrage*, 157–1; Gordon et al., eds., *The Selected Papers of Elizabeth Cady Stanton and Susan B. Anthony*, Volume 2, 168n5.

44 Du Bois, *Black Reconstruction in America*, 676. The best account of the Klan remains Allen W. Trelease, *White Terror: The Ku Klux Klan Conspiracy and Southern Reconstruction* (New York: Harper and Row, 1971). The most useful general account of terror in Reconstruction is George C. Rable, *But There Was No Peace: The Role of Violence in the Politics of Reconstruction* (Athens, GA: University of Georgia Press, 2007).

far the South was to be reconstructed squarely on the table. But the Klan itself was preceded by less coordinated attacks on freedpeople in the form of riots and night-riding, and it was succeeded by more of the same. The casualties came at the hands of the Klan, the Knights of the White Camellia, the Knights of the White Carnation, the White Leagues, the Red Shirts, the Knights of the Rising Sun, the Order of Pale Faces, the Knights of the Black Cross, the Southern Cross, the White Liners, and nameless mobs and individuals. From the New Orleans and Memphis Riots after the war to the Ellenton, South Carolina riots late in 1876, the violence proved varied and mobile, but unabated; 20,000 casualties is a conservative estimate.[45]

In some locales, deaths arrived by the scores, as at Ellenton and at the Colfax Massacre in Louisiana in 1873, in which forty-eight died while in custody as prisoners. Humiliations also came, as freedpeople with the temerity to vote, claim land, organize as workers, drill as militia members, parade as veterans, quit jobs, or stand up as domestic servants to their employers had to be brought to heel, especially through whippings and sexual violence. In some counties, the Knights of the White Camellia practiced what the classic history of Reconstruction-era terror called "nonviolent terrorism"—patrolling at night as if slavery had not ended and writing threatening letters—though the prospect of violence was what gave such intimidation force.[46] The extent and variety of terror ought not

---

45 Trelease, *White Terror*, esp. xliii, xliv, 51, 82–3, 88, 93–4, 131, and 136; Du Bois, *Black Reconstruction*, 474–5 and 679; Carl N. Degler, *The Other South: Southern Dissenters in the Nineteenth Century* (New York: Harper and Row, 1974), 250; on casualties, see also Albion W. Tourgee, *The Invisible Empire: A Concise History of the Epoch* (Ridgewood, NJ: Gregg Press, 1968 [1883]), 20, 51, and 53; Shawn Leigh Alexander, ed., *Reconstruction, Violence, and the Ku Klux Klan Hearings*, forthcoming from Bedford, introduction. On Ellenton as a climax of terror, see Lou Falkner Williams, "Federal Enforcement of Black Rights in the Post-Redemption South: The Ellenton Riot Case," in *Local Matters: Race, Crime, and Justice in the Nineteenth-Century South*, eds. Christopher Waldrep and Donald G. Nieman (Athens, GA: University of Georgia Press, 2001), 172–200; Du Bois, *Black Reconstruction*, 464–6.

46 LeeAnna Keith, *The Colfax Massacre: The Untold Story of Black Power, White Terror, and the Death of Reconstruction* (New York: Oxford University Press, 2008), xv and passim; Nicholas Lemann, *Redemption: The Last Battle of the Civil War* (New York: Farrar, Straus and Giroux, 2006), 22 and passim.

to tempt us to view the racial and class violence as desperate, formless, or aimless. Instead, it was consistently focused in its targets and its goals, seeking the restoration of Democratic Party rule, the suppression of civil liberties and labor rights, and the assertion of control over the bodies and voices of those who had just won freedom.

Anti-Black and anti-worker to be sure, the spread of Klan and Klan-like violence was above all anti-Jubilee. It had much to reverse. White supremacist terror featured a surplus of violence, even beyond what a guerrilla war designed to make Northern Republicans lose heart when faced with implacable and violent opposition required. Such a surplus recalls C.L.R. James's insistence that the surplus of repression responds to the depth of challenge presented by insurgencies.[47]

However, even at its most excessive, white conservative terror from 1865 to 1876 could include a striking amount of finesse in its dealings with the North. At one tense point in Tennessee in early Reconstruction, for example, Klan leader General Nathan Bedford Forrest threatened that if the militia were called out to prevent predations on Republicans, the Klan's clout would become clear. Its 45,000 members in the state, and more than a half a million across the South, he claimed, could bring a government to its knees.[48] Yet Forrest also had another voice, one denying before Congress any role in or knowledge of the Klan. Not only did Forrest, who in the Civil War established as good a claim as any high-ranking Confederate to being a war criminal, remain at large and a player in Southern politics despite his connections to the Klan, he also managed to put together railroad investment schemes appealing to Northern capital. The claim to know how to get things done—Forrest had been a consequential slave trader before the war and was a labor contractor after it—made the appeal of figures like Forrest a double one. They could be the Republicans' murderous night-riding opponents, but they also stood

---

47 Du Bois, *Black Reconstruction*, 674; for James, see Anna Grimshaw, "The Revolutionary Vision of C.L.R. James" (1991) at marxists.org.

48 Trelease, *White Terror*, 45.

ready to be the useful junior partners in Southern enterprises dominated by Yankee and British capital if Black rights were jettisoned.[49]

At a policy level, the tendency of Democrats restored to power in the South—most states saw only very short periods of Republican rule—mirrored Forrest's ability to at once play the bad cop and the good cop. Though opposed to a Republican Party that was associated with forwarding the interests of Northern capital, the restored Democrats often sold off the region's publically owned mineral and timber assets at bargain-basement rates to capitalists from outside the region. C. Vann Woodward's classic history of the New South wonderfully called this transfer of assets the Southern version of the nation's "Great Barbecue," a huge transfer of natural resources into private hands justified by the need to foster internal improvements. Such barbecues had long been a feature of planter rule in the antebellum South, distributing a little feast for poor whites around election time. But the postbellum Great Barbecue, Southern-style, came after the election and gifted investors as the Southern Democrats repaired ties with Northern elites. It fixed the South as a semicolony of the Northeast's elites but made perfect sense if restoration of white supremacy and control over labor dictated matters.[50] In that morally indefensible terrain, the strategy of white supremacist "Knights" to salvage manhood and political control could seem like a successful guerrilla campaign, whatever the actual costs to the region and its people.

The targets of terror were thus many. Local people who wished to live differently gave vigilantes sites to make their marks in ways that only sometimes also had formal political goals. Indeed, some of the most deci-

---

49 Paul Ashdown and Edward Gaudill, *The Myth of Nathan Bedford Forrest* (Lanham, MD: Rowman & Littlefield, 2006), 62–3, and Scott Reynolds Nelson, *Iron Confederacies: Southern Railways, Klan Violence, and Reconstruction* (Chapel Hill, NC: University of North Carolina Press, 1999), 135–7; Michael W. Fitzgerald, "Extralegal Violence and the Planter Class: The Ku Klux Klan in the Alabama Black Belt During Reconstruction," in *Local Matters*, eds. Christopher Waldrep and Donald G. Nieman, 163–4; David R. Roediger, *How Race Survived US History: From Settlement and Slavery to the Obama Phenomenon* (New York: Verso, 2008), 112–17; Trelease, *White Terror*, 259–60.
50 C. Vann Woodward, *Origins of the New South, 1877–1913* (Baton Rouge, LA: Louisiana State University Press, 1999 [1951]), 31, 23–106, and 291–320.

sive reactionary political achievements of the terrorists seem so devoid of planning for a specific result as to call into question any rigid distinctions of the sort that historians make between political action and "pre-political" protest.[51] The terrible 1866 Memphis Riot, for example, occurred just after Andrew Johnson's conservative administration's political decision to decommission almost all African-American troops in the federal army. Even so, the remaining Black troops might have played a role in protecting Black Southerners' rights. Instead, the white violence in Memphis was seen as evidence that demobilizing Black troops was right, as it allegedly avoided provoking white anger. The remaining Black troops not forced out of the regular army were often speedily sent west to prosecute (anti-) Indian wars and later to further US occupation of the Philippines. Even the seemingly unfocused racial terror in Memphis thus solidified a signally important victory for white supremacy, a lesson that could hardly have been lost on Forrest and the others who founded the Klan, with Tennessee as its center, shortly after the riots.[52]

Rare instances of authorities' use of Black militias, which became important forces in parts of the South, to suppress Klan terror succumbed to a similar logic. Opposition to their presence could unite whites across party lines. In response to terrorism in Arkansas, African Americans were briefly brought into the formal efforts to restore order and rights. But after protests from whites, they were quickly forced out. In North Carolina, at a critical point in 1869, the governor sent a white militia force to respond to a string of atrocities centering on bootlegging and politics. Their purpose was, as the historian Allen Trelease wrote, "to disband the local Negro

---

51 For an overdrawn distinction between "political" and "pre-political" protest and even "people's protest," see Eric J. Hobsbawm, *Primitive Rebels: Studies in Archaic Forms of Social Protest in the Nineteenth and Twentieth Centuries* (New York: Norton, 1965), 2, 22, and 110–23.

52 Hannah Rosen, *Terror in the Heart of Freedom: Citizenship, Sexual Violence, and the Meaning of Race in the Postemancipation South* (Chapel Hill, NC: University of North Carolina Press, 2009), 63 and 23–86; Kevin R. Hardwick, "'Your Old Father Abe Lincoln Is Dead and Damned': Black Soldiers and the Memphis Race Riot of 1866," *Journal of Social History* 18 (Fall 1993), 109–28; Roediger, *How Race Survived US History*, 130 and 135.

militia in order to placate Conservatives." Similar dynamics applied in Mississippi in 1875 and in South Carolina in 1876.[53]

By far the best investigation of white terror responding to Jubilee resulted from congressional inquiries into the Klan, producing thirteen bulging volumes of testimony dating from 1871 and 1872. As the most widespread and centralized expression of violence, the Klan inevitably became the most studied such force. Because Klan violence was so ritualized, performative, and even didactic, vigilantes often fully rehearsed their grievances against those being brutalized, making testimony especially revealing. The hearings were intensely political, with a majority Republican report and a minority Democratic report drawing opposite conclusions. The Klan's careful choices of targets ensured as much as they reflected a desire to restore Democratic rule against a fragile coalition of freedmen and mostly poor whites voting together against conservative interests. Organizing across color lines in the Republican electoral vehicle of the semi-secret Union Leagues or Loyal Leagues, such a coalition became the *bête noire* of the early Klan and other vigilantes from 1866 to 1868. Testimony in the congressional hearings by supporters of the Klan cast its actions as a response to Union League provocations. In a remarkably muddled pairing, the Klan sometimes referred to the Union League as a "nigger KKK," but when Republicans largely defunded the leagues after the 1868 elections, white terror continued apace.[54]

The maintenance of white terror underlined the political core of the mission of the Klan, whose clandestine threats, especially against white Republicans in the South, were at times scarcely distinguishable from those openly issued by bodies associated with the Democratic Party, which

---

53 Trelease, *White Terror*, 191, 163–4, and 190; Michael W. Fitzgerald, *The Union League Movement in the Deep South: Politics and Agricultural Change During Reconstruction* (Baton Rouge, LA: Louisiana State University Press, 1989), 67–70; Rable, *But There Was No Peace*, 157–8 and 165–8. For a more optimistic view of the Arkansas events, see Degler, *The Other South*, 251.

54 Trelease, *White Terror*, xxxi and 86; Fitzgerald, *The Union League Movement in the Deep South*, 9–13, 35–42, and 60.

promised to shun and destroy opponents.[55] Thus, the historian George Rable's identification of the Klan and other vigilante groups as the "military arm" of the Democrats captures an important reality. The choice of those being victimized bespoke the goals of the organization, but so did the choice of those being enlisted. They were "members of the better as well as the lower grades," according to one contemporary account. The great horses on which Klan leaders rode during nighttime raids symbolized the leadership of the prominent. However, at times the antebellum practice of paying poor whites to patrol at night to police the slave system and the wartime practice of the rich paying for substitutes to serve in their place reportedly also applied to the Klan's night rides.[56] Recreating a cross-class alliance of whites under new circumstances was the "positive" goal of the Klan, amid many negative ones.

Republican political activists often bore the brunt of the "crime-storm of devastating fury" produced by the Klan. As the anti-racist judge Albion Tourgee wrote in 1883, freedpeople were first and foremost the victims, but "white men who acted with the blacks politically" were also singled out, as were white defectors from the Klan or from the Democrats. Again, the pre-Klan activity of mobs anticipated the pattern of more formalized violence. In the horrific massacres of the New Orleans riot of 1866, the violence was against Blacks and radical whites attempting to deliberate together in the Mechanics Institute. One Floridian testifying to the committee investigating the Klan summed up its goal as "to kill out the leading men of the Republican Party" in its areas of strength. Merely voting for Republicans could occasion disabling beatings, and, as South Carolina's Willis Johnson testified, "getting out" the vote was more serious still. When John Childers of Alabama was told the Klan "had a coffin made for me," he finally became a Democratic voter. Black political leaders who

---

55 Du Bois, *Black Reconstruction*, 474.
56 Tourgee, *The Invisible Empire*, 16 ("lower grades") and 23; Rable, *But There Was No Peace*, 95; for a formulation similar to Rable's, see Eric Foner, *Reconstruction: America's Unfinished Revolution, 1863–1877* (New York: Harper and Row, 1988), 425.

refused bribes to cross over to support the Democrats reported being in special jeopardy.[57]

Professing support for Radical Republicanism in public in particular invited reprisal. The leader of a Mississippi Republican club was disemboweled in front of his wife. Wholesale massacres punctuated the process, most dramatically in Jackson and Marianna counties in Florida in 1869, a time and place in which perhaps 150 people were killed to break Republican power. Tuscaloosa, Alabama, editor Ryland Randolph, perhaps the loosest cannon among the public figures of the Klan, took pains to emphasize that whites were likewise the targets of violence. In late August 1868, he editorially singled out a local Black Republican who had written a political letter to the newspaper in Montgomery as "a candidate before the Ku Klux Klan for *grave* honors." The next month Randolph featured a cartoon in which two whites hung from a tree, a mule labeled KKK having moved and left them dangling. One of the executed had a carpetbag—Northern Republicans who moved South were derogatorily called "carpetbaggers"—with "Ohio" written on it, again with reference to a specific local figure. The other was a "scalawag," as white native Southerners supporting Republicans were called with similar unfriendliness. Carpetbaggers and scalawags who were educators seemed to present a particular menace in the Klan's eyes.[58]

Terror worked in reshaping electoral politics. In the atmosphere of

57 Du Bois, *Black Reconstruction*, 674; Tourgee, *The Invisible Empire*, 23 ("acted"); Fitzgerald, *The Union League Movement in the Deep South*, 222–3; Alexander, *Reconstruction, Violence, and the Ku Klux Klan Hearings*, forthcoming; Joint Select Committee to Inquire into the Condition of Affairs in the Late Insurrectionary States, *Testimony Taken by the Joint Select Committee to Inquire into the Condition of Affairs in the Late Insurrectionary States,* Volumes 1–13, (Washington, DC: Government Printing Office, 1872) [*KKK Testimony*]; See testimony of Emanuel Fortune, 13: 94–5, testimony of Willis Johnson, 3: 326–30, testimony of John Childers, 10: 1725 in *KKK Testimony* and *KKK Testimony*, 13: 94–5. I benefited greatly from reading Professor Alexander's excellent documentary history in manuscript form.

58 Alexander, "Introduction," *Reconstruction, Violence, and the Ku Klux Klan Hearings*, forthcoming; on education and terror, see also Tourgee, *The Invisible Empire*, 57, 86–7, and 53–4 (on Randolph); Foner, *Reconstruction*, 428; see Fitzgerald, *The Union League Movement in the Deep South*, 108–9, for the importance of schoolteachers in Republican activism in Alabama and Mississippi.

intimidation surrounding the 1868 presidential election in New Orleans, 21,000 registered Republicans produced a mere 276 votes for their party's ticket. In Yazoo, Mississippi, after especially brutal attacks on Republicans, a 1,800-vote Republican majority in the 1873 election was transformed into a 4,404-to-7 Democratic landslide in 1875. In Alabama's Greene County after the 1868 election, it was reported that all whites who had voted for Ulysses Grant were run off.[59]

However, politics in a far broader sense than the electoral realm also animated the Klan and its milieu. The attempt was to turn back Jubilee, as historian Allen Trelease wrote, in "every walk of life." Opponents of the Union League charged, and not without reason, that freedpeople and their allies used political meetings to build labor organizations. Livestock, ranging freely but often owned by better-off whites, disappeared from the countryside at times.[60] The restoration of white property, some of it now legally held by freedpeople, became a preoccupation of night riders. In Demopolis, Alabama, the Klan routed Eliza Lyon's family, murdering her husband Abe for the crime of having saved several hundred dollars. Lyon fled with her two children, leaving money and other property in the hands of the mob. Disputes over sharing of crops brought mobs to the doors of other Black families. Land ownership particularly drew attacks on both persons and property, and to own a good horse or mule invited the charge of "getting above your business," as Mississippi beating victim William Coleman put it. One victimized Alabama family was given two weeks to move on and told, "White folks wants to work this land."[61] Owning one's own labor and contracting for its sale, so fundamental to the ideology of

---

59   Du Bois, *Black Reconstruction*, 474; James S. Allen, *Reconstruction: The Battle for Democracy* (New York: International Publishers, 1937), 200–1; Foner, *Reconstruction*, 561 and 559–63; Fitzgerald, *The Union League Movement in the Deep South*, 223.

60   James Melville Beard, *K.K.K. Sketches, Humorous and Didactic* (Philadelphia: Claxton, Remsen and Haffelfinger, 1877), 18–28; Trelease, *White Terror*, xlvi; Fitzgerald, *The Union League Movement in the Deep South*, 168–9 and 228–9; Fitzgerald, "Extralegal Violence and the Planter Class," 158–9.

61   See testimony of Eliza Lyons, 9: 1262–4, testimony of William Coleman, 11: 482–4, testimony of Augustus Blair, 9: 675–7.

white self-rule in the United States, was similarly attacked. The Memphis
Riot again established patterns very early. One reason soldiers became
subject to such fierce attack was that they were accused of subverting
planter and Freedmen's Bureau plans to force urbanized freedpeople to
contract to return to plantation labor. In parts of Georgia, Alfred Richardson testified, almost any wage dispute could end in a Klan attack.[62]

The mixed nature of expressed motives for violence by the Klan warns
against oversimplifying matters by suggesting that either politics or the
control of land and labor was fundamental to the violence. Freedpeople
often reported their families being attacked because they were prosperous
and because they supported the Radical Republican ticket. Georgia leg-
islator Abram Colby, for example, suffered for his political views but also
because his property offended and attracted Klansmen. The attacks on
freedpeople's schools and the widespread burnings of African-American
churches, both features of terror from the Memphis Riot forward, singled
out symbols of Black progress and self-activity and sites of Black political
organizing. Literacy and numeracy also meant a measure of control over
economic life. Scipio Eager died at the Klan's hands because, as his brother
recalled, he "was too big a man [who could] write and read and put it
down himself."[63]

The connection of literacy with manhood and independence is particularly suggestive of the ways that gender wove its way into terror at every
turn. Disarming freedpeople, another feature of Klan terror presaged by
the Memphis Riot, had many practical rationales. It disempowered Black
militias, made the self-defense very often practiced by those whom the
Klan attacked more difficult, and kept families from hunting, thereby
putting them more in need of employment from whites, but it also powerfully enacted a symbolic emasculation at a time when literal castration

62 *KKK Testimony*, 6: 12; Hardwick, "Memphis Race Riot," 116 and 111–17.
63 See testimony of Scipio Eager, *KKK Testimony*, 7: 669; Foner, *Reconstruction*, 428; Rable, *But There Was No Peace*, 39 and 97–8; Fitzgerald, *The Union League Movement in the Deep South*, 58–9.

FALLING APART 179

of a victim by the Klan could also occur.[64] Both male and female victims of the Klan also told of being made to disrobe in the presence of attackers, as slaves had been before potential buyers, even when rape was not part of the attack.[65] Similarly, the litany of beatings of freedwomen for the offense of "sassing" white women responded to a desire to boss domestic servants without being questioned. Such a rationale thus responded to a specific crisis in gender, race, and labor relations explored by Thavolia Glymph's extraordinary work. At the same time, it expressed a nostalgia and hatred quite transcendent of calculating market relations. John Childers, himself brutalized for reasons of electoral politics by the Klan, lost a daughter to a most private violence. The daughter, hired out to care for a small child, supposedly allowed the child's cap to be lost. She was beaten so severely by her white employer that she died, at age nine, after just over a week.[66]

Sexual violence against freedwomen reasserted the power of white men in multiple ways. The political use of rape was very much about a degradation of freedwomen that hearkened back to the racialized sexual dangers of slavery. In the Memphis Riot, white-on-Black rapes singled out women tied to African-American soldiers. The victims' associations with accusations of vagrancy had already resulted in their being branded as prostitutes by local authorities, making them vulnerable long before the riot. In the riot itself, their exploitation staked out the limits of irrationality. White supremacists worried that Black men menaced the city and its white

64 See testimony of George Roper, 9: 689, testimony of Henry Kidd, 9: 868, and testimony of B.F. Tidwell, 13: 122, in *KKK Testimony*. Michael W. Fitzgerald, "The Ku Klux Klan: Property Crime and the Plantation System in Reconstruction Alabama," *Agricultural History* 71 (Spring 1997), 193–4; Fitzgerald, *The Union League Movement in the Deep South*, 228; Alexander, *Reconstruction, Violence, and the Ku Klux Klan Hearings*; on castration, see Rosen, *Terror in the Heart of Freedom*, 198–9.

65 See testimony of Joe Brown, 6: 502, and testimony of Samuel Tutson, 13: 54–9, in *KKK Testimony*, 6: 502 and 13: 54–9; (on nudity) Rosen, *Terror in the Heart of Freedom*, 211–14.

66 Thavolia Glymph, *Out of the House of Bondage: The Transformation of the Plantation Household* (Cambridge, UK: Cambridge: University Press, 2008), 97–136; See testimony of Alfred Richardson, 6: 12, testimony of Caroline Smith, 6: 400–3, testimony of Sarah Ann Sturtevant, 6: 462–5, and testimony of John Childers, 10: 1722–4, in *KKK Testimony*.

women even as they countenanced rapes of Black women. Rapists of two
of the women required that the victims serve a dinner afterward. The
women themselves, as Hannah Rosen's remarkable study shows, were to
be cast back to the "status quo ante" of the period before Jubilee. In an
1871 rape in Meridian, Mississippi, the offender acted as if he were in a
brothel—he was in fact in an African-American home—and proceeded
to choose partners. As Rosen writes, "Constructing black homes and
communities as spaces for white men's pleasure" framed many of the
Klan-era rapes. The Meridian rapist followed his rape by averring that he
was in town to fight the pro-Republican Union League.[67] The personal,
or perhaps the inhuman, was political in every sense. Similarly, in testimony to Congress on the Klan, the many rapes accompanying KKK night
rides betrayed mixed motives. The rapes served to drive freedpeople from
land and to discourage voting Republican. The spectacles were often
public. Sometimes they were gang rapes, suggesting that they bound per-
petrators together as white men and perhaps as secret-keepers.[68]
Constructing Black womanhood as a space "for white men's pleasure"
perversely reconstructed white manhood.

A longing for the restoration of slavery as the ordering principle of
society made terror especially potent and unpredictable. One pro-Klan
spokesperson testified to Congress that night-riding was simply and consciously a continuation of the tradition of patrolling to police slaves at
night. The form of protest very often centered on whippings and at times
on confronting those who resisted whippings.[69] That there was no going
back to slavery put limits on the violence. Planters needed labor and
opposed some terrorist actions that were seen as bound to drive freedpeople away, to make it impossible to attract new labor, and to advantage

67 Rosen, *Terror in the Heart of Freedom*, 40–3, 57–8, 68–70 ("status quo ante"), and 210–11;
Hardwick, "Memphis Race Riot," 121–2.
68 *KKK Testimony*, 5: 1861 and 13: 60; Rosen, *Terror in the Heart of Freedom*, 202–21.
69 See the testimony of William M. Lowe, *KKK Testimony*, 9: 873 and 877. On whipping and on
confronting resistance to whipping, see Fitzgerald, *Union League*, 154 and 219.

white workers by removing Black competition. During periods of intense need for agricultural labor, terror tended to recede. Such limits led to the frequent dissolution and reconstitution of white supremacist organizations.[70] But if terror could not always unify all whites, it could put the forces of Jubilee on the defensive and force increasing reliance on the Republican Party as the hope of protection.

THE TROUBLE WITH REPUBLICANS

If a Rainbow Coalition of women, freedpeople, and workers was to exist in electoral politics, it needed a force to sponsor the inclusion of most of its members as voters. As it was, women had no right to the ballot and African-American men only precariously gained such a right with 1867 legislation and constitutional change in 1870. Whether change in the latter case could be enforced on the ground, and for how long, depended on having allies. For women's suffrage advocates, despite the support of Train and other Democrats for the 1867 suffrage referendum in Kansas and despite a brief moment of championing Salmon Chase, a veteran Republican and Free Soil politician, as an egalitarian, possible Democratic nominee for president in 1868, there never was any serious Democratic alternative as a political home.[71]

For all of their hesitancy, the Republicans remained the party of reform and kept alive the embers of feminist-antislavery alliance. The chilly reception of the Stanton/Anthony women's suffrage forces at the 1868 Democratic convention created a desire to never repeat the experience. The Democrats remained, to adapt Alexander Saxton's useful terminology, the party of "hard racism" against Blacks and "hard sexism"

70 Reynolds, *Iron Confederacies*, 136–7; Fitzgerald, "Extralegal Violence and the Planter Class," 160–5; Fitzgerald, *Union League*, 229, probes the seasonality of terror well.
71 DuBois, *Feminism and Suffrage*, 108–10; Dudden, *Fighting Chance*, 154–60.

against women.[72] The brief women's suffrage attempts to work with the Democratic Party to enter electoral politics in the end amounted to a way to end alliances with abolitionists and Republicans, not a sustained effort to find a new home in the two-party system. Kansas Republicans accelerated the split when they opposed the 1867 women's suffrage campaign on male supremacist grounds and when national leaders responded to the attacks on women's rights so belatedly and weakly.[73] Despite all the appeals to Democrats by feminists and despite the demagoguery of Republican opponents and half-hearted friends of women's suffrage in the Kansas referendum campaign, the main source of positive votes endorsing women's suffrage remained, even in Kansas, the state's antislavery forces, overwhelmingly Republican. Stanton began a period of embracing third-party efforts, but by the 1872 presidential election, the leadership of the NWSA was back in support of the Republican ticket.[74]

The contradictory Republican Party was not only necessary to imagining a political Jubilee but also positively attractive for a time. Du Bois's *Black Reconstruction* featured headnotes presaging the content of each chapter. In one, devoted early in the book to "Looking Forward" to the course of Reconstruction as a whole, he offered a portrait of the forces inside the Republican Party. The chapter was to concern:

How two theories of the future of America clashed and blended just after the Civil War: the one was abolition-democracy based on freedom, intelligence, and power for all men; the other was industry for private profit directed by an autocracy determined at any price to amass wealth and power.

---

72 Saxton, *The Rise and Fall of the White Republic*, esp. 148–53.
73 Dudden, *Fighting Chance*, 125–32.
74 Goldsmith, *Other Powers*, 310–33; DuBois, *Feminism and Suffrage*, 125; Dudden, *Fighting Chance*, 130–1.

These impulses, he added, stood as "uneasy and temporary allies." Within the "abolition-democracy" forces, Du Bois included elements of the "new labor movement." The warring ideals did not represent two wings of the Republicans; instead the two "lay confused in so many individual minds."[75] The Republican Party was a poor people's party, a vehicle for the rich, and a place where some believed reform and development might briefly cohabit.

The irresistible dead-end that the Republicans offered to Jubilee was both specific to its time and predictive of a century and a half of left electoral politics to come. In a remarkable 1872 speech on the "Impending Revolution," the sex radical, feminist, and leader of the International Workingmen's Association, Victoria Woodhull, reflected on how hard it was to function in a political order structured around "saying that minorities shall have no voice." She spoke particularly on Massachusetts, but the problem she raised was a broad one with which activists today will be all too familiar. The building of vast social movements mobilizing much of the population could register hardly at all within two-party, winner-take-all politics. When Woodhull offered her remarks, the problem registered less acutely because, in living memory, the two-party system had broken down twice, with the collapse of the Federalists and then of the Whigs. The Republican Party, not twenty years old, had ruled for almost all of its existence and had acted as a political vehicle for antislavery initiatives. The hope was that the party system was malleable, so much so that Woodhull would herself run for president on a third-party ticket the same year as her speech. But in the long run, the party system would never again break down, and the problem of reconciling social movements with the two existing parties would be enduring.[76]

As Woodhull figured it, Massachusetts's eleven congressmen would have justly included four Democrats, a party assumed to be of no interest

75 Du Bois, *Black Reconstruction*, 182 and 183–236.
76 Victoria C. Woodhull, *A Speech on the Impending Revolution* (New York: Woodhull, Claflin & Co, 32.

to reformers despite recent efforts by Stanton and Anthony to use it as a vehicle for women's suffrage. Nevertheless "like the hard-shell Baptists" it had, according to Woodhull, its own constituency and its own regrettable consistency. Those who sought change were "under the present system, compelled to congregate together" as Republicans. Indeed, she regarded them as so much the life of the party—and non-movement-based "straight Republicans" so without mass support—that if a system of "minority representation" applied, the Republican Party in Massachusetts "would be abolished." Woodhull reckoned—she believed at the time that the Fourteenth Amendment, properly interpreted, provided the vote to women—that "Woman Suffragists cover about half the Republican Party." The further complication hinged on passionately held dual loyalties. Many of the suffrage supporters "are Spiritualists and Temperance men, while "as many more are Labor Reformers." Fractions proliferated: "Those whom are more Labor Reformers than anything else are perhaps two-sevenths," and the same fraction applied to Woman Suffragists. The "more Temperance men than anything else" category putatively made up one-seventh of the electorate. Ultimately, Woodhull convinced herself that the legislature should have included "four Democrats, two Spiritualists, two Labor reformers, two Woman Suffragists, and one Temperance man." She outlined a plan of constitutional reform designed to make such representation possible, one that made predictably little headway among legislators elected within the existing electoral rules and schemes of party organization. Only if a major party backed their voting rights would there be any political participation for women and Black men. If any Rainbow Coalition of women, African Americans, and workers were to operate politically, there was no sidestepping the Republican Party.[77]

---

77 Woodhull, *Speech on the Impending Revolution*, 32 and 33. For Woodhull's adherence to spiritualism, a belief that the spirit world was accessible to the living, often associated with reform causes, see Miriam Brody, *Victoria Woodhull: Free Spirit for Women's Rights* (New York: Oxford University Press, 2003), 82. On spiritualism, radicalism, and reform, see Ann Braude, *Radical Spirits: Spiritualism and Women's Rights in Nineteenth-Century America* (Boston: Beacon Press, 1989), and John Patrick Devaney, *Paschal Beverly Randolph: A Nineteenth-Century Black-American Spiritualist, Rosicrucian,*

However utopian, Woodhull's speech on minority representation raised the political problem of the forces of Jubilee in sharp relief. The Republican Party was difficult for supporters of emancipation to leave, and it gestured just enough toward other reform causes that feminists and in some states eight-hour campaigners made it their homes. The Democrats, unreliable as allies in any case, were sufficiently tied to Southern racism and Confederate sympathies that entering strategic alliances with them tarnished reform credentials badly, as the experiences of Stanton and Anthony showed. Even proposing new radical parties, such as efforts to ally labor with currency reform, risked being seen as draining away reform votes and abetting the election of reactionaries. An astonishing range of figures specifically identified postwar Republicans as a labor party. This was true of Black leaders like Frederick Douglass and Isaac Myers, for example, but also of the white Texas radical Albert Parsons, soon to be the most famous nineteenth-century martyr of the labor movement. Karl Marx's close US associate, the German-American Civil War officer and revolutionary Joseph Weydemeyer, was the Republican county auditor in St. Louis just after the war when he wrote his penetrating articles on the eight-hour day, emancipation, and new prospects for the working class.[78] Indeed, one valuable way for the voluminous recent scholarship on Marx and Abraham Lincoln, to deepen would be to consider whether, in supporting Lincoln, Marx was identifying with a war effort, a bourgeois party that had come into revolutionary opposition to slavery, or a party that functioned in some places briefly as a labor party.[79]

---

and Sex Magician (Albany, NY: State University of New York Press, 1996). On the Fourteenth Amendment as a proposed feminist basis for voting rights, see Allison L. Sneider, *Suffragists in an Imperial Age: US Expansion and the Woman Question, 1870–1929* (New York: Oxford University Press, 2008), 30–2.
78 Roediger, *How Race Survived US History*, 104–5; Karl Obermann, *Joseph Weydemeyer: Pioneer of American Socialism* (New York: International Publishers, 1947), esp. 128–40; Weydemeyer, "The Eight-Hour Movement," *St. Louis Daily Press* (August 8, 1866); Philip Foner and Ronald Lewis, eds., *The Black Workers: A Documentary History from Colonial Times to the Present, Volume Two: The Black Worker during the Era of the National Labor Union* (Philadelphia: Temple University Press, 1978), 416.
79 On the Marx scholarship concerning Lincoln and the Civil War, see Robin Blackburn, ed., *An Unfinished Revolution: Karl Marx and Abraham Lincoln* (New York: Verso, 2011); Kevin Anderson,

Du Bois's formulation of the issue in *Black Reconstruction* equally captured the sense of possibility the Republicans briefly offered as a vehicle
for Jubilee and the reason that pursuing that possibility would end in
tragedy. *Black Reconstruction* toyed with the idea that the Republicans in
a state like South Carolina had created a labor government. He first called
his chapter on that state from 1868 to 1876, "The Dictatorship of the
Black Proletariat in South Carolina." He came to regard that position as
not "correct" and offered instead the somewhat more modest conclusion
that Black labor "dictated the form and methods of government" within
limits set by their own "ignorance, inexperience, and uncertainty" and by
modifications of their will made by "their own and other leaders." While
this position was roundly mischaracterized and subjected to critique by
scholars from the 1930s forward, it at least confronts the key contradictory
elements at play—first that Black elites in politics often were cautious,
ineffectual, and even conservative during Reconstruction and second that
the moments in which governments based on the votes of the nation's
poorest people did effect change gave Republicans great appeal among
freedpeople and some poor whites. Similarly, and South Carolina is again
the best example, those moments also made Southern conservative and
Northern liberal whites believe that they were seeing a US version of the
Paris Commune.[80]

Where economic policy was concerned, there was little doubt from the
war forward which mind of the Northern Republicans would dominate

---

Marx at the Margins: On Nationalism, Ethnicity, and Non-Western Societies (Chicago: University of
Chicago Press, 2010), esp. 32–7; Philip Foner, *American Socialism and Black Americans: From the Age
of Jackson to World War II* (Westport, CT: Greenwood, 1977), 39–44.
80   W.E.B. Du Bois, *Black Reconstruction in America* (1992), 381 and 381n; David Levering
Lewis, *W.E.B. Du Bois, 1919–1963: The Fight for Equality* (New York: Henry Holt, 2000), 373,
nicely rehearses the reception of *Black Reconstruction* on this score, though it captures Du Bois's
own arguments less well; Heather Cox Richardson, *The Death of Reconstruction: Race, Labor,
and Politics in the Post-Civil War North, 1865–1901* (Cambridge, MA: Harvard University Press,
2001), 64–97. Eric Foner, *Reconstruction: America's Unfinished Revolution* (New York: Harper
Perennial, 2002 [1989]), 116 and 546–7; Thomas Holt, *Black over White: Negro Political Leadership in South Carolina during Reconstruction* (Urbana, IL: University of Illinois Press, 1997),
3 and passim.

the party's policies. Private profit trumped "abolition-democracy." In arguing for support for workers after the war, Wendell Phillips urged that "the same aid be given to co-operative efforts that has heretofore been given to railroads and other enterprises."[81] Such a hope was not remotely realized, even where aid to the neediest of the working poor, recently freed, was concerned. The largesse given by the federal government to a few score of railroads assumed fantastic proportions, especially concentrated in the subsidization of transcontinental lines, begun under Lincoln. In all, land grants to the railroads reached over 131 million acres, with coal and iron rights adhering to the bounties in land. The 1864 Pacific Railway Act, for example, granted 12,800 acres per mile of railroad built. States kicked in an additional 44 million acres. The total bounties would have provided "forty acres and a mule" not only for every ex-slave family but for every individual freedperson. Meanwhile, the Southern Homestead Act of 1866 failed utterly as an alternative to confiscating Rebel planters' land. The policy held out the hope that public lands in the South might satisfy the land hunger of the emancipated, but the lands were marginal and in need of clearing. Timber companies moved to the head of the line in obtaining government grants. In relatively unsettled Florida, 3,000 African-American families negotiated the homestead process, but only a thousand families bothered to apply in the entire rest of the South. In most of the cotton South, according to an 1876 government report, only one Black family in twenty owned land. That year, the Republican-dominated Congress repealed the Southern Homestead Act to further expedite exploitation of resources by mining and timbering interests. The value of land given to railroads easily reached half a billion dollars; the main appropriation for the Freedmen's Bureau budget—by no means all of it providing for the

---

81 Wendell Phillips, *Speeches, Lectures and Letters*, (Boston: Lee and Shepard, 1894), 151–2, as cited in Brian Greenberg, "Wendell Phillips and the Idea of Industrial Democracy in Early Postbellum America," in *The Struggle for Equality: Essays on Sectional Conflict, the Civil War and the Long Reconstruction*, eds. Orville Vernon Burton, Jerald Podair, and Jennifer L. Weber (Charlottesville, VA: University of Virginia Press, 2011), 143.

needs of ex-slaves—for the critical year of 1866–1867 did not reach
$695,000. Total expenditures over the life of the agency probably fell short
of $18 million. The Bureau itself was gone by 1872. In many ways, as
Du Bois noted, it was gone with the passage of the Fifteenth Amendment, as equal rights became an argument against targeted economic
redress.[82]

On the land question in the South, Republicans offered little beyond
homesteading of marginal public lands. The commitment to property and
order, and a belief that wage labor would be central to the tutelage of
freedpeople as modern citizens, left little room for enthusiasm for plans
to confiscate the estates of disloyal planters. During the more than three
years after Lincoln's assassination, the Andrew Johnson administration
reneged on commitments to make permanent the land grant to ex-slaves
made by General Sherman and proved equally disinclined to use "abandoned lands" to fully fund the Freedmen's Bureau and to satisfy the
demand for "forty acres and a mule." Thaddeus Stevens, the most insistent
Republican advocate of land reform as a strategy to recompense ex-slaves,
punish rebellion, permanently defeat the planter class, and fund Southern
state governments capable of meeting the needs of the poor, remained a
lonely voice. His plans regarding confiscation were roundly rejected across
party lines.[83]

In 1866, Stevens managed to bring his plan to use "forfeited lands" to
transform the South to a vote in the House of Representatives. Stevens

---

82 Richard White, *Railroaded: The Transcontinentals and the Making of Modern America* (New
York: Norton, 2012), 24–6; Foner, *Reconstruction*, 246, 404, and 568; Paul Skeels Peirce, *The Freedmen's Bureau: A Chapter in the History of Reconstruction* (Iowa City, IA: State University of Iowa
Studies in Sociology, Economics, Politics, and History, 1904), 106–10; for a remarkable appreciation
of the Freedmen's Bureau and its limits, see W.E.B. Du Bois, "The Freedmen's Bureau," *Atlantic Monthly*
87 (March 1901), 354–65. Reflection on the fate of the Bureau moved Du Bois to a very early incar-
nation, in the essay's last line, of his famous observation that "The problem of the twentieth century
is the problem of the color line."

83 Du Bois, *Black Reconstruction*, 197–9; Gerald David Jaynes, *Branches Without Roots: Genesis of
the Black Working Class in the American South, 1862–1882* (New York: Oxford University Press,
1986), 10; Foner, *Reconstruction*, 245–6.

attached his proposal to a Senate bill securing freedpeople's rights to the land given during the war, though only for three years rather than as permanent title. A large majority of the Republicans voted against Stevens's sweeping proposals. Even the staunch Radical Republican from Pennsylvania William "Pig Iron" Kelley, the perfect embodiment of the twin pulls on Republicans that Du Bois observed, voted in opposition. New York's leading pro-Johnson newspaper could crow that the "real strength of the Jacobins in the House" had become clear. The loosely organized Radical Republican bloc coalescing in opposition to Johnson's policies and to the draconian repression instituted in the Black Codes, passed after the war by readmitted Southern states, never held a majority among Republicans in the House and was less strong still in the Senate.[84] Where land reform is concerned, it is far from certain whether a push for a Radical Republican majority would have changed matters. The inability of the profit-oriented and market-worshipping Republican leadership to imagine a South not fully dedicated to commodity production dovetailed with the belief that wage labor taught such good values that it should precede economic independence for freedpeople and with longstanding ideologies of white supremacy justifying settler title to land to ensure that ex-slaves would seldom secure land.[85]

Ironically, such decisions to leave Jubilee incomplete made enthusiastic support for the Republicans seem even more imperative for freedpeople for a time. What the party did offer was direct federal aid and political rights, which freedpeople hoped would have social implications. There certainly was no viable alternative in the Democrats. Without resources, ex-slaves relied on direct but erratic aid from the Freedmen's Bureau to sustain a bare life through much of the early postwar period. It was precisely on defunding the Bureau that President Johnson staked much of his challenge to Republicans in Congress. Readmitted but not reconstructed,

---

84 Foner, *Reconstruction*, 246 ("Jacobins") and 238–51; Edward Magdol, *A Right to the Land: Essays on the Freedmen's Community* (Westport, CT: Greenwood, 1977), 158–9.

85 Montgomery, *Beyond Equality*, 240.

Southern states passed Black Codes denying the civil rights and coercing the labor of freedpeople beginning in 1865. The Freedmen's Bureau, the army on the ground, and the Republicans in Congress provided hope of redress.[86] When the Civil Rights Act of 1867 enfranchised Black men in the South, overthrowing the Democrats and ending the most coercive elements in labor relations seemed possible, even if land reform was not. As planters realized their own need for labor, and their lack of resources to pay for it, sharecropping arrangements became more widespread. Freedpeople saw such arrangements as an advance in their autonomy over contract labor. But to prevent—or as it turned out to delay—such a system from devolving into new forms of coercion, the presence of Republican lawmakers, sheriffs, judges, and jurors was highly desirable. The great achievement of freedpeople in eliminating gang labor arrangements, so reminiscent of slavery, came during the brief periods of Republican rule. When the South was "redeemed," the white supremacist Democrats regaining power state-by-state instituted repressive new labor regulations.[87]

The Republicans' most noteworthy contribution to Jubilee lay in initiating a fundraising campaign for Southern organizing that briefly sustained Union Leagues in the region. In 1867, the party's national congressional leadership issued the call for funds to increase a meager presence in the region, as the policies of President Andrew Johnson were being challenged by a coalition led by Radical Republicans. Replacing Johnson's "Presidential Reconstruction" with "military Reconstruction" meant contesting elections, policing civil rights violations, continuing the Freedmen's Bureau, and forwarding new democratic state constitutions. For the

---

86 Du Bois, "The Freedmen's Bureau," 354–65; Foner, *Reconstruction*, esp. 245–51. On the gaping holes in the safety net provided by the Bureau and the desperate situation the freed faced, see Jim Downs, *Sick from Freedom: African-American Illness and Suffering during the Civil War and Reconstruction* (New York: Oxford University Press, 2012), 62–87.

87 Jaynes, *Branches Without Roots*, 7, 147, 173, 175, and 180; Fitzgerald, *The Union League Movement in the Deep South*, 50–1; Harold D. Woodman, "Post–Civil War Southern Agriculture and the Law," *Agricultural History* 53 (January 1979) 319–37.

electoral campaigns, funds went south to create, revivify, and expand the Union Leagues. Such bodies, originally Northern wartime organizations, had sprung up in Unionist areas of the South after the war, first enrolling as supporters whites in hilly and mountainous areas.[88] New resources allowed expansion into plantation areas and recruitment of Black members. Slavery had created opposition to planters among whites and Blacks but allowed no hint of a space in which a biracial culture of formal opposition could mature. Though only briefly funded, and opposed in Mississippi and elsewhere by Freedmen's Bureau officials and military authorities, the Union League created the possibility of oppositional coalitions, producing electoral victories even in areas in which freedmen did not constitute a majority of voters. The League provided spaces for cross-racial communication and common efforts, sometimes enlisting whites who still supported colonization of Blacks to another country but nevertheless worked in interracial electoral alliances. White activists fought for Black voting rights and often entered into the defense of freedpeople facing terror or economic victimization.[89]

The League also helped to move freedpeople's politics beyond the local level and outside electoral politics. Black activists ensured that League activities quickly spilled over the narrowly electoral channels for which the funding was intended. For the newly freed, the Leagues provided a venue for organizing Black militia companies, for coordinating refusals to sign coercive annual labor contracts, and for mounting processions to show strength. These included marches that defied bosses by taking off from work and tramping to polling places on election days. The lack of a distinct boundary between political rights and labor rights was further illustrated

---

88 Fitzgerald, *The Union League Movement in the Deep South*, 9–36 and passim; Foner, *Reconstruction*, 283–7; Degler, *The Other South*, 203–7 and 124–263. For the longer roots of Southern Unionism and Republicanism, see Thomas B. Alexander, "Persistent Whiggery in Alabama and the Lower South," *Alabama Review* 25 (1948), 229–69.

89 Fitzgerald, *The Union League Movement in the Deep South*, 102–9 and passim; on the importance of creating such basic frameworks for socialization and communication across the color line, see Rachleff, *Black Labor in Richmond*, esp. 136–7.

by the use of the League by freedpeople to form labor unions and other
organizations of agrarian insurgency. As Michael Fitzgerald's important
study of the Union Leagues carefully puts it:

> It would not do to overstate the point: The League was not a union,
> nor did the Republican Party engage in labor organizing. The League
> leadership primarily focused on winning elections, and the labor
> activities happened at the local level. Nevertheless, the League's
> general affinity for labor activism is evident.

Indeed, the particularly strong Alabama Labor Union, the first US farm-
workers union, was organized in 1870 largely out of the energies of the
League and the Colored National Labor Union.[90]

At the same time, Republican leaders' opposition to land redistribution
tragically helped to put its entire strategy in jeopardy. The inspired coalition of white Southern scalawags and African-American voters formed
mainly around a shared opposition to planters' power, itself rooted in land.
Potentially, and in some cases manifestly, whites who had chafed under
the hegemony of slave-masters had an interest in seeing the estates of great
land-owners dismantled. Whether in deference to the few large planters
who became Republicans or a general commitment to property, Repub
licans did not pursue such a course. With redistribution foregone,
Republican governments were tempted to support high tax policies.
Delivering public goods like education was one justification for taxes but
so was the idea that planters would be unable to pay such taxes and land
would be forced onto the market. However, many white yeoman farmer
Republicans held enough land to also fear bankruptcy through tax delin-
quency. The poorest whites, often with some land but largely outside the
cash economy, were especially hard put to come up with the money to pay

---

90 Fitzgerald, *The Union League Movement in the Deep South*, 7, 66–7 and 168–9; Jaynes, *Branches
Without Roots*, 295. On the persistence of the Alabama Labor Union, see Foner, *Organized Labor and
the Black Worker*, 43–4.

taxes. Tax policy thus drove wedges into the Republican ranks along what were easily cast as racial lines.[91]

Commitments to property, markets, and profit also subverted any possibility that the Republicans would meaningfully be the party of the eight-hour working day. In the North, there was far less reason for workers inspired by Jubilee to forgive such limitations of the GOP. In the states where eight hours became the standard by law after the war, and in the case of the ill-fated 1868 federal law for government (and, until the Supreme Court ruled otherwise, government-contracted) work, Republicans often voted for the reforms and at times could claim a leading role in their passage. The state laws passed with astonishing speed as distinct products of revolutionary time. Although in Connecticut in 1866 it was Democrats who used eight hours as part of a populist campaign that won control of state government, early endorsement by prominent Republicans conditioned successes in most states. The National Labor Union (NLU) had scarcely endorsed the eight-hour standard before leading Republican congressmen and governors from Massachusetts, Illinois, California, Wisconsin, and Ohio pledged support for eight-hour laws. Grassroots pressure in the form of petitions changed some hesitant Republicans' minds on the shorter working day.[92] Women's rights advocates soon were every bit as enthusiastic about the shorter day, making it central to feminist demands.[93] When Illinois workers celebrated an eight-hour law in 1867, they had every reason to believe that, as John Jentz and Richard Schneirov have written, they were "part of a great nineteenth-century movement that had just abolished

---

91 J. Mills Thornton III, "Fiscal Policy and the Failure of Radical Reconstruction in the Lower South," in *Region, Race, and Reconstruction: Essays in Honor of C. Vann Woodward*, eds. J. Morgan Kousser and James McPherson (New York: Oxford University Press, 1982), 349–94.

92 Montgomery, *Beyond Equality*, 230–334 and esp. 310–22, on the federal law; David R. Roediger and Philip S. Foner, *Our Own Time: A History of American Labor and the Working Day* (New York: Verso, 1989), 101–9.

93 Philip S. Foner, *Women and the American Labor Movement from Colonial Times to the Eve of World War One*, 129–30.

slavery."[94] They could reasonably view Republicans as the agents of both abolition and of eight hours.

It was too good to be true. As David Montgomery has shown, the Republicans loved the loopholes making eight-hour laws unenforceable as much as the reform itself. The most telling such loophole followed the declaration of eight hours as a legal day's work with the proviso that such would apply only in the absence of contracts to the contrary—exactly the agreements on which employers would insist. Such a stance had precedents in earlier ten-hour legislation, and William Sylvis and other labor leaders at times accepted that laws without an enforcement provision were all that were on offer, supporting them as setting a public goal workers would then enforce by direct action. But in the postbellum United States, the proviso regarding contracts strikingly captured the Republican Party's commitment to justice as an abstraction and to markets, contracts, and profits in the concrete. Many workers demanded an actual eight-hour Jubilee. Fierce contestation followed, especially in Illinois, where the Republican governor had championed and signed the legislation, when the law went into effect on May 1, 1866. Workers struck and demonstrated to enforce an eight-hour day and the Republican mayor of Chicago decisively repressed militant manifestations of their movement.[95]

A fierce campaign of lobbying and other concerted action by large industrial capitalist concerns of all types, perhaps the first such campaign of its kind in the United States, opposed enforcement of the eight-hour law in Illinois, but the ideological commitment to markets and profits undermining Republican support for shorter hours came largely from other quarters. The journalists Horace Greeley and Edwin L. Godkin typified two strands of such ideology. Greeley, the most famous Repub-

---

94 John B. Jentz and Richard Schneirov, *Chicago in the Age of Capital: Class, Politics, and Democracy during the Civil War and Reconstruction* (Urbana, IL: University of Illinois Press, 2012), 109.

95 Montgomery, *Beyond Equality*, 306–11; Jentz and Schneirov, *Chicago in the Age of Capital*, 81–116 ; Adam Tuchinsky, *Horace Greeley's New-York Tribune: Civil War–Era Socialism and the Crisis of Free Labor* (Ithaca, NY: Cornell University Press, 2009), 195 (Sylvis).

lican not to hold high office, editorialized frequently on eight hours in his *New-York Tribune*, in large part because his state was a battleground on the issue. His support mattered enormously and eight-hour theorist Ira Steward courted it in more-or-less friendly exchanges with Greeley. The latter approved eight hours in principle and was active in some of the first organizations to raise the issue. He lauded the demand when an "eight-hour picnic" in New York in 1865 drew 50,000 participants. But Greeley opposed the means to secure eight hours. Long an opponent of strikes, he also declared against eight-hour laws as violations of the law of supply and demand. The *Tribune* regarded a legislatively fixed "Eight-Hour rule" as one that could not succeed, especially if the goal were to keep wages the same.[96]

Although critical of the wage system at times, Greeley was certain that "the main route to capital accumulation was industriousness and self-denial," as a recent account puts it, so that any seemingly free gifts won through class struggle— whether land for Southern slaves or eight-hour guarantees to wage workers—could only be debilitating. His own doubts and vacillations were at times forgotten, as when he told labor to credit the Republicans with the passage of an eight-hour law in New York in 1867. The fact that Democrats had as good a claim as Republicans to supporting the loophole-laden bill—striking workers pressuring the lawmakers had better claims than either— -also went unremarked.[97]

Godkin, editing the journal *The Nation*, was more insulated from electoral strategizing than Greeley. He represented in perhaps its purest form the emerging articulation of a distinctly bourgeois Republican ideology, ably discussed in a recent study by Adam Tuchinsky. Godkin "embraced the market unreservedly, depicted it in scientific terms, and believed it was

---

96 Tuchinsky, *Horace Greeley's New-York Tribune*, 188 ("rule" and "picnic") and 186–211; Jentz and Schneirov, *Chicago in the Age of Capital*, 100.
97 Tuchinsky, *Horace Greeley's New-York Tribune*, 176–7; James C. Mohr, *The Radical Republicans and Reform in New York during Reconstruction* (Ithaca, NY and London: Cornell University Press, 1973), 137 and 115–39.

an ideal and natural framework" for organizing economies and societies. He "seized the mantle of laissez-faire liberalism and marshaled it on behalf of an industrial system." From such a vantage, eight-hours legislation looked like a threat to everything and even, in Godkin's darker moments, a reason to doubt democracy itself. That is, if workers could use the state to protect themselves in the marketplace, democracy seemed to Godkin to subvert the greater good of society, now defined frankly in terms of production and profit. Somehow believing a ten-hour day was "natural," Godkin mocked eight-hour campaigns in the first volume of *The Nation* as "forc[ing] men to restrict their working day to eight hours . . . on the ground that he needs the rest of his time for reading, society and music." For what Godkin saw as frivolous reasons, "the capitalist is . . . launched into a sea of uncertainty." Godkin's ideas were influential especially in defining Republican positions on eight hours in Massachusetts. There, a GOP labor commission report had endorsed eight hours in 1865, a position seconded the following year by the Republican state convention. In 1867, a second commission changed Republican policy, clarifying that any eight-hour program had to be voluntary and had to respect the "right of individual property." Otherwise, in this view, "communism" threatened. For a time, the divisions over the hours of work in Massachusetts roughly fell on Radical versus conservative lines, with the former group providing whatever support existed among Republicans for labor's central demand. Similarly, in the vote on the 1868 federal eight-hour law, the dozen Republicans who not only provided decisive votes for the measure but also took the minority position that pay should not be reduced on an eight-hour schedule were all Radicals.[98]

It eventually became clear that the unwillingness to embrace eight hours meaningfully cut across divisions in the party. Godkin and Greeley led

---

98   Edwin L. Godkin, "The Eight Hour Movement," *The Nation* 1 (October 26, 1865), 517–18; Tuchinsky, *Horace Greeley's New-York Tribune*, 180 ("embraced"), 192–3, and 210; Montgomery, *Beyond Equality*, 240 and 247–8 ("natural"); Michael Sandel, *Democracy's Discontent: America in Search of a Public Policy* (Cambridge, MA: Harvard University Press, 1998), 189–90.

forces that were soon to describe themselves at the "Liberal" wing of the Republican Party and then as a separate political tendency, the Liberal Republicans, but in 1866 they were fragilely within the party's Radical wing. The editor of the *Chicago Tribune*, a leading Radical Republican, offered outspoken opposition to even a symbolic eight-hour law. Thaddeus Stevens professed studied disinterest in the issue. Charles Sumner opposed the 1868 federal legislation limiting hours of work for government employees. The Radical philosopher Elisha Mulford understood property as "communion with God," and after an initial burst of Jubilee-minded desire to support eight hours, many Republicans turned to Mulford's theology where the claims of the propertied on the worker's time were concerned. The best of the party proved, as David Montgomery has acerbically put it, "radical only for Louisiana" and, it might be added, not where land was concerned or for long even in Louisiana.[99]

By the time Greeley ran as the Liberal Republican candidate in the 1872 presidential election, his desire for a tendency in which he could be the left wing had generated a rightward split from a party already moving in a conservative direction. The rightward-drifting Liberal program included joining in the attack on Reconstruction governments, seeking alliance with Democrats, withdrawing protection for Black civil rights in the South, and all the while seeking to move putatively classless and raceless issues of development and government corruption to the center of what would pass for political discussion. Liberal Republicans won some German Americans, formerly the very backbone of radicalism, to the abandonment of liberation even for Louisiana. Indeed, Missouri's Carl Schurz, formerly the most encyclopedic congressional documenter of White Southern terror, was won to the Liberal Republican capitulation to that terror. The

---

99 Montgomery, *Beyond Equality*, 240 (for Mulford), 245, 269 ("Louisiana"), 318, 336, and 378–80; for a modern conservative homage to Liberal Republicanism, see Moreno, *Black Americans and Organized Labor*, 32–7; see also Jentz and Schneirov, *Chicago in the Age of Capital*, 94–6; David A. Zonderman, *Uneasy Allies: Working for Labor Reform in Nineteenth-Century Boston* (Amherst, MA: University of Massachusetts Press, 2011), 108 and 96–162.

Liberals lost soundly in 1872, but their program proved premature by only one election. The backward motion of history proceeded almost as rapidly as revolutionary time had. By the Compromise of 1877, without any leftward splits in opposition, the two-minded Republican Party described by Du Bois was single-minded. It provided at the national level little refuge for any of those inspired by Jubilee.[100]

---

100 Montgomery, *Beyond Equality*, 379–86; Tuchinsky, *Horace Greeley's New-York Tribune*, 212–41; Alison Clark Efford, *German Immigrants, Race, and Citizenship in the Civil War Era* (New York: Cambridge University Press, 2013), esp. 181–5 and passim.

Afterword:

Dreams Deferred:
Social Tragedies and Hidden Histories
in the Longer Run

All good causes are mutually helpful.
Frederick Douglass (1888)

In 1909, a souvenir postcard celebrated the centennial of Lincoln's birth by imagining his issuance of the Emancipation Proclamation. In it a towering Lincoln comes to the aid of supine slaves. Four decades earlier, women's rights advocates had made badges showing slaves striking the blows that contributed to emancipation. Suffragists, themselves also displaced from the postcard's drama, knew in 1865 of their own roles in abolition and in the petition campaign that energized support for a Thirteenth Amendment. Working-class soldiers heard of and witnessed the movement toward freedom and into combat by slaves and dreamed of their own Jubilee. The shorthand of Lincoln as emancipator triumphed, impoverishing all of these movements, even as it reflected their inability to build strong traditions of mutual support and common memory. This afterword weighs what was lost and what survived and offers a few words on what we can learn in terms of strategy and humility.[1]

---

1 The postcard is in Louise Michele Newman, *White Women's Rights: The Racial Origins of Feminism in the United States* (New York: Oxford University Press, 1999), 13; Theodore Stanton and

Of course, grand aspirations and inspiring memories did not disappear overnight, but the shifting terrain of struggle quickly suggested how much was lost by the early 1870s. To judge the full weight of the tragedy, human examples involving the struggles of Victoria Woodhull and Albert and Lucy Parsons deserve brief elaboration. In each case, Frederick Douglass's estrangement from those organizing and being victimized speaks volumes not because he was the worst practitioner of solidarity of his time but because he was among the best. The stories of missed connections show how the causes inspired by Jubilee kept resurfacing, sometimes linked together by common oppressors, but without the contagion of inspiration that had seemed possible a short time before.

In the early 1870s, the free-love advocate, socialist, and suffragist Victoria Woodhull offered a broad vision of what freedom would mean for white women and, she hoped, for all. The fate of her vision showed what had become possible by virtue of emancipation and what had become impossible as the spirit of Jubilee receded. Woodhull gained fame as an orator and essayist, as a stockbroker, and for her testimony before a congressional committee, where she addressed women's suffrage in 1870. Her rationale for free love and women's political power hinged critically on enabling women to defend themselves and their children against abuse, a fact of her own life. As she wrote in 1871 in a passage considering marriage and prostitution together:

> Thousands of poor, weak, unresisting wives are yearly murdered. Who stand up in the spirit-life looking down on the sickly, half made-up children left behind, imploring humanity . . . to look into this matter . . . to the very bottom, and bring out into the fair daylight all the blackened, sickening deformities that have so long been hidden.

Harriot Stanton Blatch, eds., *Elizabeth Cady Stanton*, Volume 2 (New York: Arno, 1969), 95. See also David Blight, *Race and Reunion: The Civil War in American Memory* (Cambridge, MA: Harvard University Press, 2001), esp. 300–98.

Even Thomas Nast's vicious 1872 *Harper's Weekly* caricature of Woodhull as "Mrs. Satan," literally a bat out of hell, illustrates that she appealed to followers as a defender of women from alcoholic and raging husbands.[2]

At a time when women's suffrage threatened to become a single-issue movement, Woodhull's quixotic 1872 presidential campaign raised a range of expansive anti-"slavery" demands. She proceeded frequently by analogy with the slave's emancipation, reminding readers that the slave-holders had convinced most of the nation that "slaves were better off as slaves" within recent memory. Just as the "anti-slavery revolution came," more revolutions were to come. She based her case that women already possessed the right to vote on the view that the Fourteenth and Fifteenth Amendments established female citizenship so that states putatively acted illegally in turning women away from the polls. Part of her reasoning also held that marriage was a form of servitude and that discrimination on the grounds of previous servitude was illegal. In an attempt to recapture a bygone day of Jubilee, Woodhull shared the presidential ticket in 1872 with Douglass. Both were nominated by the Equal Rights Party, which explicitly rejected inequality based on race or sex. Woodhull, who did not meet the constitutional age requirement stood for the presidency and Douglass, a staunch Republican, was the vice-presidential choice. Woodhull opposed any split from Douglass, and he specifically thanked her for her support for the Fifteenth Amendment. The two were also in alliance on the wrong side of the question of Haiti

2 Alma Lutz, *Created Equal: A Biography of Elizabeth Cady Stanton, 1815–1902* (New York: Octagon Books, 1974), 205–15, including discussion of how Anthony and Stanton increasingly broached questions of abuse. Sarah Burns, *Painting the Dark Side: Art and the Gothic Imagination in Nineteenth-Century America* (Berkeley, CA: University of California Press, 2004), 182–4, includes impressive analysis and a reproduction of Nast's cartoon. See also the extraordinary collection by Madeleine B. Stern, ed., *The Victoria Woodhull Reader* (Weston, MA: M & S Press, 1974), 1–2, and (the volume is irregularly paginated), 2–4 in the section on "Political Theory." For Woodhull's consistent pairing of free love—which for her ideally ended in monogamy and was the opposite of "lust"—and protection from abuse see Woodhull, "A Speech on the Principles of Social Freedom" (New York: Woodhull, Chaflin & Co, 1871), 16–17 ("unresisting wives"), and 32. I am indebted to Peter Rich of the University of South Carolina for an appreciation of Woodhull's connection of free love and domestic violence, and for help with sources.

in 1870 and 1871, supporting US annexation of the island against an opposition combining opposition to empire with doubts about the racial "character" of Haitians.[3]

Woodhull's almost-as-famous sister and coconspirator, Tennessee Claflin, was so popular in Black New York that she was elected commander of an important African-American militia there. She accepted the post by explaining how important militias could be in fighting repression of working-class movements. The militia unit had recently marched with Fenians at the invitation of the great Irish revolutionary O'Donovan Rossa, and other African-American militia forces had participated in a grand 1871 International Workingmen's Association (IWA) commemoration of the Paris Commune. In and beyond Section 12 of the IWA, Woodhull's forces cultivated ties with labor organizations. Elizabeth Cady Stanton and other leading suffragists declared themselves in support of Woodhull's presidential candidacy (though Susan B. Anthony and the National Women's Suffrage Association did not), making Woodhull the focal point of all the forces inspired by Jubilee for a fragile moment before her prosecution and persecution on obscenity indictments partly engineered by other reformers. In the face of charges against her, support evaporated. Douglass did not even acknowledge the unsolicited vice-presidential nomination by deigning to decline it. Jubilee for all had proven for over a decade to be a remarkably enticing idea, but revolutionary time also had ended abruptly and divisively and defied Woodhull's efforts to revive it.[4]

---

3 Amanda Frisken, *Victoria Woodhull's Sexual Revolution: Political Theatre and the Popular Press in Nineteenth-Century America* (Philadelphia: University of Pennsylvania Press, 2004), 7, 49, 54–84 and 175n64; Woodhull, "A Speech on the Principles of Social Freedom," 32–5; Woodhull, "Sociology: The Naked Truth; or, the Situation Reviewed!", *Woodhull and Chaflin's Weekly* (January 25, 1873), as reprinted in *The Victoria Woodhull Reader*, ed. Stern, unpaginated. In the same volume, see Woodhull, "Tried as if by Fire; or, The True and the False Socially" (New York: Woodhull & Chaflin, 1874), 41–2. On Haiti and its connections to women's suffrage, see Allison L. Sneider, *Suffragists in an Imperial Age: US Expansion and the Woman Question, 1870–1929* (New York: Oxford University Press, 2008), 36–53.

4 Timothy Messer-Kruse, *The Yankee International: Marxism and the American Reform Tradition, 1848–1876* (Chapel Hill, NC: University of North Carolina Press, 1998), 200 and 198–205; Philip S. Foner, *American Socialism and Black Americans: From the Age of Jackson to World War II* (Westport,

The fate of Lucy and Albert Parsons, who remade their lives out of Jubilee, was more tragic still. On November 11, 1887, the state of Illinois executed Albert Parsons and three others by hanging. Outrageously accused and unfairly tried after the bombing of police at a labor demonstration in Haymarket Square in Chicago in May 1886, Parsons died with the words "Let the voice of the people be heard" on his lips. With his partner, Lucy Parsons, Albert had tried to keep living in revolutionary time long after Jubilee. He had returned from successful hiding to stand trial with his co-defendants, leaders of the anarchist and eight-hour movements in Chicago. What brought Albert Parsons to the gallows and Lucy to defiant grief reminds us of the force of Du Bois's insistence on Reconstruction as a magnificent drama, an awful tragedy, and a central part of the story of "our labor movement."[5]

Jubilee made the heroism, and the love, of Albert and Lucy Parsons possible and its unraveling made their fate remorselessly logical. Both Lucy and Albert Parsons began their political lives as strugglers for freedom in Reconstruction Texas. They found each other in the heady possibility of Jubilee. Albert, the brother of a Confederate general, served in the Rebel army as a teenager. Transformed by Jubilee, by 1868, he edited a Radical Republican newspaper and once took a bullet in the leg after his attempts to register Black voters and collect taxes for Republican administrations. Lucy, probably of African, American Indian, and Mexican ancestry and likely born a slave, was also a Radical Republican and later remembered witnessing Klan horrors in the Waco area, scene of mass murders and gang rapes of African Americans in the postbellum

CT: Greenwood, 1977), 37–9; Barbara Goldsmith, *Other Powers: The Age of Suffrage, Spiritualism, and the Scandalous Victoria Woodhull* (New York: Harper Perennial, 1999), 310–33; Frisken, *Victoria Woodhull's Sexual Revolution*, 55–84.

5 W.E.B. Du Bois, *Black Reconstruction in America, 1860–1880* (1998), 727, for "our labor movement" and for the first epigraph. The second epigraph is from Frederick Douglass's 1888 speech to the International Council of Women in Washington, DC, available at blackpast.org. Parts of this section incorporate material from Dave Roediger, "Strange Legacies: The Black International and Black America," in *Haymarket Scrapbook*, eds. Roediger and Franklin Rosemont (Chicago: Charles H. Kerr Publishing Company, 1986), 93–6.

years.[6] When Parsons abandoned what he considered to be the "labor party" of the Republicans in Texas for the Marxist-influenced Workingmen's Party in Chicago, he was quickly catapulted into the leadership of the 1877 general strike in Chicago. The struggle, part of a nationwide railroad workers' uprising, had the eight-hour day as a central demand and unevenly involved impressive Black-white solidarity. But despite Wendell Phillips's activism on labor's behalf after the defeat of the workers in 1877 and despite Elizabeth Cady Stanton's bitter commentary noting that federal troops broke the strike in decisive instances, just after their complete withdrawal from protecting civil rights in the South, no new effort at a Rainbow Coalition arose.[7]

Enemies of freedom understood well how different oppressions could be made to intersect. Lucy's race and Albert's race-mixing were issues during the time of the Haymarket trial, and the *Waco Daily Press* headline before Albert's execution read: "BEAST PARSONS. His Sneaking Snarl From Some Moral Morass in Which He Hides. Miscegenationist, Murderer, Moral Outlaw, For Whom the Gallows Wait." Chicago press accounts portrayed Lucy as an animal and the Parsonses' children as "anarchist sucklings." Hate mail to Lucy ranted, "Your parentage was engendered in the jungle along with the hyena."[8]

---

6 Carolyn Ashbaugh, *Lucy Parsons: American Revolutionary* (Chicago: Charles H. Kerr Publishing Company, 1976), 13–15, 64–6, 86, 99–100, 267–8, and 274. Lucy Parsons, ed., *The Life of Albert R. Parsons* (Chicago: Lucy Parsons, 1903 [1889]), 15; Paul Avrich, *The Haymarket Tragedy* (Princeton, NJ: Princeton University Press, 1984), 6–19 and 42–3.

7 David R. Roediger, *How Race Survived US History: From Settlement and Slavery to the Obama Phenomenon* (New York: Verso, 2008), 104–5; Ezra Hervey Heywood, *The Great Strike* (Princeton, MA: Cooperative Publishing Company, 1878), 5; David Stowell, *Streets, Railroads and the Great Strike of 1877* (Chicago: University of Chicago Press, 1999), 39–40; Philip S. Foner, *Organized Labor and the Black Worker* (New York: International Publishers, 1976), 103; David Roediger, "'Not Only the Ruling Classes to Overcome, but Also the So-Called Mob': Class, Skill and Community in the St. Louis General Strike of 1877," *Journal of Social History* 19 (Winter 1985), 213–39. For Stanton, see Ann D. Gordon, "Stanton and the Right to Vote: On Account of Race or Sex" in *Elizabeth Cady Stanton, Feminist as Thinker*, eds. Ellen Carol DuBois and Richard Cándida Smith (New York: New York University Press, 2007), 121.

8 Ashbaugh, *Lucy Parsons*, 60, 99–100, and, for the headline, 86, and "'Rattler' to Mrs. Lucy Parsons" (January 28, 1889), typescript in Carolyn Ashbaugh Papers, Charles H. Kerr Company Archives at the Newberry Library in Chicago.

Nonetheless, only in response to the most outrageous acts of racist terror did the anarchist wing of the labor movement hesitantly and inadequately address the issue of Black freedom. The International Working People's Association, in which the Parsonses took leading roles as both anarchists and Marxists, championed the rights of African Americans in its 1883 Pittsburgh Manifesto but seldom found ways to act on such rhetoric. Lucy Parsons's "The Negro: Let Him Leave Politics to the Politician and Prayers to the Preacher" was the fuller of only two pre-Haymarket articles in the anarchist paper *Alarm* on the issue. In it, Lucy reacted to a series of lynchings that took the lives of thirteen Blacks in the Carrollton, Mississippi area. Writing a month before Haymarket, she advised African Americans, "You are not absolutely defenseless. For the torch of the incendiary, which has been known to show murderers and tyrants the danger line, beyond which they may not venture with impunity cannot be wrested from you." However, at the time, Lucy displayed little sense of racial oppression. She absolutely denied that "outrages" were "heaped upon the Negro because he is black." "Not at all," she wrote. "It is because he is poor. It is because he is dependent." Lucy, probably after moving to Chicago in the mid-1870s, began the practice of not saying that she had any Black ancestry.[9]

Albert, meanwhile, wrote frequently on the comparison between chattel and wage slavery but without attention to the continuing role of white supremacy. His words sometimes suggested a retrospective hatred of Black slavery, as in an 1884 riposte against Jefferson Davis's contention that Africans benefited from being enslaved to Southern Christians: "How thankful the slave must have been to be rescued from a barbarian master and sold to a Christian one." But Parsons generally accepted Davis's contention that wage slavery was a more efficient way to exploit Black workers than chattel slavery and noted no special problems for Black workers

---

9 *The Alarm* (April 3, 1886) and Philip S. Foner, *American Socialism and Black Americans* (Westport, CT: Greenwood, 1977), 79–80.

arising from the heritage of slavery. His presence as an early Chicago leader in the Knights of Labor, the most egalitarian US organization on race and gender matters, did not lead Parsons to revisit issues of racial justice.[10] Albert and Lucy Parsons could cling to revolutionary time but not to a heady optimism that allowed in the 1860s for the belief that the various axes of oppression could give way as a result of allied efforts. Their movement's extraordinarily advanced positions on the oppression of Indians reflected remarkable searching into the meaning of civilization and at times intense personal experiences. But it could generate no meaningful campaigns of solidarity.[11]

The positions taken by T. Thomas Fortune, "the most noted man" in African-American journalism at the time, are suggestive of the gulf between even a militant, pro-labor Black editor and the best of the labor movement. Fortune, editor of the *New York Freeman*, had since 1884 developed an increasingly apt critique of racial and class relations in the United States and the world. He used ideas from Marx and from Henry George to argue for Black-white labor unity and enthusiastically supported the Knights of Labor even as he lambasted racism within that organization.[12]

Fortune also advocated Black self-defense, sometimes in language not less explosive than that of Lucy Parsons. Writing in the *AME Church Review* in January 1886—a year when he also attempted to make alliances with Irish nationalists—he began with a discussion of the "essential

---

10 Parsons, ed., *The Life of Albert R. Parsons*, xiii and 16; *The Alarm* (October 11, 1884); David R. Roediger, "Albert R. Parsons: The Anarchist as Trade Unionist," in *Haymarket Scrapbook*, eds. Roediger and Rosemont, 31–3; Peter Rachleff, *Black Labor in Richmond, 1865–1890* (Urbana, IL: University of Illinois Press, 1989 [1984]) remains the best account of Reconstruction, the Knights, and race in the South.

11 *The Alarm* (November 8, 1886); Franklin Rosemont, "Anarchists and the Wild West" in *Haymarket Scrapbook*, eds. Roediger and Rosemont, 101–2. In the same volume, see also Steven Sapolsky, "The Making of Honore Jaxon," 103–5.

12 Emma Thornbrough, *T. Thomas Fortune: Militant Journalist* (Chicago: University of Chicago Press, 1972), 95; Jean M. Allman and David Roediger, "The Early Editorial Career of Timothy Thomas Fortune," *Afro-Americans in New York Life and History* 6 (July 1982), 39–52; Foner, *Organized Labor and the Black Worker*, 51–2.

element in which the Afro-American character was most deficient . . . the dynamite element." That element was required to build a movement that "resists an injury promptly." On another occasion he offered a strategy for ending Southern terror against Blacks: "The only way to stop it is for colored men to retaliate by the use of the torch and dagger." When the May 1, 1886, strikes began, Fortune wrote of them as part of a long conflict inspired by "the capitalist, landowner and hereditary aristocrat against the larger masses of society . . . the disinherited proletariat of the world."[13]

Nonetheless, in the wake of Haymarket, Fortune did not comment on the arrests in Chicago, editorializing instead on behalf of tax-reform as a solution to the "pernicious aggregation of capital in the hands of a limited number of men," and castigating strikes for higher wages and shorter hours as "absurd." Four months later he would reprint a significant editorial passage from the *Detroit Plaindealer*, a Black weekly: "In the North men are condemned to suffer the extreme penalty of the law for urging men on by anarchistic utterances to the destruction of life and property. In the South they murder and outrage a people and yet go escaped of justice." Fortune added that "the Anarchists are hunted down and punished by the officers of the State," who ignore outrages in the South. Elsewhere in the *Freeman*, the Chicago correspondent nevertheless praised the "great verdict" handed down against the Haymarket defendants.[14]

Frederick Douglass shared much with the Parsonses, but not Lucy's grief.[15] In the extremely broad-based and transnational defense campaign on behalf of the Haymarket defendants, Douglass remained silent. When reports of African-American anarchist activity in Boston surfaced in 1892, he argued

---

13 Fortune, "Civil Rights and Social Privileges," *AME Church Review* 22 (January 1886), esp. 119; *New York Freeman* (December 6, 1884; July 4, 1885; and May 1, June 19, and December 4, 1886); Allman and Roediger, "Fortune," 49–50. See also Shawn Leigh Alexander, *An Army of Lions: The Struggle for Civil Rights before the NAACP* (Philadelphia: University of Pennsylvania Press, 2012), 10 (Irish).

14 *New York Freeman* (May 8, September 11, and August 28, 1886).

15 Roediger, *How Race Survived US History*, 106. See also William S. McFeely, *Frederick Douglass* (New York: W.W. Norton and Company, 1991), 123–6 and 219–23.

for anarchist tactics without any expression of sympathy for the fate of anarchists being victimized. As he remarked: "If the Southern outrages on the Colored race continue the Negro will become a chemist [that is, a maker of explosives]." He could not envision Black–radical labor cooperation, only that "Anarchists have not a monopoly on bomb-making, and the Negro will learn." Similarly, the *Boston Republican*'s sympathetic editorial treating the use of "dynamite, the dagger or the bomb" by fellow Blacks who were deprived of other recourse added, "We do not encourage dynamiters and bomb-throwers where no cause exists for indulging in such a warfare, as is the case of the Chicago anarchists a few years ago."[16] Ironically, the most meaningful expression of abolitionist support for the Haymarket prisoners came from a figure relatively isolated from ongoing struggles. John Brown Jr., son of the great martyr to the slave's freedom, sent Catawba grapes from northern Ohio to the jail four days before the executions, reminding the condemned of his father's solace at having been "permitted to die for a cause."[17]

In other instances, embers of glimpsed possibilities of solidarity smoldered longer. While major women's suffrage voices stayed still in the Haymarket defense campaign and the strongest voices for working women—Parsons and Mother Jones—had little use for the demand for women's suffrage, Florence Kelley and others saw continuing possibilities. Kelley, the daughter of the Radical Republican William Kelley, combined Marxism and feminism insistently and, especially in the 1890s, to some effect.[18] Frederick Douglass, in an act of great political flexibility and courage, quickly returned to the women's rights platforms from which he had been so roundly denounced in the late 1860s. He mended fences with

16 See Foner, *American Socialism and Black Americans*, 80–1 for the quotations.

17 Louis Ruchames, Jr., ed., "John Brown, Jr. and the Haymarket Martyrs," *Massachusetts Review* 5 (Summer 1964), 765–8. On the complex relations of Brown's martyrdom to the Haymarket defense campaign, see Rebecca Hill, *Men, Mobs, and the Law: Anti-Lynching and Labor Defense in US Radical History* (Durham, NC: Duke University Press, 2009), 60–83.

18 Meredith Tax, *The Rising of the Women* (Urbana, IL: University of Illinois Press, 2001 [1980]), 63–90; Kathryn Kish Sklar, *Florence Kelley and the Nation's Work: The Rise of Women's Political Culture, 1830–1900* (New Haven, CT: Yale University Press, 1997).

the Elizabeth Cady Stanton faction of the movement, appearing at the NWSA's meeting in 1878, for example, and later cordially met with Woodhull in England. Near his life's end, he held that women's suffrage exceeded even abolition in its import. On the day he died, Douglass attended a women's rights meeting. By some accounts, his last act was to reenact a scene from the proceedings after he returned to his home.

Not every personal bond and radical hope born in the general strike of the slaves that Douglass had championed died with the end of revolutionary time, but pace and possibility changed. The upsurge of freedom gave the United States its central democratic demands for the half century before women's suffrage was achieved nationally, the seventy-five years until the eight-hour day became law, and the century and more until a new round of civil rights legislation reestablished some of what briefly applied in Reconstruction. While Douglass held in an 1888 speech on the emancipation of women that "all good causes are mutually helpful," tragic divisions prevailed, including racism, anti-immigrant prejudice, and class prejudice among suffragists.[19]

Where the actual goals of Jubilee among freedpeople were concerned, much was tragic but not all was lost. There was no restoration of slavery, but neither was there redistribution of land. Freedpeople faced powerful old and new adversaries with very few resources, but sharecropping preserved some autonomy over one's own labor. When not caught in webs of debt peonage, freedpeople could quit and move, as Lucy Parsons did precociously and as millions of African Americans would do by the middle of the twentieth century. There was tragic movement "back toward slavery"

---

19 "Death of Fred Douglass," *New York Times* (February 21, 1895); Gordon, "Stanton and the Right to Vote," 121–5; McFeely, *Frederick Douglass,* 132–3; Douglass, "The Emancipation of Women" Speech at the Twentieth Annual Meeting of the New England Woman Suffrage Association, Boston, May 28, 1888" in "Frederick Douglass, "The Woman's Suffrage Movement: Address before the Woman Suffrage Association, April, 1888" in *Frederick Douglass on Women's Rights,* ed. Philip S. Foner (Westport, CT: Greenwood, 1976), 116 and in the same volume, his "The Woman's Suffrage Movement: Address before the Woman Suffrage Association, April, 1888," 114; see also 90–103 for Douglass's lack of any long-term estrangement from women's rights agitation. See also Aileen Kraditor, *Ideas of the Women's Suffrage Movement, 1890–1920* (New York: W.W. Norton, 1981 [1968]), esp. 43–74 and 123–218.

but not the wholesale retreat suggested by historian Theodore Allen's contention that "slavery in all but name" had been reinstituted.[20]

The fantastic motion and creativity of slaves made it possible for a time for white Union forces to hear appreciatively the African-inspired ring shout and spiritual "Say Brother," and to transform the tune into the fierce praise of a revolutionary when they created the war song "John Brown's Body" to its tune. Julia Ward Howe would soon adapt the tune in composing the celebrated patriotic anthem "Battle Hymn of the Republic," and Ralph Chaplin would later make it the basis for the international labor classic "Solidarity Forever." That so much of the best of a nation and of what it gave to the world's struggles for freedom lay in African aesthetics and slave self-activity is entirely apropos. But that basis of classic freedom songs in a ring shout remains also almost entirely unappreciated, only recently returned to our knowledge in the writings of John Stauffer and Benjamin Soskis. Our received history sometimes so shies away from its own brutalities and tragedies that in doing so, it also renders invisible our better connected selves.[21]

That Victoria Woodhull's passion and Lucy Parsons's problems could not be shared by Frederick Douglass and vice versa constitute profound human tragedies. That freedom for all could not have been an immediately realizable goal is understandable in terms of the crises that ripened after the Civil War, and rotted after 1870. Separated social movements too often became unable to support, or even know, each other even as they gained precious little by going it alone.

In closing, we might reflect on the sad reality that the actual gains made as a result of the understandable and seemingly pragmatic decisions of the groups involved to get what they could while they could proved short-lived and fragile. The Black manhood suffrage that Douglass hoped would allow for defense against racial terror lasted not two decades in the postbellum

---

20 Du Bois, *Black Reconstruction*, 670–710; Theodore W. Allen, *The Invention of the White Race*, Volume 1: *Racial Oppression and Social Control* (New York: Verso Books, 2012 [1994]), 144.

21 John Stauffer and Benjamin Soskis, *The Battle Hymn of the Republic: A Biography of the Song that Marches On* (New York: Oxford University Press, 2013), Chapter 1.

South, and in most places quite less than that. The alliances with white supremacist Democrats and appeals to class, race, and anti-immigrant prejudice that some feminists hoped would boost women's suffrage did not deliver speedy results. The caste and craft unionism to which labor leaders gravitated as an alternative to freedom for all proved disastrously suited to organizing even white male workers in an industrial economy. As uncharted and seemingly utopian as attempts to build a movement relentlessly pursuing a common sense of Jubilee while revolutionary time waned undoubtedly were, the narrow, commonsense alternatives each group pursued also offered no refuge from oppression.

We cannot call revolutionary time into being, but knowing the story of Jubilee encourages us to cherish such time and the alliances of mutual interest and mutual inspiration that grew in it. Much was arrayed against the unity of those alliances as ordinary time returned. When Wendell Phillips expressed solidarity in June 1869 with Indian attacks on the building of the Transcontinental Railroad, he supported a resistance little appreciated by most freedom fighters of the period. Writing in the abolitionist *National Anti-Slavery Standard*, he grounded his deliberately provocative stance in an appreciation of both longstanding exploitation and militant resistance. He prized sovereignty and resistance over Indian citizenship, which he saw as potentially empty for Native Americans and other people of color in the US context and apt to encourage illusions. His words reflected the internationalism and optimism of Jubilee. "Every blow struck on those rails," he hoped, "is heard round the globe. Haunt that road with such dangers that none will dare use it." For a moment, as revolutionary time was waning, Phillips poignantly questioned the strategic prioritizing of citizenship that had left him (and his opponents) willing to forsake alliances for electoral gains. He somberly wrote during the very push for the Fifteenth Amendment:

> At present citizenship means little. Heaven forbid that we should betray the Indian to such protection as "citizenship" gives to the Georgia negro . . . No, we are thankful the Indian has one defense

that the negro never had. He is no citizen and has the right to make war. Well may he use that last right, and never yield it till "citizenship" means more than it does now.[22]

In this astonishing self-questioning, Phillips committed an error he seldom made during Reconstruction, actually underestimating the value that citizenship and the franchise could confer. Phillips had, after all, more or less supported Republican initiatives that led to the specific spelling out of constitutional provisions that excluded women from voting and "Indians not taxed" from citizenship. His bending of the stick for a moment in the opposite way is of interest not because it got things right; there was no easy solution as to how to support equality without fetishizing the abstract power of citizenship as something greater than material gains, such as land, and solidarity with other excluded groups. Indeed, Phillips soon returned to more mainstream initiatives for Indian citizenship while continuing to defend Native land rights and to denounce atrocities committed by the United States. But in that moment of profound solidarity and profound self-questioning, Phillips offers us, if not a solution, then certainly another vantage for thinking through the politics of difference and of citizenship in moments of victory and defeat.[23]

---

22 Angela F. Murphy, "Wendell Phillips on the Transcontinental Railroad" on the Universal Emancipation (July 2012) website at universalemancipation.wordpress.com.

23 Ibid., and Irving H. Bartlett, *Wendell Phillips: Brahmin Radical* (Boston: Beacon Press, 1961), 380–1; James Brewer Stewart, *Wendell Phillips: Liberty's Hero* (Baton Rouge, LA: Louisiana State University Press, 1986), 292–3. For a searching connection of African Americans' nominal Constitutional freedom and anti-Indian policy, see Mahmoud Mamdani's "Settler Colonialism: Then and Now," Edward Said Lecture (Princeton University, December 2012), available at misr.mak.ac.ug; see also James D. Anderson, "Race-Conscious Educational Policies Versus a 'Color-Blind Constitution': A Historical Perspective," *Educational Researcher* 36 (2007), 249–57. For a contemporary intervention on rights of some at the expense of others, see Chandan Reddy, *Freedom with Violence: Race, Sexuality, and the US State* (Durham, NC: Duke University Press, 2011).

List of Illustrations

page 74: Winslow Homer, *Our Watering-Places—The Empty Sleeve at Newport*

Winslow Homer, *Our Watering-Places—The Empty Sleeve at Newport*. *Harper's Weekly,* August 26, 1865. Wood engraving, illustration: 9 ⅛ x 13 ⅝ in. Brooklyn Museum, Gift of Harvey Isbitts, 1998, 105.91.

page 83: Thomas Waterman Wood, *A Bit of War History: The Veteran*

Thomas Waterman Wood, *A Bit of War History: The Veteran*. 1866. Oil on canvas, 28 ¼ x 20 ¼ in. The Metropolitan Museum of Art, Gift of Charles Stewart Smith, 1884, 84.12c.

page 84: Thomas Nast, *Pardon and Franchise*

Thomas Nast, *Pardon and Franchise*. *Harper's Weekly,* August 5, 1865.

page 91: "Southern Currency"

"Southern Currency." Circa 1863. Pictorial Envelope. PR-022-3-1-48. Collection of the New-York Historical Society.

page 101: Winslow Homer, *Near Andersonville*

Winslow Homer, *Near Andersonville*. 1865–1866. Oil on canvas: 23 x 18 in. New Museum, Newark, New Jersey, Gift of Mrs. Hannah Corbin; Horace K. Korbin Jr.; Robert S. Corbin; William D. Corbin; and Mrs. Clementine Corbin Day in memory of their parents, Hannah Stockton Corbin and Horace Kellogg Corbin 1966 (66.354). Photo © Newark Museum/Art Resource, NY.

page 103: Timothy H. O'Sullivan, *Slaves, J.J. Smith's Plantation, South Carolina*

Timothy H. O'Sullivan, *Slaves, J.J. Smith's Plantation, South Carolina*. 1862. Albumen silver print: 8 ⁷/₁₆ x 10 ¾ in. The J. Paul Getty Museum, Los Angeles.

Acknowledgments

Much help made the completion of this project possible in time for the sesquicentennial of the 150th anniversary of the Thirteenth Amendment. Reduced teaching time was provided by the University of South Carolina Distinguished Visiting Professorship in the Department of History in spring 2012 and by the Illinois Program for Research in the Humanities Fellowship in the academic year 2012–2013. Funds from the University of Illinois Research Board subsidized research assistance and the inclusion of the many illustrations in the book.

The opportunity to present the work at various stages of incompletion energized my writing and the feedback from audiences at lectures and seminars made this a better and bolder book. Venues for such presentations included the Newark Museum, the Marion Thompson Wright Lecture Series at Rutgers University in Newark, University of San Diego, American University of Beirut, the Missouri History Museum, Logan Community College, University of Latvia, St. Ambrose University, University of Illinois Working-Class History Group, University of Alabama, Oakland University, University of Dayton, University of Kansas, Monmouth University, the *Historical Materialism* conference in London, and University of California, Los Angeles. The organizers of these lectures deserve special thanks. They include Clement Price, May Fu, Alex Lubin, Matt Childs, Jennifer Hamer, David Cochran, Toyin Fox, Sharony Green, Robin Kelley, Jordan Camp, Barnes Bradshaw, Sherrie Tucker, Zachary Sell, Caroline Merithew, Graham Cassano, Keri Manning, Annette Windhorn, Hettie Williams, and Alberto Toscano. *The Construction of Whiteness*, a University of Mississippi Press collection I coedited with Stephen Middleton and Donald Shaffer, afforded an opportunity to try out the ideas of this book at article length.

Research assistance from John Carlos Marquez, Michael Staudenmaier, and Bao Bui enriched the book. I also benefited greatly from reading a prepublication copy of Shawn Leigh Alexander's excellent forthcoming documentary history of congressional hearings on the Ku Klux Klan. Thanks to JoAnn Zeise, Peter Rich, Evan Kutzler, Antoinette Burton, Dianne Harris, Edward Blum, Bruce Levine, and John McKivigan for sharing advice and unpublished materials. Thavolia Glymph's visit to Illinois highlighted our sesquicentennial of emancipation celebrations at University of Illinois and deepened my sense of what is at stake in insisting on the self-emancipation of slaves. Among those not fully persuaded by my approach, Ellen DuBois offered especially valuable critique. The music created by freedpeople, especially as rendered by Paul Robeson and by Odetta, was a soundtrack for my writing. Members of the 2012–2013 fellows seminar of the Illinois Program for Research in the Humanities offered patient criticisms of a very early draft. Elizabeth Esch offered valuable commentary on the ideas and the writing. My agent, Geri Thoma, and both Clément Petitjean and Sebastian Budgen at Verso likewise deserve thanks.

Training in my early career as an historian prepared me, in specific and in ineffable ways, to write this book. My dissertation and my first book concerned the working day in United States history, written in collaboration with Philip S. Foner, who provided voluminous research materials bearing on the struggle for an eight-hour working day, a drama so central to the story of Jubilee. Foner also, a little unexpectedly, offered challenging criticisms to the role of Marx and Marxists in the United States in the 1860s and 1870s, especially where race is concerned. Such heterodox radicalism animated my early work on St. Louis in Reconstruction and this book as well. My first academic job, as an editor under John Blassingame for the Frederick Douglass Papers Project at Yale University, also took me to questions central to this study, especially regarding Douglass's theorizing of what the early Civil War was and what it could become. Thomas Alexander, who taught me Southern history as I taught Southern history at the University of Missouri, was an especially gentle source of great inspiration.

Projects such as this would be impossible were it not for the fabulous collections of writings, speeches, and letters of central figures in the story being told. Extending collection of such materials beyond presidents and others with enormous formal political power is a difficult task. For this book, my debts are great to the Frederick Douglass materials gathered and published by Philip S. Foner and later by the Frederick Douglass Papers Project, to the Freedmen and Southern Society Project, to the massive documentary history of Black workers assembled by Foner and Ronald Lewis, and to the work by Ann Gordon and others on the papers of Elizabeth Cady Stanton and Susan B. Anthony.

My two mentors during graduate study at Northwestern University, George Fredrickson and Sterling Stuckey, made this little book possible. Fredrickson taught by example that it was possible to write across a range of disparate topics over a career, telling stories that needed to be told, for audiences inside and beyond academia, in part by combining excellent historical scholarship by others with knowledge of key primary sources. His elegant small book on the history of racism and his adventuresome, late-in-life appraisals of Abraham Lincoln stayed much on my mind as I wrote. Stuckey's emergence in his later career as a leading expert on Herman Melville and his insistence on telling stories spilling across centuries and continents similarly modeled the possibility of avoiding over-specialization. He presented me with a wonderful example of the fact that writing subtle and sophisticated history does not mean giving up on political engagement and a willingness to write at times against the grain of current consensus among historians. Perhaps above all, he taught me to reread and to return to such classic works as those of Douglass and W.E.B. Du Bois, confident of finding new things there. Mentors who were not my teachers in an academic setting, especially George Rawick, C.L.R. James, Susan Porter Benson, and Martin Glaberman, also very much prepared me to see self-organization by working people as logical and decisive in critical periods of historical change.

Index

Page numbers in *italic* refer to illustrations

Sylvis, William, 120, 145, 160–4 passim, 194

taxation, 21, 192–3, 203, 207
temperance, 130, 137, 184
tenant farming and sharecropping. *See* sharecropping and tenant farming
ten-hour workday, 19, 113–14, 123, 124, 194, 196
Tennessee, 149, 171, 173. *See also* Memphis, Tennessee
terrorism, 55, 169–81 passim, 197, 205, 207, 208. *See also* domestic violence
Texas, 166, 203, 204
theology, 44, 49
third parties and third-party candidates, 163, 183–5
Thirteenth Amendment, 17, 27, 44, 90, 134–5, 138, 199
Thirteenth Amendment (pro-slavery) (proposed), 27, 28
Tilton, Theodore, 133
tragedy, 21–2, 44, 54, 148, 200; Du Bois view, 10, 15, 186, 203
Train, George Francis, 144, 145, 154, 157, 181
Transcontinental Railroad, 19, 43, 107, 113
Trelease, Allen, 173–4, 177
Troup, Alexander, 166, 168
Truth, Sojourner, 3–4, 14, 132, 141, 144, 156
Tubman, Harriet, 31, 37–8, 77
Tuchinsky, Adam, 195–6
Twain, Mark: "A True Story," 54
two-party system, 182, 183
typographical unions, 20, 162, 166–9 passim

Underground Railroad, 77, 88
Union army, 27; aid to slaves, 89; Black troops, 3, 5, 40, 42, 43, 54–5, 56; "contraband" use, 37, 55–6; "direct-action abolitionism" by, 42–3, 88; land policy of, 60, 61, 188; slave aid to, 88–9, 92. *See also* Black soldiers
Union League, 153, 174, 177, 180, 190–2 passim
unions, 20, 119, 128, 161–9 passim, 192; segregation in, 20, 121, 159–63 passim. *See also* labor movement; National Labor Union
unpaid labor, 18, 132
US Bureau of Refugees, Freedmen, and Abandoned Lands. *See* Freedmen's Bureau
US Congress, 28, 183–93 passim, 197; Black suffrage, 143; constitutional amendments, 27, 157; KKK hearings, 171, 174, 180; land

policy, 60–3 passim, 187, 188–9; military pensions, 76–7; women's suffrage, 131, 157, 200
US Constitution: amendments, 17, 27, 44; proposed amendments, 27, 28, 145, 157, 158. *See also* Fifteenth Amendment; Fourteenth Amendment; Thirteenth Amendment
USS *Planter*. *See Planter* (ship)
US Supreme Court, 26, 193

Van Evrie, John H., 82
Vanity Fair, 27–8, 93–6 passim
Vedder, Elihu, 92–3, 96–8, 97, 98; *Jane Jackson, Formerly a Slave*, 98
veterans, Black. *See* Black veterans
veterans, disabled. *See* disabled veterans
veterans' pensions, 76–9 passim
Veterans Reserve Corps. *See* "Invalid Corps"
violence, domestic. *See* domestic violence
violence, sexual. *See* sexual coercion and violence
violence against children, 56, 179, 200
violence against freedpeople, 175–80 passim, 205
violence against slaves, 53, 55, 57, 87, 88, 96; returned "blow for blow," 96, 97
Virginia, 37, 38, 42, 53, 58, 63–4, 149
volunteerism, 18, 108
voting rights. *See* suffrage

wage labor, 59–60, 112, 119–23 passim, 178, 205
war journalism, 1–5
War of 1812, 7, 9
Washington, DC: emancipation in, 29
Weydemeyer, Joseph, 112, 115, 185
"White blindspot," 119, 120, 148
whiteness, 13, ability/disability and, 68, 69, 70, 78; Douglass challenge to, 31; emancipation from, 13, 67–103 passim, 112
White poor. *See* poor Whites
White riots. *See* race riots
Whites, LeeAnn, 84
White supremacists and supremacy, 61–2, 82, 149, 169–81, 189; in women's movement, 152–3
Williams, Raymond, 148
Wisconsin, 76–7, 87, 114, 193
Woeful Afflictions: Disability and Sentimentality in Victorian America (Klages), 71–2
women "camp-followers." *See* "camp-followers"